CONTENTS

TABLES AND FIGURES

Tables

Figures

RETHINKING DEMOCRACY AND THE EUROPEAN UNION

Edited by Erik Oddvar Eriksen and John Erik Fossum

Routledge
Taylor & Francis Group

LONDON AND NEW YORK

PLYMOUTH UNIVERSITY
9009276225

First published 2012
by Routledge
2 Park Square, Milton Park, Abingdon, Oxon OX14 4RN

Simultaneously published in the USA and Canada
by Routledge
711 Third Avenue, New York, NY 10017

Routledge is an imprint of the Taylor & Francis Group, an informa business

© 2012 Erik Oddvar Eriksen and John Erik Fossum for selection
and editorial matter; the contributors for their contributions

The right of Erik Oddvar Eriksen and John Erik Fossum to be identified
as editors of this work has been asserted by him in accordance with
sections 77 and 78 of the Copyright, Designs and Patents Act 1988.

All rights reserved. No part of this book may be reprinted or reproduced
or utilized in any form or by any electronic, mechanical, or other means,
now known or hereafter invented, including photocopying and recording,
or in any information storage or retrieval system, without permission in
writing from the publishers.

Trademark notice: Product or corporate names may be trademarks or
registered trademarks, and are used only for identification and
explanation without intent to infringe.

British Library Cataloguing in Publication Data
A catalogue record for this book is available from the British Library

Library of Congress Cataloging in Publication Data
A catalogue record for this book has been requested from the Library of Congress

ISBN: 978–0–415–60557–1 (hbk)
ISBN: 978–0–415–69072–0 (pbk)
ISBN: 978–0–203–13808–3 (ebk)

Typeset in Bembo by
Swales & Willis Ltd, Exeter, Devon

NOTES ON CONTRIBUTORS

Ben Crum is Associate Professor at the Department of Political Science at Vrije Universitet Amsterdam. His research focuses on the political theory of European integration and global governance. Over the last decade, his work has reflected in particular upon the challenges of democracy and constitutionalisation in the European Union (EU), with a special focus on the rise and fall of the EU Constitutional Treaty. His recent publications include 'Accountability and Personalisation of the European Council Presidency', *Journal of European Integration* (2009), 'The Multi-level Parliamentary Field: A Framework for Theorizing Representative Democracy in the EU' (co-authored with John Erik Fossum), *European Political Science Review* (2009) and 'The Benelux Countries: How Politicization Upset a Pro-integration Coalition' (co-authored with Peter Bursens) in Maurizio Carbone (ed.) *National Politics and European Integration* (2010).

Erik Oddvar Eriksen is Director and Professor of Political Science at ARENA – Centre for European Studies, University of Oslo. His main fields of interest are political theory, democratic governance, public policy and European integration. He is the scientific co-ordinator of the FP6-funded Integrated Project *Reconstituting Democracy in Europe* (RECON) (2007–2011). Recent publications include *Making the European Polity: Reflexive Integration in the EU* (editor) (2005), *Law, Democracy, and Solidarity in a Post-national Union* (co-edited with Christian Joerges and Florian Rödl) (2008), *The Unfinished Democratization of Europe* (2009) and 'Bringing European Democracy Back in – or How to Read the German Constitutional Court's Lisbon Treaty Ruling' (co-authored with John Erik Fossum), *European Law Journal* (2011).

John Erik Fossum is Professor of Political Science at ARENA – Centre for European Studies, University of Oslo. His main fields of interest include political theory, democracy and constitutionalism in the EU and Canada, Europeanisation and transformation of the nation state. Fossum is co-architect behind, and substitute coordinator for, the FP6-funded Integrated Project 'Reconstituting Democracy in Europe' (RECON) (2007–2011). Recent publications include *The European Union and the Public Sphere* (co-edited with Philip Schlesinger) (2008), 'Europe's American Dream', *European Journal of Social Theory* (2009), 'The Multilevel Parliamentary Field – A Framework for Theorising Representative Democracy in the EU' (co-authored with Ben Crum), *European Political Science Review* (2009), *The Constitution's Gift: A Constitutional Theory for the European Union* (co-authored with Agustín J. Menéndez) (2011) and *Law and Democracy in D. Neil MacCormick's Legal and Political Theory* (co-edited with Agustín José Menéndez) (2011).

Yvonne Galligan is Professor of Comparative Politics at Queen's University Belfast and Director of the Centre for Advancement of Women in Politics. Her research focuses on gender politics, comparative political representation, and gender and public policy in national and EU contexts. Recent publications include *Gender Politics and Democracy in Post-socialist Europe* (co-authored with Sara Clavero and Marina Calloni) (2007), 'STV – A Gender-proportional System?', in Manon Tremblay (ed.) *Women and Legislative Representation: Electoral Systems, Political Parties and Sex Quotas* (2008), 'Constituting and Reconstituting the Gender Order in Europe' (co-authored with Sara Clavero) in *Perspectives on European Politics and Society* (2009) and 'Women's Leadership in the European Union' (co-authored with Fiona Buckley) in Karen O'Connor (ed.) *Gender and Women's Leadership* (2010).

Magdalena Góra is Associate Professor of Political Science at the Institute of European Studies, Jagiellonian University in Krakow. She holds a PhD in Political Science from Jagiellonian University with a doctoral thesis on the Polish foreign policy toward Israel. Her main academic interests are processes of collective identity formation after the EU enlargement as well as changes in foreign policy and international relations in Central and Eastern Europe in the context of European integration. Her publications include 'Between Old Fears and New Challenges: The Polish Debate on Europe' (co-authored with Zdzisław Mach) in Justine Lacroix and Kalypso Nicolaïdis (eds) *European Stories* (2010), *Collective Identity and Democracy – The Impact of EU Enlargement*, RECON report (co-edited with Zdzisław Mach) (2010), 'Challenges for Democracy in Central and Eastern Europe', in Robert Posłajko (ed.) *Liberty and Society in an Enlarged Europe* (2010).

Ulrike Liebert is Professor of Political Science and Director of the Jean Monnet Centre for European Studies at the University of Bremen. Her research focus is on problems of democracy and integration in the new Europe, European political sociology and comparative democratisation. Recent publications include 'Europe in Contention: Debating the Constitutional Treaty' (editor), *Perspectives on European Politics and Society* (2007), *The New Politics of European Civil Society* (co-edited with Hans-Jörg Trenz) (2010), 'Contentious European Democracy: National Intellectuals in Transnational Debates' in Justine Lacroix and Kalypso Nicolaïdis (eds) *European Stories* (2010) and *European Economic and Social Constitutionalism after the Treaty of Lisbon* (co-edited with Dagmar Schiek and Hildegard Schneider) (2011).

Christopher Lord is Professor of Political Science at ARENA – Centre for European Studies, University of Oslo. His main fields of interest include the study of democracy, legitimacy and the EU. Recent publications include *A Democratic Audit of the European Union* (2004), 'Two Constitutionalisms? A Comparison of British and French Attempts to Legitimise the Constitutional Treaty', *Journal of European Public Policy* (2008), 'The EU's Many Representative Modes: Colliding? Cohering?' (co-authored with Johannes Pollak), *Journal of European Public Policy* (2010) and 'Polecats, Lions and Foxes: Coasian Bargaining Theory and Attempts to Legitimate the Union as a Constrained Form of Political Power', *European Political Science Review* (2011).

Zdzisław Mach is Professor of Sociology and Anthropology at the Jagiellonian University Krakow and Director of the Institute of European Studies. His research interests cover identity issues such as nationalism, minorities and ethnicity, the development of European citizenship, migration and the reconstruction of identity, the ethnic origin of nation and construction of identities as well as the development of the idea of Europe. Recent publications include 'Social Dimension of the Constitutional Treaty: European Identity and Citizenship' in Zbigniew Maciąg (ed.) *European Constitution and National Constitutions* (2009), *Collective Identity and Democracy – The Impact of EU Enlargement* (co-edited with Magdalena Góra) RECON report (2010) and 'Between Old Fears and New Challenges: The Polish Debate on Europe' (co-authored with Magdalena Góra) in Justine Lacroix and Kalypso Nicolaïdis (eds) *European Stories* (2010).

Agustín José Menéndez is Profesor Contratado Doctor Permanente at the Department of Basic Public Law at the University of León and RECON fellow at ARENA – Centre for European Studies, University of Oslo. His main research fields are European constitutional law, European social and tax policy, legal theory and the theoretical basis for fiscal law. He is co-editor of *Arguing Fundamental Rights* (with Erik Oddvar Eriksen) (2006), co-author of *The Constitution's Gift: A Constitutional Theory for the European Union* (with John Erik Fossum) (2011) and the author of *Justifying Taxes: Some Elements for a General Theory of Democratic Tax Law* (2010).

Helene Sjursen is Professor of Political Science at ARENA – Centre for European Studies, University of Oslo. Her fields of interest include the EU as an international actor, the EU's foreign and security policy, and EU enlargement. Her recent publications include 'What Kind of Power? European Foreign Policy in Perspective', *Journal of European Public Policy* (Special Issue editor) (2006), *Questioning EU enlargement – Europe in Search of Identity* (editor) (2006), and 'Norge og EU – Rett og Politikk', *Nytt Norsk Tidsskrift* (co-edited with John Erik Fossum) (2008).

Hans-Jörg Trenz is Professor at the Centre for Modern European Studies at the University of Copenhagen and Research Professor at ARENA – Centre for European Studies, University of Oslo. His main fields of interest are the emergence of a European public sphere and of a European civil society, European civilization and identity, migration and ethnic minorities, cultural and political sociology, social and political theory. Recent publications include *The New Politics of European Civil Society* (co-edited with Ulrike Liebert) (2010), 'In Search of the Popular Subject: Identity Formation, Constitution-making and the Democratic Consolidation of the EU', *European Review* (2010) and 'Social Theory and European Integration', in Adrian Favell and Virginie Guiraudon (eds) *Sociology of the European Union* (2011).

PREFACE

In 2007 we embarked on a big collaborative research project (RECON) in order to examine the critically important question of how to reconstitute democracy in Europe. See http://www.reconproject.eu.

The project was fashioned in the wake of the Laeken (2001–2005) Constitutional Treaty process and the ensuing debates on the legitimacy of the European Union (EU), which were given added impetus from the negative ratification referenda in France and the Netherlands. The basic questions we asked were: What democracy for Europe? Can there be democracy without the state, and can there be a constitution without a people, or nation? Is there a need for a new democratic theory, or is there only need for democratic reforms in order to make the EU democratic? To that end we established three ideal typical models of European democracy, pointing to intergovernmental, supranational and transnational governing structures. In what direction do developments within the multilevel EU point? The complexity of the European project that gives rise to different and divergent developmental trajectories within the various institutional orders and policy areas was reflected in the project. Work on the project, which is not yet finalized, has taken us into uncharted terrain both in empirical and in theoretical terms.

We have benefited greatly from working together with a large group of scholars – political scientists, sociologists, legal scholars, philosophers, media researchers and social anthropologists across all of Europe and beyond. The RECON project has 21 partner institutions, and more than 120 researchers have been involved. We have also received much help and many contributions from scholars not formally affiliated with RECON. Thank you all very much.

In this book we have set out to take stock of core aspects of RECON's research agenda – with particular focus on the development and refining of the analytical scheme, an important undertaking unto itself, as this book shows. What do developments within the EU's institutional and constitutional realms tell us about the prospects for democracy? What form of civil society is emerging and how does it contribute to a common identity and a European public sphere? What do developments within policy areas such as foreign and security policy and gender policy tell us about the nature of the EU? And how does the EU compare with other cosmopolitan developments? What does the uniqueness of the European political project consist in?

Europe has recently been struck with crisis, the deeper systemic effects of which we can still not tell. But it does appear from the crisis response that the situation for European democracy is bleaker than when we embarked upon this project in 2007. This in no way detracts importance from addressing this most pressing problem for Europe, and also for the world: What are the prospects for democracy, and hence for collective action, beyond the nation state?

We are grateful for the funding of this project from the European Commission's Sixth Framework Programme for Research and from the Norwegian Research Council. We are also grateful for administrative support from ARENA. The same goes for the administrative staff of RECON, Geir Kværk and Marit Eldholm. We are also indebted to excellent assistance from Kathinka Louise Rinvik and Solveig Mork Holmøyuik.

Erik Oddvar Eriksen and John Erik Fossum
Oslo, June 2011

1

INTRODUCTION

Reconfiguring European democracy

Erik Oddvar Eriksen and John Erik Fossum

The last months have seen newspapers filled with headlines on the European crisis, the imminent collapse of the European Union's (EU) common currency, the euro, and the repercussions that these events may have. At the time of writing, it is not clear what the outcomes will be. Whether the euro will survive, be reshaped, or collapse, are questions that remain shrouded in uncertainty. The same applies to the fallout for the EU, whether it will continue to survive, and, if so, in what form or shape that will be.

Social science is notoriously bad at prediction. Rather than trying to assess likely outcomes, at this stage we are better served by trying to clarify what is really at stake here. Is the core issue the financial crisis and the viability of the Monetary Union? If so, one might assume that the issue belongs in the realm of political economy, and the main question is that of how we may best manage capitalism in a context of highly integrated national economies. Is the core issue now facing Europe rather fundamentally a political one and pertaining to the nature and viability of the EU? A recent article predicts 'Europe's return to Westphalia'.[1] It argues that the root of the problem is not economical but deeply political and that what is missing is 'trust and political will'.

The author of the article questions the ability of central political decision-makers such as France's president Nicolas Sarkozy and Germany's chancellor Angela Merkel to make good on their commitment to protect the euro, a commitment that the leaders stress is ultimately political. Sarkozy noted in January 2011 that: 'The euro is Europe [. . .] We will never let the euro be destroyed [. . .] It is not simply a monetary or an economic issue. It has to do with our identity as Europeans.'[2] Sarkozy thus framed the issue as a key determinant for the future of the European *community*, and, he added, this is a community that we identify with.

This statement suggests that what is at stake is the future of the EU as a community of identification. But if so, what kind of community is it? The problem here is that Europeans do not agree among themselves on the basic contours of the community that Sarkozy refers to; they do not even agree on *whether* it is a community to identify with in the first place. On this, also, the academic views and positions range remarkably widely. Some have presented the EU as a special sub-type of international organisation (Moravcsik 1998, 2001), others have conceived of it as a European super-state in the making (Morgan 2005), and others again have tended to consider it as an experiment in supranational or transnational democracy (Bohman 2007a).

One central issue is the magnitude of *state transformation* that the European integration process unleashes; the other is the *democratic implications* that this process will have. Some see integration as producing democratic problems and undercutting democracy as we know it; others underline the democratic benefits that integration brings along. Positions then naturally diverge on the implications of EU dismantling, with some applauding and others lamenting this.

Thus, to get a clear view of what is at stake we need a better understanding of what the EU is, what it does to the member states, and what this entails for democracy. If the EU really does not transform the member states, as we should expect from an international organisation that is an instrument of the member states, an EU collapse will hardly threaten the viability of the member states. This reading presupposes that there is no real identity at stake in relation to the EU and runs against what Sarkozy has claimed. If instead the EU is better understood as a major vehicle in transforming the members from nation states to subunits of a European federal state, then an EU collapse will have significant effects.[3] A frequently voiced argument here is that European states' identities and even state-ness have come to resonate with their *European-ness*; national law has become so entangled in EU law practice that the states are no longer conventional 'nation states'. The claim is that Europe has already travelled such a distance down the EU integration path that a reversal back to a Europe of *independent* nation states will represent a transformative project of near-revolutionary proportions (not to speak of the possible fallouts from the process itself if it does not unfold amicably). There is a clear danger that Europe will be thrown back to the disgraceful power politics of an international order locked up in xenophobic nationalistic struggles for influence and dominance, and/or driven by religious zeal.

The need for democracy

More fundamentally, the present European economic crisis raises a normative claim of democracy. It raises a question of authorisation: Who is authorised to make binding collective decisions? It also raises fundamental questions of accountability: Who can be put to account, through which forums, and through which institutions? What sort of consequences should those responsible face? These are questions also raised by Amartya Sen who underlines that the appropriate response requires rearranging the eurozone. Fundamental action is necessary because democracy itself is at stake here: 'Stopping the marginalisation of the democratic tradition of Europe has an urgency that is hard to exaggerate'.[4]

At the bottom of every crisis and every political disaster lies the question of justification: Why should we suffer from others' mismanagement? Why should we pay
for others' recklessness and misbehaviour? Citizens and states all over Europe (and
beyond) are deeply interwoven and affect each others' well-being and freedom in
profound ways. People require answers, and they require that the rules they are
supposed to follow are also abided by those in power. Only a system of democratic
rule can ensure proper authorisation, compliance and accountability.

A major issue at stake in the debate on the EU is therefore that of whether
democracy is possible and sustainable at the EU level, and what form this might
take. The problem we face here is that the EU is highly complex and quite intrac-
table. The EU's complexity manifests itself in numerous issue-specific debates that
are not well connected together. This makes it more difficult to get a clear overarching view of what the overall status of democracy in the EU is. Consider the
constitutional dimension (which will be addressed in more detail in Chapter 4). A
closer look at this debate yields not clarification but added confusion. Many (notably Eurosceptics) insist that the EU neither has, nor does it need, a constitution
(Milward 1992).[5] Others see the EU as a failed constitutional project, which came
to an end when the Dutch and the French rejected the Constitutional Treaty in
2005.[6] The European Council, the main body in charge of EU treaty changes, has
underlined that the Lisbon Treaty, even if comprising a good deal of the substantive
contents of the Constitutional Treaty, is not a constitution in a relevant sense, and
hence should be qualified by national constitutional law as an ordinary international
treaty.[7] The above positions (unfit for a constitution or a case of constitutional
failure) appear in marked contrast to the well-established and already decades-old
opinion of legal scholars and practitioners to the effect that the European Union
already has a constitution.[8] This puzzling situation puts the Laeken constitution-
making effort (2001–2005) in a strange light: Why try to constitutionalise something that already is a constitution? The puzzle does not end here: there is also
deep confusion over the constitutional status of the Lisbon Treaty. Can the Lisbon
Treaty be understood as a mere international treaty if it is substantively very similar
to the Constitutional Treaty? With these questions unresolved we are also not clear
on the proper constitutional grounding of democracy in Europe.

The upshot of this is that it is impossible to discern any one single overarching
position or view of democracy in the EU. The debate is multidimensional and covers different positions on what the EU is, as well as different conceptions or theories
of democracy. Thus, to get a proper handle on what is at stake, we have to try to
get a better sense of the main positions in this debate. In the following section we
will outline three major positions on the future of European democracy that cut
across ideologies and academic disciplines.

Which European democracy?

The first, dominant position takes as its key premise that *the nation state remains
the main container of democracy*. Proponents of national democracy understand

globalisation and Europeanisation as *undermining* the salience of the nation state as the embodiment of democratic government. Conservative Eurosceptics see European political integration as synonymous with the factors that drain out the essence of nationhood.[9] Social democrats and communitarians claim that the European integration process sustains a neo-liberal supranational order, an order that undercuts both the systems of risk regulation and the measures of solidarity that were such characteristic traits of the European welfare state (see Greven 2000; Miller 1995; Offe 2000, 2003a; Scharpf 1999; Streek 2000).[10] Taken together, these factors are seen to sustain a system of multi-tiered democratic deficits. Many students of democracy go further and argue that the democratic deficit is not merely a contingent matter relating to the effects of globalisation, but refers to a lack of core civic democratic components such as a common European public sphere (Grimm 2004). Some underline the structural character of the problem: it highlights built-in limitations in the *size* of representative democracy. Robert A. Dahl (1999), for instance, has argued that, beyond a certain scale and scope, representative democracy cannot work; thus, extending representative democracy to the European level lengthens the democratic chain of legitimation and *heightens citizens' alienation*. The most obvious solution is to roll back integration. But can the rolling back of European integration *rescue* national democracy under conditions of interdependence and globalisation?

The merit of this solution is disputed by other analysts who argue that the main challenge to national democracy does not emanate from European integration, but instead from *decisional exclusion* as a result of denationalisation and globalisation. Dahl's argument about a 'reasonable threshold' of size can also be countered:

- *The right size of the republic* is not clear, as already the American federalists recognised.
- *The current interdependent international affairs* subject the individuals to foreign decision-making.
- With the deprivation of any form of direct international representation, 'the relative weight of each individual's vote should be even more severely discounted' (Marchetti 2006: 302).
- Public deliberation and the mediation of participation through various public spheres may outweigh the loss of direct influence (Bohman 2005: 33).

Moreover, the real democratic problem is political neglect and lack of ability to act on global problems. Many of the decisions affecting national citizens are made elsewhere; or the necessary collective decisions are not made at all. Indeed, these processes reveal decreasing steering capacities on the part of the nation state (see Nielsen 2004).[11] When framed in this light, analysts such as Jürgen Habermas (2001a, 2004) have cast European integration not as the nemesis of democracy, but as a means of *uploading* democracy to the European level. Many representatives of both positions take the nation state as their frame of reference and discuss the prospects for democracy in these terms. Proponents of a European federal state (e.g., Mancini

1998; Morgan 2005) would for instance argue that instituting democracy at the supranational level is the best assurance for sustaining democracy also at the member state level. Within such a configuration, the member states could no longer be sovereign nation states. Some argue that the only viable way out of the present crisis is to integrate further. But will the member states relinquish national identity, and can a European federation develop an acceptable and viable European identity? The answer hinges, at least in part, on how central to democracy is the claim to the effect that, without a collective identity, there can be no democracy.

The second position is made up of transnationalists and multilevel governance scholars who argue that the challenge facing Europe is neither to rescue the nation state nor to upload state-based democracy to the EU level. The EU is seen as a *sui generis entity*, a possible *alternative* to the nation state model.[12] Further, some analysts hold the EU up as a type of polity that has prospects for developing democracy *beyond* the nation state.[13] Ruggie (1993) sees the EU as a case of unbundling of state authority and with this a change in the constitutive principle of territorial sovereignty. Transnationalists and multilevel governance scholars portray the EU as made up of a host of *new governance structures* that combine to make up an alternative to a government above the nation state. To them, sovereignty resides with the problem-solving units themselves (see, for example, Bohman 2007a; Cohen and Sabel 1997, 2003; Dryzek 2006; Gerstenberg 2002). A variety of supranational organisations, transnational 'private global authorities' and governance networks engage in rule-making and regulation beyond the state. They are based upon the private law framework of legal institutions but claim legitimacy, serving the public interest. Dense transnational networks and administrative systems of coordination have been intrinsic to the legitimacy of the EU, and some see these as amounting to a form of *transnational constitutionalism* (Fischer-Lescano and Teubner 2006; Joerges *et al.* 2004). This debate focuses on the conditions under which decision-making in such issue areas can be deemed to be legitimate. If the self-governing collectivity is part of several communities – national, international and global – the locus-focus of democracy becomes a puzzling matter (Held 1995: 225).

The crucial question that this debate brings forth is whether the state form and a collective identity are necessary preconditions for democracy to prevail, or whether a leaner structure made up of legal procedures and criss-crossing public discourse can ensure democratic legitimation. In short, can democracy prevail without state and nation?

The third 'cosmopolitan' position in the debate focuses on Europe as a particularly relevant site for the emergence of *cosmopolitanism* (Archibugi 1998; Beck and Grande 2005; Delanty and Rumford 2005). Scholars from different disciplines draw variously on transnationalism; on the notion of the EU as a new form of community; and on the EU's global transformative potential through acting as a 'normative power' or 'civilian power' (Manners 2002; Sjursen 2007). Even though cosmopolitanism 'is not part of the self-identity of the EU' (Rumford, 2005: 5), scholars nevertheless recognise the EU as a part of, and as a vanguard for, an emerging democratic world order. It is seen to connect to the changed parameters of power politics through which sovereignty has turned conditional upon respecting democracy and human rights. It can be posited as one of several emerging regional-cosmopolitan entities that intermediate between the nation state and the (reformed) United Nations (UN), and which become recognised as a legitimate independent source of law.

Some, notably Cohen and Sabel (2003, 2006) and Bohman (2007a), opt for a 'cosmopolitanism restrained', which blends elements of cosmopolitanism with regional transnational governance. They argue for the normative validity of a *poly-centric system of directly deliberative polyarchy* modelled on the European system of governance. This entails a model of direct participation and public deliberation in structures of governance wherein the decision-makers – through 'soft law', bench-marking, shaming, blaming and so forth – are connected to larger strata of civil society. The EU is seen as a multilevel, large-scale and multiperspectival polity based on the notions of a disaggregated democratic subject and of diverse and dis-persed democratic authority.

Filling in the holes

This brief overview underlines that the problems and challenges facing Europe are not only political: contemporary Europe raises important academic questions. One pertains to the need to clarify the type of entity that the EU is. The intellectual challenge stems from the fact that we cannot confine the analysis to familiar forms of state, but must include new forms of multilevel governance and the prospect of the EU forming a regional subset of an emerging cosmopolitan order. The second issue pertains to clarifying the status of democracy and constitution in Europe. Two questions are here deeply entangled. One pertains to the appropriate *level* for locat-ing democracy in Europe, which revolves around whether the EU level can itself sustain democracy, or whether democracy is still mainly located at the member state level. The other pertains to the appropriate *form* of democracy. This is not merely over the form of representative democracy but more profoundly over the very salience of representative democracy, with the main contender being transna-tional deliberative democracy.

What is fundamentally at stake in Europe is the future of democracy. The basic question that this book addresses is: What democracy for what type of Europe? The book is aimed at: (a) conceptual clarification of the meaning and status of democracy in Europe today; and (b) the development of an analytical framework that makes democratic stock-taking possible over a range of institutional realms and policy fields. This framework operates with upscaled (supranational) and downs-caled (state-based) versions of democracy; therefore it is relevant to integration and disintegration alike.

With regard to (a), the book fills a gap in the literature in that it offers an analyti-cal framework that captures the main positions in the debate on the character of the EU as a political system; discerns the democratic implications of a given polity choice; and provides an overarching framework to establish the democratic quality and the empirical salience of the different options available to the EU. It consists in three democratic polity models (audit democracy, federal multinational democracy and regional-European democracy). This framework is comprehensive; it is designed to capture whatever democratic potentials the EU construct might have. Further, precisely because the framework is comprehensive, it also means that we can dismiss as undemocratic those traits that deviate from all three models. The broad framework thus gives us a better sense of what the EU is; where it is heading; and whether it is heading in a democratic direction or not (because there is no assurance that integration will be matched by democratisation).

The book makes a contribution to the intellectual battle over the character of the EU and the putative democratic merits of this complex political configuration. This is important in broader global terms because the EU is the most advanced attempt at creating democracy beyond the nation state and is really the canary in the coal-mine for this question.

This undertaking will clarify whether it is possible to devise a democratically viable constitutional and institutional framework for the EU that continues to rely on state-based democratic theory. The undertaking would also clarify the main alternative, namely whether we need to abandon state-based theory and instead configure a new theory of democracy that is suitable to the EU's transnational character. Devising such an analytical framework is important also to make sense of the many conceptual, institutional and policy innovations we find in Europe, many of which sit uneasily with established understandings of democratic politics and hence have been difficult to assess in relation to democratic principles and standards.

On (b), the book also fills a major gap in the literature by linking the debates in a range of institutional realms and policy domains to the broad debate on the character of the EU polity and EU democracy. Each of the chapters on the various institutional realms and policy domains or issue areas applies, and suitably clarifies, three democratic polity models within its particular domain. In several instances this is a matter of 'uncovering' or rendering explicit what is at stake for democracy within a given field, with security and foreign policy the most obvious such challenge because of the traditionally strong executive dominance and correspondingly weak democratic controls here. Each chapter has been written by one or several specialists in the given field, thus ensuring that key themes in debates over domains ranging from security and foreign policy on the one hand to gender justice on the other are properly reflected and linked up with the broader debate on the character of the EU polity and EU democracy.

The analytical approach

In order to address the question of what democracy for what Europe, we start by establishing the core components of democracy, and set out the basic requirements for a democratic polity (Chapter 2). These requirements must be sufficiently broad to encompass the possibility of non-state-based democracy, and the most relevant forms of state-based democracy. Deliberative democracy lends itself particularly well to this undertaking because it does not confine democracy to the state, nor to the notion of a pre-political people, but rather grounds it in the rights that free and equal subjects grant to each other when they want to govern common affairs through positive law. Deliberative democracy's de-substantialised concept of popular sovereignty, in which citizens' political opinion and will-formation bear the burden of legitimation, enables us to consider also supranational and multinational entities in democratic terms.

The second step is to apply these basic requirements to the complex and contested multilevel EU configuration. When applying the democratic criteria to the EU, one must take into account that the EU is variously understood as made up of intergovernmental, supranational and transnational principles and structures, respectively. There is no single model of democracy that can simultaneously encompass all these three sets of organisational principles: they make up very different configurations of opinion and will-formation processes. Thus, we do not get at one single viable solution, but rather at *three models* of European democracy. Each of these represents a possible solution to the democratic challenges facing Europe. Each model is original and is developed through applying the democratic principle to a set of organisational parameters. Taken together the theoretical architectonic, composed as it is of three models, offers a comprehensive framework for assessing Europe's democratic challenges. All three models are set up to address the distinct challenge facing Europe, namely that of forging viable democracy in a situation where states are not only highly interdependent but deeply imbricated in each other.

The first model expands the standard intergovernmental position so that national democracy is supplemented with a limited set of EU-level democratic structures. This model posits that viable democracy in the EU can operate through a combination of *audit democracy* at the Union level and representative democracy at the member state level. The second model posits that democracy in the EU is best served through establishing the EU as a *multinational* federal state. The third posits that European democracy can be reconfigured through the EU serving as a regional *post-national* Union with an explicit cosmopolitan imprint.

With these models spelled out, we get a far better sense of the democratic challenge facing EU-Europe. As noted earlier, a critical issue pertains to whether what is at stake is the need to develop a new theory of democracy, or rather to modify existing conceptions of democracy to sit with the distinct traits of the European experience.

The different chapters in the book spell out the democratic polity models across EU institutions and policy fields, with due attention to what research has shown to be distinct EU features. At this point it is useful to mention three features that raise particularly thorny issues.

First is that the EU is marked by complex authority structures. Integration has proceeded along different tracks, as manifested in the EU's three-pillared structure (which the Lisbon Treaty formally abolishes but in practice only modifies). The persistence of the pillar structure testifies to the fact that the EU has developed unevenly across policy fields and institutional realms. Accordingly, representative arrangements and lines of accountability vary with institutional site and across policy field.

This is hardly surprising given a second feature, namely the sheer institutional and socio-cultural complexity of the multilevel configuration that makes up the EU. There are huge discrepancies in the size of the member states (from Germany to Luxemburg); significant vertical institutional incongruence, through federal (Germany, Belgium and Austria), quasi-federal (Spain and the UK) and various forms of unitary arrangements at the member state level; and a great amount of horizontal institutional heterogeneity, at the Union level through different systems of representation and accountability (entrenched in supranational and international structures), and far more so at the member state level (various forms of presidential systems and parliamentary systems).

These features if anything serve to amplify the importance of a third and different feature, namely that the debate on the EU is becoming increasingly specialised. What is the EU, what are its core characteristics, and what is it good for? When there is no agreement on the overarching character of the polity, the different debates in the various institutional realms and issue areas can operate with widely different implicitly or explicitly articulated conceptions of the EU polity and EU democracy.

What is therefore important to keep in mind is that the EU's complexity, its contested character and the presence of a range of loosely connected sub-debates must have direct bearings on the research strategy. In applying the three democratic polity models to the various parts of the EU (institutional and policy fields), we take the specifics and the complexity of the EU into consideration.

These comments serve to underline that it is necessary to pay special attention to how the democratic polity models can be transposed to the various parts of the EU. With reference to one of the dimensions that will be assessed in the book, does EU democracy presuppose constitutionalism and, if so, in what form? Does the process of entrenching democracy at the EU level:

- unfold according to a familiar state-based model of democratic constitutionalism;
- instead draw on a novel and innovative democratic constitutionalism; or
- is it a process of democratic institutionalisation without a clearly articulated constitutionalism – that is, democratisation without having settled the classical constitutional question?

What would a democratic polity look like in the different institutional arrangements and policy fields of the Union?

These questions require us to pay attention to the specific – and distinct – constitutional character and institutional development of the EU. As noted, analysts are deeply divided on this issue. This shows that the application of the democratic polity models to the EU cannot simply be a 'top-down' exercise: it has to have a certain 'bottom-up' character where the specific developments in the relevant institutional realms or policy fields are given due attention. What might a non-state foreign policy look like? What form would qualify as democratic?

As we apply the democratic polity models across the EU's institutions and policy fields, we will also be able to shed further light on how the Lisbon Treaty will reconfigure the EU. The main purpose of this transposition is, however, to set out the analytical framework that is needed for a systematic assessment of the democratic character of the EU from the vantage point of three democratic polity models for European democracy. Moreover, from these examinations, the book also contains a set of findings across a broad range of EU domains that further testify to the relevance of the framework.

Chapter outline

The book is divided into 11 chapters, where Chapters 1, 2 and 3 make up the overarching analytical framework. Chapter 2 sets out the three democratic polity models (audit democracy, federal multinational democracy and regional-cosmopolitan democracy). The three models are discerned from applying the baseline model of democracy to the EU's complex structures. They contain a set of more specific indicators for better discerning model traits in the complex multilevel configuration that makes up the EU. The framework thus provides three distinctly different models of European democracy. At this stage we posit that the third model, regional-European government, holds the greatest potential. This model requires modifying, albeit not profoundly altering, democratic theory. We conclude by arguing for the need to test this model out more properly against the complex EU.

Chapter 3 supplements the first in that it develops a system of democratic audit that is explicitly tailored to each of the three democratic polity models. The basic audit criterion is 'public control with political equality', which can be adapted to state and non-state forms of democracy; thus it sits with all three democratic polity models. The chapter also provides preliminary findings from the application of this system of democratic audit to the EU.

Chapters 4–10 are devoted to the application of the three democratic polity models to a range of institutions and policy fields. Chapter 4 applies the three democratic polity models to the EU's constitutional dimension. The basic question it addresses is a subset of the book's overarching question applied to the constitutional realm, namely: What constitution for what Union? It examines the status of the EU as a constitutional construct in relation to the three democratic polity models. It finds that the EU has a constitution of sorts – a material constitution with a set of fundamental rights and representative arrangements but which nevertheless falls short of being a formal democratic constitution and has limited affinity with the first two polity models. The chapter underlines that the EU was forged on the basis of a distinct form of constitutionalism.

Chapter 5 applies the three democratic polity models to the EU's representative dimension. It starts by identifying a number of key features that set the EU political system apart as a distinct – unique – representative system. The EU's representative structure is neither structured as a traditional federal two-channel system nor as a loose inter-parliamentary network, but rather along the lines of a 'multilevel parliamentary field'. The chapter then 'unpacks' this notion along the lines of the three democratic polity models and examines which model conception of the EU sits best with it – to find that it is the third, the regional-cosmopolitan one.

Chapter 6 is concerned with the question of gender justice in the EU and the incorporation of gender as an essential aspect of decision-making. The chapter defines what is meant by gender democracy, establishes a set of criteria and outlines these in relation to the three democratic polity models. As such, the chapter fills several important gaps in the existing literature. It helps to direct the research on gender politics in the EU to the critical area of democracy, which has been understudied. Further, by programming the gender dimension along the lines of the three democratic polity models, the chapter takes the debate on gender and democracy further.It offers an analytical framework that is not only adapted to the democratic theory debate but also pins this down to tangible institutional forms and policy issues.

Chapter 7 focuses on civil society and public sphere, both of which are central democratic requirements. It is therefore important to establish what configuration of civil society and public sphere is emerging in Europe, and what this contributes to the EU's democratic character and legitimacy. To that end, the chapter establishes how civil society and public sphere should be conceptualised under each of the three democratic polity models, and it provides a set of criteria for assessing patterns of political communication. The chapter also seeks to shed empirical light on the patterns and dynamics of public engagement with the EU. It therefore reports on the results from a range of empirical studies of national parliamentary discourses on EU treaty ratification, print media coverage of EU treaty reform, and print media-based election campaigns.

Chapter 8 focuses on the development of a European foreign, security and defence policy, and the status of democracy therein. It points out that in principle there is no reason to single this issue area out as distinct, although it is clear that the partition of the world into sovereign states has subjected democracy to the Janus-faced character of the state. The democratic principles, autonomy and accountability, are pinned down to four specific criteria, namely constituency, legitimacy, core function and executive power. The RECON framework helps to fill one important *lacuna* in the literature, namely the lack of a proper conceptualisation of the foreign policy actor. The chapter demonstrates that the EU is moving beyond the first intergovernmental model in terms of integration but also that this integration has not been matched with democratisation. This chapter also sheds light on the character of the broader international context and whether it is moving beyond Westphalia, which is of vital importance to the prospects for a regional-cosmopolitan Europe.

Chapter 9 focuses on the reconstruction of collective identities in contemporary enlarged and enlarging Europe. It examines the relationship between democratic polity building and collective identity formation, and adopts a discursive conception of collective identity construction to that end. This entails that democracy should not be construed as something that is based on pre-political identities but should instead be thought of 'as a way of discursively constructing the collective identity of the people'. The three democratic polity models are presented as narrative templates for establishing the possible constituents of a given form of European democracy. The ensuing research effort is one of reconstructing 'how people narrate their belonging, how and by whom such narratives are amplified and what effects they have on stabilising or de-stabilising the collective bonds and drawing the boundaries of the social bonds' (Chapter 9: p. 168). The chapter concludes that collective identity is necessary for democracy because it gives expression to popular sovereignty and serves to stabilise and objectify the social relations that sustain that narrative.

Chapter 10 focuses explicitly on the third democratic polity model, with particular emphasis on the assertion that this is a model with a cosmopolitan imprint. The rationale for this is the frequently asserted notion that the EU is a cosmopolitan vanguard. The question that this chapter addresses is whether it makes sense to discuss the question of cosmopolitan vanguard only in relation to the regional-democratic model or whether states could also be cosmopolitan vanguards. To that end, the chapter discusses Canada as a possible state-based cosmopolitan vanguard. It establishes a set of criteria for assessing degree or magnitude of cosmopolitanisation along state and non-state lines, and holds these up against Canada and the EU. It is suggested that only certain types of states are likely to become cosmopolitan vanguards.

In the conclusion we assess whether it is possible to discern a clear image of democracy in the EU across these examinations. We discern some lessons that help to specify in particular the regional-democratic model further.

Notes

1 Philip Stephens (2011) 'Europe's return to Westphalia', *Financial Times*, 23 June. Available at: http://www.ft.com/cms/s/0/e019ba34-9dc9-11e0-b30c-00144feabdc0. html#axzz1QdxwydYx
2 See World Economic Forum news release, 'Euro will never be abandoned says France's President Nicolas Sarkozy', 27 January 2011. Available at: http://www.weforum. org/news/euro-will-never-be-abandoned-says-france%E2%80%99s-president-nicolas-sarkozy?fo=1
3 A number of analysts have picked up on European and broader international developments to underline that the EU is not a state but is more than a mere association of sovereign states. Many present it as a system of multilevel governance embedded in transnational governance arrangements and networks (e.g., Hooghe and Marks 2003; Jachtenfuchs and Kohler-Koch 2003).
4

> The process has to begin with some immediate restraining of the unopposed power of rating agencies to issue unilateral commands. These agencies are hard to discipline despite their abysmal record, but a well-reflected voice of legitimate governments can make a big difference to financial confidence while solutions are worked out.

(Amartya Sen [2011] 'It Isn't Just the Euro: Europe's Democracy Itself Is at Stake', *The Guardian*, 22 June. Available at: http://www.guardian.co.uk/commentisfree/2011/jun/22/euro-europes-democracy-rating-agencies

5 For an overview of UK Eurosceptics, see Grimm 1995, 2005; Holmes 1996.
6 'The objectionable aspect was its form: an idealistic constitution . . . The new document was an unnecessary public relations exercise based on the seemingly intuitive, but in fact peculiar, notion that democratisation and the European ideal could legitimate the EU' (Moravcsik 2005: 3; see also 2006). The negative referenda have been held up as the ultimate proof of the hopelessly flawed character of the project of giving the European Union a democratic constitution worthy of its name. In autumn 2004, 68 per cent of those polled supported the idea of a European Constitution (Eurobarometer 62 [2005] 'Public opinion in the European Union', p. 149. Available at: http://ec.europa.eu/public_opinion/archives/eb/eb62/eb_62_en.pdf). Opinion polls showed that a majority of decided Europeans (49 per cent versus 16 per cent, including in France [48 per cent versus 17 per cent] and the Netherlands [63 per cent versus 11 per cent]) supported the draft Constitutional Treaty (Eurobarometer [2005] 'The future constitutional treaty: First results', p. 8. Available at: http://ec.europa.eu/public_opinion/archives/ebs/ebs214_en_first.pdf
7 'The constitutional concept, which consisted in repealing all existing Treaties and replacing them by a single text called "Constitution", is abandoned' (European Council, 2007).
8 'Legally speaking, it was clear from the outset that the 1957 EEC Treaty, like the 1951 ECSC Treaty before it, established a special, supranational organisation of a constitutional character' (Pernice 2009: 369). Pernice refers to the explanatory memorandum to the 1957 German law ratifying the EEC, which described the Community as a 'European body of constitutional nature.' On the salience of the constitutional dimension, see also notably Stein 1981; Weiler 1999.
9 For a selection of Eurosceptical writings, see Holmes 1996; Hooghe 2007; Hooghe and Marks 2007).
10 Siedentop (2000) gives this argument a special twist. While supporting a European federal state, he argues that the present integration process is an unhappy marriage of French *étatisme* and neo-liberal economism. This mixture threatens to undercut the prospect for democracy in Europe.
11 Bartolini (2004) sees this in the weakened power of centres' ability to control peripheries. Against this view we find analysts who argue that European integration *strengthens* the state. See, notably, Milward 1992; Moravcsik 1994.
12 Hooghe and Marks (2003) outline two models of multi-level governance, among which 'MLG II' is the one closest to the non-state approach to governance.
13 See notably Schmitter 1996, 2000. See also Hoskyns and Newman 2000; Preuss 1996; Weiler 1999, 2001; Zürn 1998.

2

EUROPE'S CHALLENGE

Reconstituting Europe or reconfiguring democracy?

Erik Oddvar Eriksen and John Erik Fossum

Introduction

The European Union (EU) is widely held to harbour a democratic deficit. This raises the issue of *forging* a viable democracy at the supranational level. This must however also be considered in relation to the question of *sustaining* national democracy within an altered European and global context. The point is that the European integration process has reshaped the workings of the member states' democratic orders to such an extent that we must take the EU's influence directly into account to understand the character and the quality of member state-based democracy. The EU, initially a creature of the member states, has contributed to transforming them, directly through legally binding actions and, more indirectly, through unleashing processes of mutual learning and adaptation. European states' identities and even state-ness have thus come to resonate with their *European-ness*, as national law has become so entangled in EU law practice that the member states no longer operate as independent nation states. To dismantle the EU to forge a Europe of wholly independent nation states today will be a transformative project of near-revolutionary proportions.

How then to ensure democracy in Europe? Many supporters of integration argue that supranational democracy is necessary to handle the problems of interdependence. The standard solution they propose is for the EU to develop into a federal European state, where the nation states are transformed into member states akin to (German) *Länder* or provinces. Critics counter this by arguing that European integration is the problem, because it contributes to the hollowing out of national democracy. They see the issue as one of *rescuing* national democracy from the throes of European integration.[1] Both of these proposals see the issue of democracy in Europe foremost as a *political* challenge. The solutions are well known; the issue is to find the will or the means to apply them.

But is the main challenge merely political? If we for instance look at the German Federal Constitutional Court's ruling on the compatibility of the Treaty of Lisbon with the Basic Law (30 June 2009), the plaintiffs presented the EU as a state-based federation whereas the German Constitutional Court presented the EU as an association of sovereign states. Hence there is struggle over the facts of the matter as well as of the concept of democracy.

Much of the scholarly community has long argued that the European integration process reshapes state sovereignty and that this has profound democratic implications. It challenges the idea of state sovereignty safeguarding constitutional rule, and thus the protection of the citizens' rights and interests, which in turn enables and justifies democracy. Properly entrenching democracy in Europe is therefore not merely a political challenge: it requires explicit attention to democratic theory. But what kind of a theoretical challenge is this? Is it a matter of adapting state-based democratic theory to the more complex European setting, as would be the case with the intergovernmental and federal solutions that were mentioned earlier? Or does the EU require major changes in democratic theory? This is precisely what transnationalists and cosmopolitans claim: they argue that Europe's experiment challenges democratic orthodoxy, which holds the nation state as *the* institutional-communal mainstay of democracy (see, for example, Bohman 2007a; Cohen and Sabel 1997, 2003; Dryzek 2006). The question they pose is whether democracy in its nation state trappings is an adequate foundation for Europe. To properly appreciate what a democratically viable EU entails in today's transnational world, James Bohman argues, requires revamping democratic *theory* (Bohman 2007a).

The question is thus whether we must abandon or whether we can still rely on state-based democratic theory. Is it possible to devise a democratically viable constitutional and institutional framework that continues to rely on state-based democratic theory? Such a solution could be labelled *reconstituting Europe* because it would entail changing the existing order in Europe. Or, rather, is it necessary to reconfigure a new theory of democracy that is suitable to either the particular transnational character of the EU or to an increasingly cosmopolitanised world?

In order to address this, we need to compare and contrast the main alternative democratic solutions. What are they and how should they be compared? Our resolve has been to establish a set of minimum standards that retains core democratic tenets but is not confined to the organisational configuration of the state or to the mode of community steeped in the nation. We apply the fundamental requirements of a democratic order to the complex multilevel configuration that makes up the EU. But rather than ending up with one model of EU democracy, this yields three democratic polity models or representations of the EU (all of which are innovations on existing scholarship).

The first model posits that democracy can be reconstituted as a combination of audit democracy at the Union level and representative democracy at the member state level. The second model posits that democracy can be reconstituted through establishing the EU as a *multinational* federal state. The third posits that European democracy can be reconfigured through the EU serving as a regional *post-national*

Union with an explicit cosmopolitan imprint. Note here on the third model that when we apply our democratic criteria to the EU we end up with a democratic polity model that differs from the one that transnationalists propound. We then consider which of these models is the most robust in relation to the fundamental requirements of a democratic order; we also consider which of these is most feasible. We argue that the third model holds the greatest potential, notably because it is the model that the EU most closely resembles. This is however also the least known and institutionally developed model. Establishing its democratic merits requires further elaboration of the model; it requires a systematic mapping effort to establish the extent of EU proximity to the model and whether the EU is developing in this general direction; and it requires a resultant assessment of the overall democratic quality of this. But first of all, what makes up the bare bones of a political order?

Back to basics

Every democratic system harbours an inevitable gap between principle and practice. Every actual institutional arrangement that claims to be democratic is at most an approximation.

Real democracy has never been realised.[2] The idea of democracy as a system of self-governing citizens does not come wrapped up in an explicit and exclusive institutional package, and democratic orders always contain *non-democratic elements*. Hence the quest is for *democratisation* through constant trial and error of institutional forms, rather than for conclusive settlement through embrace of one particular institutional form of democracy.

This problem appears particularly apposite when considering such complex multilevel systems as the EU, which is of such a scale and scope as to pose serious challenges to the representative version of democracy because of the lengthened chains of electoral control. This recognition has given added impetus to the question as to whether the deliberative model of democracy can recompense for this. Under modern conditions, democratic legitimacy cannot be based on direct participation of all citizens in the making of the laws they are subjected to, because the people are never present to make the choices. What is more, it is hard to see how democratic legitimacy can be based on votes at all, because it is impossible to find a democratic method that allows for the just aggregation of individual preferences to a collective decision. The principle of majority vote represents the winners, not the common will. It does not guarantee full political equality as the prevalence of permanent minorities testifies to. Moreover, the counting of votes is a method to reach decisions, but it is one that does not test the quality of the preferences and is a poor substitute for deliberation (Goodin 2005: 12).

Finding answers to what is the right thing to do through reflecting and deliberating together is superior to finding solutions through complex rounds of bargaining over contested issues. Exchanging threats is not arguing, and adding is not reasoning. Deliberation, which denotes actors' attempts to come to an *agreement* about the definition of a situation, to reach a common *understanding* of how a given situation should be described with the help of the human language, speaks to *the quality requirement* of democracy (Habermas 1996; cp.1981). That is that decisions should be good or just. The ability to reach consensus on empirical and normative questions is seen to emanate from the obligation to provide reasons, which is 'forced' upon every participant in real discourses. Deliberation contributes to the rationality of decision-making by the pooling of information and by argumentatively testing the reasons presented. In a well-performed deliberative process the participants will find out which reasons are good enough. It will make for qualitatively good and fair decisions, insofar as the members put forward arguments and respond to counter-arguments in a rational manner. Further, deliberation will increase legitimacy when affected parties are included and given a chance to argue their case.

The epistemic interpretation of deliberative democracy holds that deliberation is a cognitive process for the assessment of reasons in order to reach just decisions and establish conceptions of the common good (Cohen 1997; Estlund 1993). The main argument for deliberative democracy is to be found in the presumption that a free and open discourse brings forth qualitatively better decisions, and that the decisions are justified to the affected parties. The theory of deliberative democracy is an answer to the requirement of the democratic Rechtstaat that political decisions should be right.

Deliberation is crucial for legitimacy and conflict handling; however, deliberative theory has not yet offered a clear account of the basic social and institutional requirements of democracy in a modern context.

The quadrangle of political order

The European integration process brings up foundational issues with renewed vigour: what are the fundamental requirements of a democratic political order? To address this first question we can start with the so-called 'magic quadrangle' (see Figure 2.1), which makes up the foundational concepts of any political order that claims to be democratic.[3]

Public discourse is at the core of the political order, because it is the medium through which members can address themselves as a collective. It refers to statements and claims supported by evidence, and justifications open to the public.

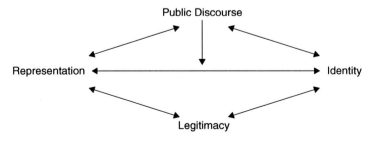

FIGURE 2.1   The quadrangle of political order

Public discourse is essential to 'the development of public knowledge, values, interpretations and self-understandings for change and innovation, as well as reproduction or transmission over time in the inventory of ideas and arguments that are available in a given public sphere' (Peters, 2005: 87–8). It takes place within more or less bounded public spheres and within a given setting or public culture, which provides framework conditions for how the public sphere operates. A public culture provides a set of actively accepted and acknowledged, as well as tacitly held, values, world views, positions and preferences that make ethical-political as well as moral agreements possible – agreements about justice and the common good. A public culture facilitates and to a considerable extent also channels discourse towards certain issues and agendas.

Public discourse is connected to political action and decision-making by a set of institutions and procedures equipped with the capability of converting goals into practical results. In modern polities, public deliberation is wed to systems of representation, because no system can accommodate the participation of all relevant stakeholders. Representation refers to procedures and processes for citizens to influence political decision-making and the actions of public officials in manners generally considered to be legitimate. The modern conception of representation can be said to be parasitic on deliberation, because no person can consider him or herself to be legitimately represented unless the terms of the representative relationship are spelled out, and the represented are offered acceptable justifications for decisions taken on their behalf. Representation may be seen as a precondition for political rationality, because it secures institutional forums removed from local pressure, in which elected members of constituencies can peacefully and co-operatively seek alternatives, solve problems and resolve conflicts on a broader basis (Mansbridge 2003).[4] However, public deliberation cannot itself determine the necessary scope of participation in the deliberative process and it is not a system of action.

Identity speaks to criteria and conditions for membership in a given community, as well as to the collective's interpretations of itself (or the collective's self-understandings). The political function of collective identity is – due to its deeper ties of *belonging and trust*, which makes ethical-political processes of deliberation possible – able to transform a collection of disjunct individuals and groups into a collective that is capable of common action. Identities may be deep or shallow; coherent or fragmented; genuine or manipulated; inclusive or exclusive. Identity formation in a modern democratic context is mediated through public discourse and the institutions and procedures that regulate interpersonal interaction. In that sense all the variants of identity straddle the line between universal principles and particular, distinctive contexts.

By legitimacy we do not simply mean the acceptance or support for an order, but that there are good reasons to be given for why a political order deserves obedience. Legitimation serves to make sure that a polity is fit to make binding decisions on behalf of a *demos*; that the policies and decisions chosen protect the integrity of the society and realise its vital values and goals in a good manner, and that therefore the citizens have a duty to comply. Legitimacy is a function of decision-makers'

compliance with norms, or fair procedure. It is the quality of pre-established procedures that generate legitimacy as they make actors comply even when political
decisions or laws are in conflict with their preferences or interests.[5] In democratic
states there is a presumed link between the normative validity of a political order
and the social acceptance of this order. Many students of modern politics today
subscribe to the tenet that democracy is the sole remaining legitimation principle
of political authority.[6]

The magic political quadrangle of political order (Figure 2.1) does not yield
universal criteria for a democratic order; rather, its foundational concepts come
close to depicting thick relationships and institutional arrangements of a democratic
nation state. Moreover, we should distinguish between democracy as a principle of
justification from it as an organisational principle.

The democratic minimum

It is important to underline that there is an inevitable gap between principle and
practice. Any actual institutional arrangement that claims to be democratic is,
as mentioned, at most an approximation to the ideal of procedural democracy.
Democracy is a contested concept – even more so in a changing world.

We therefore need to make a distinction between justifying reasons and forms of
institutionalisation. This can be generalised into a distinction between democracy
as a *legitimation principle* on the one hand and democracy as an *organisational form* on
the other. Only by adhering to democratic procedures can power holders justify
their decisions and the citizens subject them to critical tests; only by employing
these procedures can collective goals be achieved legitimately; only through these
can laws be changed and new laws enacted correctly. In other words, democracy is
not identical with a particular organisational form, but is rather a principle, which
specifies what it means to get political results right. The democratic principle is
operative as an ever-present critical and self-actualisation standard. Even though
the institutions of modern governments do not mirror this standard, the norm of
government by the people preserves its critical status as the principle through which
proponents and opponents can come to understand each other's claims.

In institutional terms then, democracy, at a minimum, requires both a *polity* and
a *forum* which refer to:

- authoritative institutions equipped with an organised capacity to make binding
  decisions and allocate resources; and
- a common communicative space located in civil society, where the citizens
  can jointly form opinions and put the power-holders to account.

This is part of what we term an *institutional* variant of deliberative democracy
(Eriksen and Fossum forthcoming). Its point of departure is that democratic legitimacy derives from the public justification of the results to those affected. Hence
the democratic principles of *autonomy* and *accountability*. But we label our theory

institutional because justification takes place according to standards the actors consent to and because we recognise that these standards can only be properly entrenched within certain institutional contexts (Eriksen 2009a). Consider autonomy that refers to the basic democratic principle that those affected by laws should also be authorised to make them. This criterion is institutionally committing. It posits that publicly authorised bodies of decision-making react adequately in the determination of the political community's development, insofar as the citizens can be seen as acting upon themselves.

With regard to accountability, it designates a relationship wherein obligatory questions are posed and qualified answers required. We term this deliberative accountability (cp. Mansbridge 2003). This principle also comes with distinct institutional requirements: it speaks to a justificatory process that rests on a reason-giving practice, wherein the decision-makers can be held responsible to the citizenry, and where, in the last resort, it is possible, to *dismiss* incompetent rulers (Bovens 2007: 107; Held 1995: 16). In other words, these principles, to be effective, presuppose representative democratic arrangements and explicit sanctioning mechanisms.

Democratic boundedness – the European conundrum

There is a recursive relationship between democratic principle and democratic practice: foundational concepts will shape our assessment of the prospects for rendering democracy possible within a given institutional-systemic context, and the context will shape the standing of each of the foundational concepts – including of how they are related. The concepts we must rely on will necessarily be bounded, with degree and character of binding varying with context. Such bounds are more easily justified the better they conform to the tenets of autonomy and accountability.

The critical issue facing Europe today is precisely what democratic boundedness entails in the contemporary context: does it presuppose the exclusive type of territorial control and recourse to force that we associate with the modern state? Or can democracy be ensured within a weaker notion of political system, akin, for instance, to Easton's definition as 'the authoritative allocation of values for society as a whole' (Easton 1971: 134)? In line with this, when outlining the third model, we conceive of the polity not as a state but as a government.

The debate over democracy in Europe, as shown earlier, is not confined to the nation state. Rather, the debate is over *which democracy for which Union?* There is contestation over how best to conceptualise democracy; over normative standards; over appropriate terminology; and even disagreement over the factual record: how best to describe the Union in institutional terms and account for it in theoretical terms.[7]

Thus, proper transposition of the foundational concepts to the European context is itself a matter of contention. One issue is 'methodological nationalism' (Beck 2004).[8] Another is the 'reification fallacy'.[9] Unreflective acceptance of nationalism can render researchers blind to a deeper knowledge of when a nation is and when it is *not*. On the other hand, simply abandoning the standards, terminology or institutional arrangements associated with the nation state will not do. The Union is made up of states; it draws its core legitimating principles from the democratic constitutional state; and it draws on national terminology (flag, anthem and own currency) in the effort to forge a European identity. One pitfall here stems from the propensity to think of the EU as n = 1, and from this to conclude that it defies comparison. The issue is not whether the EU can be compared; the issue is under what terms it is to be compared.

There is a problem, then, with embracing either position: reliance on a nation state-based vocabulary or wholesale rejection of this. To choose one of these would be to rule out the other part of the debate, and, by implication, to discard rather than consider the objections. That might prematurely shut down promising lines of argument.

Our resolve has been to try to incorporate the positions in the debate on democracy in the EU into a broader analytical framework. In other words, when applying the foundational concepts to the contested setting that makes up the European multilevel constellation, we cannot a priori settle for one but have to take several different options into consideration.

Any transposition of foundational concepts onto a given setting must contend with the two core dimensions that mark any system of governance: the territorial and the functional.[10] These can be considered as continua. The territorial dimension operates on a scale from no control to complete control of territory. The depth and character of territorial control is itself conditioned on the nature of the functional dimension, that is, the functional tasks that the system of governance undertakes. This ranges from a system undertaking a single function (such as a narrowly based international regime) to a system that undertakes all functions (best reflected in the fiction of the sovereign nation state). Certain functions such as resource acquisition are required simply to sustain a governmental entity. Exclusive territorial control requires military and police powers. Democratic systems, as we see from the foundational concepts, require institutions to ensure representation, to forge and protect conditions of membership and distinctive identities, and to ensure legitimacy by sustaining beliefs and values, and through effective discharge and fair distribution of the goods that the entity is set up to deliver. These two dimensions – territorial and functional – can be combined in different ways so as to give rise to very different political systems.[11]

Properly reconstituting democracy in Europe presupposes that the functional and normative requirements are fulfilled. But a major lesson from the European debate is that these can be combined in different institutional ways. In other words, when we apply the basic requirements of a democratic order to the complex 'constitutional essentials' of the multilevel constellation that makes up the EU, we find considerable scope for variation. The EU multilevel constellation's essentials are made up of intergovernmental, supranational and transnational governing structures, which differ with regard to the main locus of the democratic unit. Intergovernmental structures point to the national level; supranational to the European level; and transnational to structures of civil society and cosmopolitanism.

In the following pages we describe the three ideal typical models. We outline each model in a stylised form and assess each of them briefly in terms of suitability for the complex EU context.

Three models for reconstituting European democracy

The EU is a dynamic and contested entity; to grasp the debate and the choices facing Europe, we spell out three polity models. These have been developed from the three main positions in the debate on the EU: as an intergovernmental organisation, as a federation or as a transnational system of governance, but are all innovations on existing scholarship.

Model 1: Audit democracy

The first model envisages democracy as being directly associated with the nation state. The presumption widely shared by Eurosceptics is that it is only the nation state that can foster the type of trust and solidarity that is required to sustain a democratic polity. On the basis of a well-developed collective identity, the citizens can participate in opinion-forming processes and put the decision-makers to account at regular intervals, as well as continuously through public debate. The model implies that the EU must be so institutionally fashioned as to ensure that the institutions at the EU level are accountable to the member states, which continue to serve as the main vehicles for ensuring autonomy.

This model posits that the emerging structure at the European level operates as a regulatory regime deeply embedded in extensive institutional arrangements of public (or semi-public) character (Eberlein and Grande 2005: 97). The model presumes that the member states delegate competence to the Union, a competence that can in principle be revoked (cp. Pollack 2003). Although this entails a form of self-binding on the part of the member states, such delegation can come with a powerful set of controls imposed by the member states, in order to safeguard that they remain the source of the EU's democratic legitimacy. The member states both authorise EU action and confine and delimit the EU's range of operations through the provisions set out in the treaties, as well as through a set of institutions that permit each and every member state to exercise the power of veto. The model can thus be understood as a way of addressing the democratic problems that complex state interdependence and globalisation bring forth, through establishing European institutions that are accountable to the national democratic systems. The Union's *own legitimacy* would be based on its ability to produce substantive outcomes in line with the principle of Pareto optimality, which states that only decisions that no one will find unprofitable and that will make at least one party better off, will be produced, and hence lend legitimacy to international negotiations (Scharpf 1999: 237).

In accordance with the constraints of democratic delegation, that is, which issues can be delegated without severe loss of democratic self-governing ability, the EU's conferred competences would be foremost in the operation of the Common

Market. The scope for common action in other policy fields would be quite nar-row, as would be the scope for redistribution. Further, the EU would have a very limited scope for foreign and security policy, and it would be entirely subject to member states' preferences. The EU's fiscal base would be limited; it would be based on member state contributions, not EU taxing powers (see Table 2.1). The EU level would be based on a problem-solving strategy and a consequentialist notion of legitimacy (Eriksen and Fossum 2004). A problem-solving, derivative entity (from the member states) handles problems of a rather pragmatic, techni-cal–economic nature and preferences that do not invoke moral claims or affect identities. Thus conceived, the EU would be a contractual order, an institutionally unique type of international organisation or regime, where the member states are the 'masters of the Treaties'. The states not the citizens make up the 'constituen-cies', and are the sole sources of legitimacy. They act internationally, either on their own, or through their conferring powers on the Union through delegation. The 'constitutional arrangement' is a contract with the 'pouvoir constituant' structured as a juridical relationship among separate parties. It would be akin to a 'gentlemen's agreement', which presupposes individual membership and sovereignty. The sig-natories represent individual modalities of government, not a social pact among citizens. Contractually based orders do not put up normative criteria of political legitimacy (Frankenberg 2000: 260f).

The standard model understands democratic authorisation by member states to take the form of intergovernmental bodies in which the contracting partners strike bargains on behalf of nationally fixed preferences and interests (Moravcsik 1998). This model is not without its own democratic challenges. One problem is the issue of *agency drift*: what assurances do member states have that the Union – whose decision-makers need decisional freedom to solve problems rationally – operates in accordance with their interests? Another problem is integration-fos-tered technocracy and executive dominance, that is, the bypassing of democratic institutions at both the Union and member state levels. Here many see the EU's attempt to combat executive dominance, through developing and strengthening the European Parliament (EP), as a part of the problem. They see it not only as unfit to curtail executive dominance and technocracy, but also to exacerbate these problems through furthering integration.

Is the development of the EP then simply an anomaly for the delegated democ-racy model? Or can we adapt the model to accommodate the present role of the EP? Our response is a qualified yes. We can extend the delegated democracy model in such a way as to include the EP, but with it serving a more delimited function as an agent of *audit democracy*. This entails that it would, together with supranational institutions (such as a court and an executive), help member states – notably their parliaments – to supervise and control the Union's actions through providing an added forum for bringing forth relevant information on the Union's actions; to launch commissions of inquiry and include other bodies to undertake critical scru-tiny of aspects of the Union's activities; and to engage civil society actors. These institutions would be specifically mandated to hold supranational decision-making bodies to account. They would be constitutionally barred from legitimising and authorising law-making, as well as from expanding Union competencies. In other words, this would be an EP that would be confined to a delimited audit function.

Within this model the EU-level structure would remain a *functional regime* set up to address problems that the member states cannot resolve when acting independently. The ensuing model of the EU posits that the institutions at the Union level be mandated to act within a delimited range of fields. The relevant determinant for establishing which fields would reside in the EU's ability to offload and compensate for the declining problem-solving ability of the nation state in a globalising context. This pertains, in particular, to the ability to handle cross-border issues (such as economic competition, environmental problems, migration, terrorism and cross-border crime, etc.). According to Giandomenico Majone, such a regulatory regime does not need popular legitimation proper, because politically independent institutions, such as specialist agencies and Central Banks, judicial review and the delegation of policy-making powers to independent regulatory commissions, would provide the required legitimation of a unit constructed to resolve the perceived problems of the members (Majone 1998). It remains to be seen whether this model can ensure democratic legitimation. That depends on how the surveillance and accounting mechanisms in place actually square with the ratio of delegated competencies.

Reconstituting member state-based democracy

The model's core presumption is member state-based and institutionally entrenched democratic will-formation approximating the criteria of autonomy and accountability. member states must have the last word; they must be placed on the same line and have the right to veto. The requirement of unanimity prevails; there are neither trumps nor a supreme third party to resolve conflicts.

For this model to work, today's EU will have to go through a process of reconstitution, mainly through a significant *downscaling* of the system at the EU level. It will have to roll back much of the legal order, including removing much of the protective apparatus of human rights and the constraints on aggressive nationalism that have been established in the post-war period.[12] Moreover, a downscaled order would lack the organised capacity to make binding decisions, such as majority vote and court rulings. It would not be set up to solve deep conflicts, and it would be unable to reallocate resources. Within such a downscaled order, the internal democracy of the nation states may increase, because the formal conditions for sovereignty would be re-established, but the states would have limited control over the *external* factors that shape their range and freedom of action – because congruence between the actual decision-makers and the recipients would decrease. Without *input congruence*, that is, participation in the making of the decisions that affect someone, there can be no self-determination; and without *output congruence*, that is, overlap between the polity and the territory it controls, there can be no effective participation.

It is difficult to strike a viable balance between autonomy/accountability and congruence within a setting of delegated sovereignty: heightened interdependence among states means that, to ensure autonomy, the scope of the constituency must be increased. But this comes at the expense of accountability: effective democratic auditing requires supranational institutions that are able to 'open up' and render transparent the workings of intergovernmental executive bodies. Confining supranational bodies to the role of agents of delegated sovereignty, based on a bound mandate, is notoriously difficult. The members of a supranational body will need leeway and large zones of discretion in order to facilitate cogent decision-making. The EP started out as a body of national parliamentarians, and hence bore some semblance to a European-based agent of national audit democracy. Since direct elections were introduced in 1979, however, it has emerged as a legislative body proper, a body with authority to act in its own right. It is not bound up in and confined to acts of delegation by the member states (Rittberger 2005: 2).

It is also not clear that a process of rolling back the EU will adequately address the democratic challenges facing interdependent nation states: creeping juridification (the expansion of jurist-made norms to new social domains), executive dominance and technocratic governance. At a minimum, then, this model's proposal for reconstituting democracy in Europe presupposes that the member states upgrade their own political and legal institutions so as to ensure public scrutiny and democratic control of the EU. The conundrum is that the act of rolling back the EU's political structures may not rescue national democracy under conditions of (economic) globalisation where the nation state's autonomy is diminished. The model of audit democracy may ensure legal accountability, but not democratic or deliberative accountability, because issue-complexity and issue-linkage always leave discretionary room for delegates. Audit democracy would also be prone to *input-output incongruence*. Since the fate of national democracy is intrinsically linked to developments at the EU level, the other reconstituting strategy is to argue for the need to entrench democracy properly at the European level.

Model 2: Federal multinational democracy

The democratic credo posits that all political authority emanates from the law laid down in the name of the people. The legitimacy of the law stems from the autonomy presumption that it is made by the people or their representatives – the *pouvoir constituant* – and is made binding on every part of the polity to the same degree and amount. This is so to say inherent in the legal medium itself, because it cannot be used at will, but has to comply with principles of due process and equal respect for all. A legally integrated community can only claim to be justified when the laws are enacted correctly, and the rights are allocated on an equal basis. The conventional shape of such a community is the democratic constitutional state, based on direct legitimation, and in possession of its own coercive means.

A federal European state would be institutionally equipped to claim direct legitimation, and entrench this in legally binding form. Federal state structures not only heighten autonomy and accountability, but can also greatly reduce the incongruence that globalisation and complex interdependence produce.

A legally integrated state-based order is often seen as premised on the exist-ence of a sense of common destiny, an 'imagined common fate' induced by com-mon vulnerabilities, so as to turn people into compatriots willing to take on col-lective obligations to provide for each other's well-being. In some contrast, the EU is multinational. The federal model must therefore be modified to accom-modate the fact that nation-building at the EU level would be taking place *together with* nation-building at the member state (and partly even regional) level. The modified version would be a *multinational federal European state*. In its institutional design, such an entity would have to coordinate the self-government aspirations and the rival nation-building projects that would occur within the European space. In constitutional terms, a multinational federation presupposes that the principle of formal equality be supplemented with particular constitutional prin-ciples. These are intended to provide some form of 'recognitional parity', for national communities at different levels of governance (in the EU at Union and member state levels). Wayne Norman cites seven such principles: (a) partner-ship; (b) collective assent; (c) commitment and loyalty; (d) anti-assimilationism; (e) territorial autonomy as national self-determination; (f) equal right of nation-building; and (g) multiple and nested identities (Norman 2006: 163–9). This model is premised on the tenet that a uniform national identity is *not* a core pre-condition for the democratic constitutional state (Habermas 1998a, 2001b). The multinational federal state requires citizens' allegiance in the form of a *constitutional patriotism*, which portrays loyalty in political terms; it hinges on the validity of legal norms, the justification of policies and the wielding of power in the name of fairness.

The multinational federal model of democracy, as set out here, implies that the EU will be distinguished by a commitment to direct legitimacy founded on basic rights and representation and procedures for opinion and will-formation, includ-ing a European-wide discourse. The basic structural and substantive constitutional principles of Union law, as well as coercive measures required for efficient and con-sistent norm enforcement and policy implementation, will be institutionalised at both core levels of government (member state and European). The model presup-poses the establishment of schooling, symbolic measures and social redistributive means at both levels, so as to render the process of socialising the people of Europe into 'Europeans', compatible with citizens retaining distinctive national identities; a set of clearly delineated criteria for who are Europeans and who are not will also be established. There will be an onus on positively identifying Europe, and on distinguishing Europeans from others so as to make up the requisite social basis and 'we-feeling' for collective action – for regulatory and redistributive measures, and for a common European foreign and security policy. The EU will be legally recog-nised as *a state* with the right to police and military force for territorial control and protection of sovereignty, and with provisions for legal secession of any sub-unit from the Union (see Table 2.1).

Reconstituting the EU as a federal democracy

The model's core tenet is for the Union to entrench in state-based form legally binding democratic will-formation. This requires authoritative institutions at the Union (and member state) level, organised along federal lines and equipped with final word on those matters that fall under each level's respective jurisdiction.

The EU's peculiar, and distinctive, institutional structure (with great asymmetries and polycentric features), makes it difficult to meet standards of democratic legitimacy. In the EU, there is no real chance for an all-inclusive public debate among all citizens, because the civic-institutional infrastructure is deficient (Grimm 1995; Peters 2005; Trenz 2005). The 'European people' is represented in 'pseudo elections' (often also referred to as second-order elections)[13] – with low turnout and without a proper European-wide party system – and a parliament that is not a fully fledged and sovereign legislator. The upshot of all this is that the EU deviates clearly from the democratic nation state. In its present form the EU has some traits of a *multinational non-state-based federation*, with the important provisos that its 'federalism' is organised around other issues and methods of territorial control than is the case with every state-based federation, and that the EU's own vocation is *post*-national because it is set up to fight aggressive nationalism.

For the EU to comply with the tenets of this model, it would have to be reconstituted as a polity. That would not only entail *increased* competencies, but also institutional revamping, including the establishment of direct, representative, links with the citizens in *all* relevant functional domains. This could make for a European democracy that complies with the criteria of autonomy and accountability, but the feasibility is low. Under the present legal framework, such a reconstitution requires the *consent* of every member state. The recent treaty processes show that this is not easily forthcoming. Any further move in such a statist, national direction is likely to encounter strong resistance, because many are vehemently opposed to a federal 'super-state'. The German Constitutional Court, in its ruling on the Lisbon Treaty, made clear that the EU is not a nascent federal state; it also underlined that the German Basic Law cannot authorise a federal European state. In today's Europe, the resources required for such an order, for forging a common identity and for making us all good Europeans, are in short supply. The model presupposes increased congruence through lifting tasks to the European level. Insofar as this has occurred, it has been in an uneven rather than coherent manner; it has not been properly democratically authorised; and it has not been matched with adequate measures of democratic accountability.

How close to statehood the EU will need to come to comply with the federal model requires attention to the character of the states' system, because this model is premised on a system of democratic states. In today's deeply interwoven world, where states are becoming increasingly interdependent, 'democracy in one country' is not sustainable. The issue is whether democracy can be sustained through (horizontal) pressures from the system of states, or whether supranational bodies (above the state), which citizens can appeal to when their rights are threatened, are necessary. In today's world, a range of such bodies has emerged. The EU, albeit deficient, is the most elaborate case of supranational democracy.

As we will see, the EU's commitment to universal principles suggests that it has a communal vocation that is broader and more universal than even that of the multinational state. The question brought up by the EU is whether the state model can still be seen as an adequate harbinger of democracy and solidarity in today's world. This pertains to the mode of loyalty, as well as to the institutional-structural make-up that democracy requires in a globalised world. Can a move beyond Westphalia, towards cosmopolitanism, offer a better, more suitable version of democracy?

Post-national democracy

The normative yardstick of autonomy and accountability that we have derived from deliberative democracy is not confined to the nation state template and its presuppositions of sovereignty, demos, territory and nation; it can therefore also be used to establish a non-state polity's democratic character. International law has changed in a cosmopolitan direction, and the EU has pooled sovereignty in a territory it does not fully control. These developments manifest themselves in an altered conception of sovereignty: from denoting singular state territorial control to a more multidimensional and disaggregated conception (Morgan 2005; Slaughter 2004).

Transnationalists such as Cohen and Sabel (1997, 2003) and Bohman (2007a) argue for the normative validity of a *polycentric system of directly deliberative polyarchy* modelled on the European system of governance. They see the EU as a multilevel, large-scale and multiperspectival polity based on the notions of a disaggregated democratic subject, and patterns of diverse and dispersed democratic authority. Their claim is that transnational civil society, networks and committees, Non-governmental Organisations (NGOs) and public forums all serve as arenas in which EU actors and EU citizens from different contexts – national, organisational and professional – come together to solve various types of issues, and where different points of access and open deliberation ensure democratic legitimacy. Local problem-solving, the institutionalisation of links between units, and agencies to monitor decision-making both within and between units make this structure conducive to democratic governance. In his most recent work, Bohman (2007a) seeks to reconcile this with the notion of the 'democratic minimum'.[14] This notion is intended to render a normatively viable, yet not confined to the state, conception of democracy. But, as Rainer Forst has noted, this is a minimum foremost in name, because its proper realisation requires a comprehensive set of institutions (Forst 2007: 93). Bohman does not spell these institutions out, but it is clear that spelling them out would reshape his theory. The democratic minimum is less footloose and requires stronger institutional supports than those Bohman assumes. Barring such institutional supports, Bohman's conception of rule beyond the state cannot adequately deal with the challenge of weak coercive means. How can goals be realised and rights protected *without* the sanctioning capacity of the state? Would such a system be able to 'deliver'? How can it bring about changes required by justice? Further, can it ensure equal access and public accountability in the complex multilevel constellation that makes up the EU?

The crucial question that this debate brings forth is whether the state form and a state-based collective identity are necessary preconditions for democracy to prevail, or whether a leaner structure made up of legal procedures and criss-crossing public discourse can ensure democratic legitimation. In short, can democracy prevail without state and nation? However conceived of, democracy requires some minimum institutional requirements because deliberation in itself cannot bear the burden of democratic legitimation.

The minimum institutional requirements we have discerned do not require a state-type structure but they clearly *exceed beyond* and are *different* from the transnational governance networks that Cohen and Sabel and Bohman put their trust in. They draw on the theory of deliberative democracy because they see it as particularly equipped to account for the particular experimentalist form of democratisation that they identify with the EU. But this is a misnomer: the EU's democratisation unfolds along representative democratic lines with clear resemblance to national arrangements.

Model 3: Regional-European democracy

In a globalising world, the nation states suffer democratic deficits, because their citizens are in so many ways subjected to decisions taken outside their borders, beyond national control. The agenda over which the body of citizens exerts exclusive control is greatly diminished. *Decreased output congruence* underpins the case for supranational government. As noted earlier, cosmopolitans and transnational governance scholars envisage democracy *beyond* the template of the nation state and the states' system. Europe is then also held up as a particularly relevant site for the emergence of cosmopolitanism (Archibugi 1998: 198; Beck and Grande 2005; Delanty and Rumford 2005). This multidisciplinary cast of scholars draws variously on transnationalism; on the notion of the EU as a new form of community; and on the EU's global transformative potential through acting as a 'civilian power' (Manners 2002; Rumford 2005). Even though cosmopolitanism 'is not part of the self-identity of the EU' (Rumford 2005: 5), scholars nevertheless recognise the EU as a part of, and as a vanguard for, an emerging democratic world order.

Little systematic effort has however been put on specifying *how* an EU imbued with cosmopolitan norms can comply with the core democratic principles of autonomy and accountability. Our point of departure is that the core tenets of autonomy and accountability presuppose congruence between political and social space. Congruence is needed to reconcile the autonomy principle with the all affected principle. However, this need not sum up to *exclusive territorial control*. According to Robert Morrison MacIver (1928: 277), we should 'distinguish between the government and the state and regard constitutional law as binding, not for the state, but the government. It binds the legislator in the making of law itself.' *Government* refers to the political organisation of society and to the fact that a state is not merely a Hobbesian coercive order, as Weber's definition alludes to, but notably also an expression of the common will and public opinion (Arendt 1969; Hegel 1821; MacIver 1928; see also Wendt 2003). The characteristic feature of governmental power is not coercion, but the ability to act in concert and to be recognised. Political power emanates from citizens coming together in public forums and reaching agreement on the rules for social coexistence and the collective goals they should realise. Power is collective, communicative and inter-subjective by nature; it is created in the interaction between agents; it is only in operation and only strong so long as the people are assembled and agree (Arendt 1958: 200; Habermas 1996: 149). Thus, it is also possible to understand modern constitutions as disconnected from the state form, from a coercive Leviathan – insofar as they remain linked in with the project of modernity, whose normative telos is to make the addressees of the law also their authors (Frankenberg 1996). A true republic presupposes democracy, but democracy need not presuppose the state. A non-state entity can make up a system of government insofar as it performs the functions of authorised jurisdictions. By government we therefore refer to a system of authorised rule that depicts the political organisation of society, or, construed in more narrow terms, to the institutional configuration of representative democracy and the political unit.

From this we posit that whereas the Union can be set up as a non-state entity, it must nevertheless also retain some of the hierarchical attributes of government. The idea is that since 'government' is not equivalent with 'state', it is possible to conceive of a non-state, democratic polity with explicit government functions. Such a government-type structure can accommodate a higher measure of territorial-functional differentiation than can a state-type entity, because it does not presuppose the kind of 'homogeneity' or collective identity that is needed for comprehensive resource allocation and goal attainment. Such a governmental structure is based on a division of labour between the levels that relieves the central level of certain demanding decisions.

Government without a state?

The question is whether the EU has then also obtained competencies and capabilities that resemble those of an authoritative government. In fact it embraces democracy as a founding norm, has representative institutions, and the parliamentary principle has become more strongly institutionalised. Its institutional setup is complex but 'still it legislates, administers and adjudicates. The legitimacy of these processes also has to be assessed according to the same standards that one would apply to any government' (Chalmers et al. 2006: 87).

When further entrenched in this direction, the EU can be a post-national government, a system whose internal standards are projected onto its external affairs; and, further, it will be a system of government that subjects its actions to higher ranking principles – to 'the cosmopolitan law of the people'.

The problem (currently experienced by the EU) is how an entity with a nascent government order can be effective: implementing decisions against a dissenting minority, in the absence of state-type coercive measures. When it is the member states that keep the *monopoly of violence in reserve*, such an order can only be effective to the degree that actors comply on the basis of voluntary consent. But how to ensure compliance in a polity that lacks the enabling conditions of sovereignty that confer stability on social relations in the form of a 'centralized authority to determine the rules and a centralised monopoly of the power of enforcement'? (Nagel 2005:116). Proper procedures are imperative: when decisions are properly made, when they follow the authorised procedures of the constitutional state, the likelihood that they be respected is high (Tyler 1990). This model therefore seeks to graft the authorised procedures of the constitutional state onto the European level but within a more limited remit of action than the sovereign state. Precisely because it does not regulate some of the core state functions, it can operate with a broad repository of mechanisms to ensure compliance and consent. These include 'soft' mechanisms, ranging from a moral consensus on the protection of human rights; via consultancy and deliberation in transnational structures of governance and their concomitant civil society mechanisms of shaming and blaming; to institutionalised procedures for *authoritative* decision-making in intergovernmental and supranational institutions, which come with direct sanctions.

The EU's own institutions for territorial control are *at their weakest* in the core state functions: military security, taxation and police. The EU is still first and foremost a humanitarian-type power, because its own military capabilities are almost non-existent (although the member states possess very significant military capabilities) (Sjursen 2006a). But whereas the institutions at the EU-level are equipped with far weaker coercive measures than those of states, the EU nevertheless wields quite substantial influence with notable effects, because the *member states* carry out the joint decisions. Collective decision-making and implementation in the EU take place within a setting of already legally institutionalised and politically integrated orders, which help to ensure compliance.

The model of European democracy that we can discern from these observations seeks to reconcile transnational insights with institutional conditions, notably the need for a government-type organisational structure. The model, thus, posits that the EU's democratic legitimacy can be based on the credentials of crisscrossing public debate, multilevel democratic decision-making and enforcement procedures, and the protection of fundamental rights to ensure an 'autonomous' civil (transnational) society. This is the clearest manifestation thus far of democracy as a principle based on a post-conventional form of consciousness, one seen to have been generated by the struggles and processes that produced modern constitutions. Whereas such an entity holds traits that undermine the distinction between states and international organisations, it cannot do away with the modern legitimating principles that were established through democratic revolutions. The concept of government highlights the *moral authority* of the procedures entrenched in the democratic *Rechtsstaat* – as a legitimating, trust and compliance-generating mechanism. Hence, the normativity of democracy: no legitimacy without proper procedure!

Two implications follow from how we apply these insights to the EU: first, that reconfiguring democracy in Europe entails decoupling *government* as the democratic form of rule from the *state form* – as a coercive system of power relations that is sovereign because of the codes of international law. A post-national-type EU would be based on non-violent settlement of disputes, the entrenchment of institutions, rights and legal principles that subject actors to the constraints of a higher-ranking law – the cosmopolitan law of the people – that empowers the citizens to take part in law-making processes at different levels. Policy-making, implementation and law enforcement would then take place through a variety of organisations, and the EU would be a subset of a cosmopolitan order that does not hold the means of legitimate violence in reserve, but is rather embedded in a system of multilevel commitments and constraints.

Second, the model posits that the borders of the Union are not drawn on essentialistic grounds. The EU can, therefore, only justify itself through drawing on the principles of human rights, democracy and rule of law – even when dealing with international affairs. The ensuing order would not aspire to become a world organisation, but would be cosmopolitan in the sense that its actions would be subjected to the constraints of a higher ranking law and be committed to the fostering of similar regions in the rest of the world (Eriksen 2009b).

Regionally situated authoritative government within a cosmopolitan, non-state-based framework raises questions pertaining to institutional design and make-up. One particularly tricky issue is how to ensure democratic autonomy and accountability within such a system. The short answer is that this requires a polity with a *pyramidal* structure of autonomy and accountability, that is, where the global level contains certain fundamental legal guarantees, the EU level handles a limited range of functions over which it has final authority, and the member states the rest. Autonomy has a different status in this model than in the previous ones, because it cannot simply refer back to a delimited democratic constituency but must always balance the requirements of a given constituency with the universal principles embedded in cosmopolitan law. The accountability issue is also very complicated here. The many 'accounts', that such a system necessarily fosters, presuppose a more central role for civil society and the public sphere in demanding and ensuring proper justificatory accounts; hence it locates democracy more explicitly in the civil society/public sphere than is the case in the previous two models.

Reconstituting the EU as a regional democracy

This model's core presumption is that European citizens will be able to consider themselves as self-legislating citizens within the functional domain that is the exclusive preserve of the European government, that is, human rights protection, risk regulation, environmental policy and social security (see Table 2.1).

The model requires reconfiguring democratic theory. But for the EU to fully comply with this model, it needs to be reconstituted. The present-day EU does not fully comply with the standards of a proper *government*. Its enforcement mechanisms might still be too weak to qualify as a government proper. On the

other hand, the self-proclaimed democratic system of law-making and norm interpretation at the European level, constrained by the member states, has built-in
assurances that the EU not become an unchecked entity – an eventual 'world
despotic Leviathan'.

The present-day EU does not contain the balance between economic rights and
social protection (understood as a set of minimum standards) that the cosmopolitan
model sees as required for effective citizenship: to approximate such a balance there
is a need for retrenching market integration and drawing clear bounds on the operation of the market, while *extending social guarantees* across Europe. In this sense the
cosmopolitan model presupposes clear bounds on integration, whereas the Union
is marked by problems of democratically unauthorised 'creeping competence' (Pollack 1994) and *juridification*.

The debate on the EU's bounds and who should be offered EU membership
reflects on the one hand that reminiscences of primordial ties are weakly reflected
at the European level, and a similar argument holds for collective identity. On the
other hand, the debate on where to draw the borders of the EU pits cosmopolitans
against communitarians, where some of the latter argue for the need to *confine* the
Union to European Christendom. The debate on Turkish membership offers one
important take on the Union's value basis (Sjursen 2006b). There is clearly no
political consensus on a cosmopolitan vocation for the EU.

The instantiation of a regional-European version of democracy along cosmopolitan lines raises questions for cosmopolitan-democratic theorising: viable
regional-European democracy requires a form of re-balancing of the membership
in a community of compatriots with the inclusive requirements of the cosmopolitan society. Cosmopolitanism holds individuals as morally ultimate in both domestic and global contexts; they form the only legitimacy basis of political orders. But
democracy presupposes some kind of distinction between members and non-mem-
bers. Democratic sustainability requires some form of identity, and identity thrives
on exclusion, boundary-drawing and distinction. Identities are both a condition
of, and a constraint on, justice. Boundary construction, the dual processes of inclusion and exclusion, aims at establishing a particular balance between contextualised
identities, democratic practice and global justice. Further, the outline of a given
functional constituency must be considered in light of a collective identity's key
role in instilling allegiance and loyalty. What is valuable to us, what we share with
one another and not with all the others, is what makes us special; something that
arouses feelings and emotions, that we are committed to and that can motivate us
to collective action, trust and solidarity. Collective identity stems from membership
in a community of compatriots. It is rather weak in an all-inclusive society. World
citizens do not have much in common apart from shared 'humanity' (Habermas
2001b: 108).

We have seen that the EU holds traits suggestive of a nascent sub-type of cosmopolitan order. However, its effectiveness in pursuing cosmopolitan principles
hinges not only on internal resources but also on external. There are no equivalent
orders established in the world. Insofar as the EU is an agent for a cosmopolitan

world order, it faces the problem of becoming overburdened with tasks and normative expectations.

Conclusion

The basic question that this chapter has addressed is that of ensuring democracy in today's Europe. Our main concern has been to clarify what kind of a challenge this is. What is clear simply from a cursory look at the EU and the scholarly debate is that this is not simply a political challenge in the sense of applying a set of established and well-known solutions to the complex EU. This is not to deny that political factors figure centrally in every conceivable effort to entrench democracy across Europe.

The tight interweaving of states in Europe under the two headings of Europeanisation and globalisation underlined the need also to think of this as a major intellectual challenge. But what kind of intellectual challenge was this: was it that of modifying established theory of democracy to suit the complex EU, or was it more radical – namely, that of coming up with a new theory of democracy? We found the basic choice to be that of either somehow reconstituting democracy in Europe or of somehow reconfiguring democratic theory to suit the complex multilevel European configuration.

The former option was tailored to an understanding of democracy as basically tied to the constitutional state but which still had to be modified to suit the EU. This option we found encompassed two democratic polity models (audit democracy and federal multinational democracy). The first audit democracy model implied retrenching the EU in order to re-equip the member state as the stalwart of democracy within an intergovernmental (rather than a supranational) context. It sought to reconstitute democracy, through installing a system of *audit democracy* at the EU-level coupled with representative democracy at the nation state level. The basic intention was to rescue nation state democracy. Doing so would require a significant element of EU retrenchment, a major transformation of the current European political landscape. The problem is that, even if such a transformation were to be successfully carried out, it would bring up the question of what would guard against Europe becoming privy to the limitations in nationalism and the Westphalian order. In complying with this model, Europe might yet be saddled with the problem that helped spark the European endeavour in the first place. The second possible way of reconstituting democracy was through *multinational federal state* democracy. But we found that even this model could not accommodate Europe's institutional diversity, the asymmetries built into its institutional configuration, and its polycentric character. The Union does not only fall well short of this model in territorial control and contiguity; in its present form, it has also entrenched a set of institutions that clearly deviate from key tenets of this model.

This left us with the second more radical option, namely the need to somehow reconfigure democratic theory to suit the complex EU. Transnationalists argue that the question of democracy in Europe requires a new conception of the presuppositions of democracy, in effect, a new democratic theory tailored to the European circumstance of multiple demoi. This required decoupling democracy from the presupposition of a state and a fixed demos. But when doing so, we found that the minimum requirements for democracy that we spelled out earlier both exceeded and differed from what the transnationalists pinned their hopes on.

Our ensuing conception of democracy, the third model labelled regional-European democracy, is configured not as a system of transnational networks but rather in the procedures of the modern form of *government* within authorised jurisdictions. This can be understood as a regional-cosmopolitan arrangement because its viability hinges on accommodating global developments, some of which exist today: post-war legal developments in the wake of the UN, which have helped to make state sovereignty conditional on compliance with basic human rights. The post-national regional-European *government* model configuration retains many of the core tenets of the democratic constitutional state, albeit in a somewhat reconfigured form: it retains authorised jurisdiction but relaxes sovereign territorial control.

The upshot is that the search for democracy in Europe need not preoccupy itself with a radically new democratic theory but rather opt for a better specification and spelling out of what it takes to realise democratic principles under post-national conditions. The following chapters seek to do precisely that.

TABLE 2.1 Requirements for three democratic orders in Europe

Requirements	Audit democracy	Federal multinational democracy	Regional-European democracy
Sovereignty	The member states are formally sovereign entities. The Union is derived from the member states.	The Union is recognised as a sovereign state, in accordance with international law.	Polity sovereignty is multidimensional and shared among levels, subject to cosmopolitan principles of citizens' sovereignty.
Coercive capabilities	The Union level has no coercive capabilities of its own. Military and police forces are controlled at the member state level.	The Union level has state-type military and police capabilities. The member states have police functions.	Military and police authority shared among all levels.
Authoritative decision-making	• Constitutional limits on Union-level competencies • Union level: problem-solving on the basis of delegated authority • Union level: decision-making and sanctioning ability confined to	• State-based constitution delineating the competencies of the Union and the member states • Institutions for authoritative decision-making at both core levels (Union and member	• Constitutionally entrenched delineation of powers and responsibilities along both horizontal and vertical lines • Union sanctioning ability is limited

TABLE 2.1 *Continued*

Requirements	Audit democracy	Federal multinational democracy	Regional-European democracy
	Common Market matters • member states: sustain final authority in all matters, in accordance with national constitutions	states) within their respective areas of competence • Sanctioning ability available for norm enforcement and policy implementation, at both core levels of government (member state and European)	• Union subjects its actions to higher ranking principles • Authoritative law-making through democratically regulated deliberative procedures
Resource acquisition and allocation	• EU level: no independent taxing powers and limited scope for redistribution • Member states decide autonomously over tax and redistribution within their territories	• EU level: redistributive measures; independent fiscal policy and taxing ability • Member state level: redistributive and taxing powers	• EU level: no independent taxing powers and limited redistributive powers • All levels: committed to global redistribution
Membership/border-setting	The Union is open to all European states that qualify in functional terms.	The Union's borders are set in accordance with designation of Europeanness.	The Union's borders are drawn in accordance with democratic criteria for a self-sustainable democratic entity and with regard to the development of similar regional associations.
Territorial exit	Provisions for exit – subject to approval from the Union (majoritarian support required).	Provisions for legal secession of any sub-unit from the Union – subject to constitutional provisions.	The Union has provisions for territorial exit for sub-units (subject to the constraints of cosmopolitan law).
Mode of legitimation	Audit (derivative) democracy at Union level Representative democracy at member state level.	Popularly elected bodies based ons representative democracy at all levels; competencies divided in bipolar federal manner.	Popularly elected bodies within a system of legally 'hierarchicalised' competences.
Public sphere	Public sphere confined to the nation state.	European-wide public sphere.	Multiple overlapping (European and global) discourses.

Notes

1 For a selection of Eurosceptical writings, see Holmes 1996.
2 Which already Rousseau knew and which made R.A. Dahl (1971) choose the term polyarchy for modern democracy. See also Habermas 1976: 271ff.
3 See Peters 2005. There is considerable controversy as to the specific meanings of these terms; what normative standards they should embed; what institutional arrangements can carry them; how they operate in practice; and how they should be (and are) related. But such controversies are so to speak mainly internal to the quadrangle; the relevance of the quadrangle itself is largely beyond dispute.
4 Deliberation is intrinsic to the mode of representation on which parliaments are based. This principle of representation can be stated as follows: 'no proposal can acquire the force of public decision unless it has obtained the consent of the majority after having been subjected to trial by discussion' (Manin 1997: 190).
5 See further, Beetham 1991; Buchanan 2002; Habermas 1976; Weber 1921.
6 Of the long-established authorities, religion, law, state and tradition, it is only democratically enacted law that has survived the corrosion process of modernity. See Frankenberg 2000.
7 See, for example, Abromeit 1998; Beck and Grande 2005; Beetham and Lord 1998; Bellamy and Castiglione 1998; Brunkhorst 2004, 2005; Gerstenberg 2002; Grimm 1995: 282–302; Haas 1968; Habermas 2001b; Hooghe and Marks 2003: 233–43; Joerges and Neyer 1997: 273–99; Majone 2005; Milward 1992; Schmitter 2000. See also Eriksen 2009a; Eriksen and Fossum 2000a; Jachtenfuchs and Kohler-Koch 1996, 2003; Miller 1995; Moravcsik 1998; Morgan 2005; Olsen 2007; Scharpf 1999; Weiler 1999.
8 This term refers to scientific observers adopting a 'national perspective', which entails that '(s)ociety is equated with national-territorial society organised in states.' (Beck 2004: 140). Beck identifies the following errors and assumptions from this: 'subsumption of society under national state; generalisation from one society to all others; a territorial conception of culture; a misguided equation of "international" with "cosmopolitan".'
9 Jacob Levy (2004: 160) has cogently noted that 'nation' does not denote a kind of community describable apart from nationalist projects and the claim of national self-determination. Once we have a sociologically persuasive account of where a 'nation' is, we find that one way or another the political mobilisation that nationalist theory is supposed to justify is already part of how we've picked the community out. In other words the political program of nationalism is built into the category of nation to begin with; the normative argument is always circular.
10 Consider Rokkan's model of state-formation and nation-building that is based on these two dimensions. See Flora *et al.* 1999; Rokkan 1975. Schmitter (1996) was the first to apply these to the EU. See also Bartolini (2005) for a more detailed attempt to apply Rokkan's model to the EU.
11 Consider Schmitter's (2000) pairing of these into: confederation, federation, consortio and condominio.
12 Today, Union transactions are about far more than functional problem-solving – they have turned 'political'. The EU has market-correcting or positive integration measures, such as certain redistributive schemes and means of standard-setting; there is increased use of qualified majority voting; and there is a constitutionalisation process. These and other traits testify to the EU as revolving around more than the politics of the lowest common denominator. See, for example, Egan 2001; Joerges and Vos 1999. On the role and status of European law and the European Court of Justice, see, for instance, Alter 2002 and Stone Sweet 2004.
13 The main difference between first- and second-order elections is that there is less at stake in the latter. Since European elections do not produce executive changes, they are really second-order national elections (Reif and Schmitt 1980).
14 'The central feature of this democracy as I understand it is that it is a reflexive order, an order in which people deliberate together concerning both their common life and the

normative and institutional framework of democracy itself. Democracy in this view is popular control over decision-making in a specific sense: it is the interaction between communicative freedom as it is manifested in the public sphere and the normative powers by which people create and control their rights, obligations and deontic status' (Bohman 2007a: 5).

3

A DEMOCRATIC AUDIT FRAMEWORK

Christopher Lord

Introduction

Since Robert Dahl (1971), several attempts have been made to frame indicators of democratic performance (Beetham *et al.* 2008; *The Economist*[1]). This paper has two goals: first, to propose a means of anchoring indicators more clearly in normative democratic theory and, second, to ask how indicators which follow from such an approach might be adapted to the special case of the European Union (EU). Section 1 forms this introduction. Section 2 uses democratic theory to identify indicators that can be defended as minimum requirements for a definition (public control with political equality) that satisfies both main justifications for democracy (intrinsic and consequential). Section 3 then shows how context-specific models of democracy – which take account of variations in local value preferences and conditions of realisation – are nonetheless needed to avoid indeterminacy in the testing of indicators based on a normatively defended view of the democratic minimum. Section 4 demonstrates the value of this approach – and illustrates how it might be made to work – with the help of three models of EU democracy developed as part of the RECON project of which this research is a part. Section 5 concludes.

Along the way the paper aims to slay a handful of dragons. As a by-product of revisiting core justifications for democracy, section 2 offers what I believe is a novel counterargument to the view that democracy is a standard that cannot coherently be expected of the Union at all. Between them, sections 2 and 3 take on the view that democracy can be considered an essentially contested concept, suggesting, instead, that it is only a boundedly contested one. That is to say, it is only contested within the bounds of needing to agree some means of securing public control with political equality.

Deriving core indicators

For many it is important that democracy should do what the people want. Thus democratic institutions are expected to be 'responsive' or to 'aggregate' the preferences of those they represent. I do not want altogether to disparage the view that democracy has something to do with the efficient satisfaction of the public's wants. But I do want to suggest that 'utilitarian' concepts of democracy stand in a more complex and contingent relationship to democratic performance than their advocates suppose.

As I will argue in a moment, democracy is a right to join together with others as equals to exercise public control over a polity before it is a system of rule likely to produce particular kinds of policy outputs. Indicators of democratic performance should reflect that priority. They should aim to identify what *procedures* are needed to deliver public control with political equality; and, only then, test for whatever relationship between public policy outcomes and popular preferences the governed happen in any one time or place to value as part of their commitment to democracy. Among the many attempts to define indicators of democratic performance, I know of none that makes explicit this need to give priority to norms and procedures, and several that mix input and output standards, as well as measures of public satisfaction, without clarifying the contingency of the latter two and the necessity of the first.

The fundamental difficulty with taking 'policy outputs that do what the people want' as a core test of democratic performance is that it is by no means clear that such a state of affairs is either necessary or sufficient for democracy (Plamenatz 1973: 181). It is insufficient, since, as is often remarked, even a technocracy or a benign dictatorship might succeed in aligning policy outputs with citizens' preferences. It is unnecessary, since, as John Plamenatz put it, a political system may 'refuse to meet widespread popular demands (. . .) without ceasing to be democratic' (ibid.: 210). Representatives may owe the represented their 'judgement' and not their 'obedience' (Burke 1774). Yet as long as the governed have regular opportunities to recall or renew that trust, we may be quite justified in classifying as democratic a political system that for much of the time does not do what the people want. From this point of view the most encompassing definition of democracy is 'responsible government' – that is, publicly controlled government – rather than 'responsive government' (Plamenatz 1973: 210; see also Mansbridge 2003).

One way of arriving at 'public control with political equality' (Weale 1999: 14) as a definition of democracy is essentially inductive and historical. As David Beetham puts it, it is the absence of public control with political equality that people have historically complained about where democracy has, in their view, been missing (Beetham 1994: 27–8). Yet, even if historical experience had been otherwise, a moment's reflection reveals the two conditions to be necessary to any notion of rule by the people. Whereas democracy is conceivable where citizens do not rule in person, it is inconceivable where they do not control those who take decisions in their name. If, though, some of the people were to count for more than others in exercising that public control, there would be an element of rule of some of the people by others of the people, rather than a straightforward rule by the people. Hence, political equality must also be added to the definition.

The need for 'public control with political equality' emerges even more clearly if we take the discussion back to its philosophical roots in the question, 'Why should we value democracy in the first place?' Justifications for democracy are usually considered to be of two kinds. Intrinsic justifications hold democracy to be desirable in and of itself on the grounds that individuals should have as much control as possible over decisions affecting their own lives. As James Bohman (2007b: 76) summarises this view, 'democracy is an ideal of self-determination'.

In contrast, consequentialists argue that democracy is best justified as a means towards other values, such as peace, prosperity and the securing of all kinds of rights (not just democratic ones) against arbitrary rule (Ryan 1998: 392). For consequentialists, the notion that democracy can be justified as a means of reconciling collective choice with personal autonomy – to the point at which each collective choice can in some sense be seen as each individual's choice – is implausible at best, incoherent at worst (Weale 1999). Democracy, in their view, cannot be justified as a means of reconciling personal autonomy with collective choice, since it is not individuals – but majorities – who choose in modern democracy. Whereas the role of the individual as a decider in modern democracies is vanishing small – equivalent to just one vote in many millions cast on a single day out of many – the role of the individual as an objective of obedience remains very much in the evidence. Majority decisions require individuals to do many things they would sooner not do; and, even if democracies are usually less cruel than other political systems in their means of coercion, the very fact of majority endorsement is often used to justify systems of collective choice that are remarkably encompassing in their effects on individual lives and limited in the exit options they allow those same individuals (Dunn 2005: 19).

Yet, even taking these objections into account, there are important connections between democracy and individual autonomy. Democracy at least requires that the autonomously formed judgements of all individuals should be considered of equal worth in the formation of majorities. Indeed, there are certain rights to autonomous will formation – freedom of speech and of association – that democracy cannot deny without negating itself (Habermas 1996). Moreover, important though they are, there are good reasons for considering consequential justifications for democracy to be secondary to intrinsic justifications. The claim that democracy is justified by certain of its consequences begs the question, 'Who is to decide which of those consequences are desirable, when and why?' Any answer to this question that did not already assume that the only justifiable form of collective choice is one that all citizens can control as autonomous equals would, arguably, be arbitrary.

Regardless, though, of whether we are more convinced by the intrinsic or consequential arguments, the two justifications for democracy overlap in requiring 'public control with political equality'. On the one hand, only publics who can control their representatives can see themselves as authoring their own laws through the latter. On the other, it is usually public control by equally empowered individuals, which consequentialists assume when they predict that democracies will be somewhat more likely than other forms of government to be non-arbitrary and equally respecting of the rights of all.

Since, however, the concern of this chapter is with identifying means of assessing the democratic performance of the EU, it is useful to note another feature of intrinsic and consequential justifications for democracy: namely, the counter-arguments they offer to the claim that it is an absurdity approaching a category error even to apply democratic standards to a polity such as the EU, which is, after all, neither a state nor a nation. If the intrinsic justification for democracy is, in Habermas' terms (1996), that individuals should be able to see themselves as authoring their own laws through representatives, it must surely apply to the EU? Not only does the Union make laws but those laws affect life chances and the allocation of political values. In spite of some brave attempts at portraying the Union as a kind of Pareto-improving paradise, it is hard to ignore ways in which it redistributes values and resources between the states, regions, sectors, generations, sexes, adherents of different social and economic models, and, of course, holders of cherished identities (Lord and Beetham 2001).

Indeed, it seems to me that both intrinsic and consequential justifications rule out *a prioristic* assumptions about the proper locus of democracy. Unless it can be shown that democracy is impossible beyond the state – which, of course, is no more than a defeasible empirical claim and not an absolute normative prohibition – then intrinsic justifications require that publics should themselves choose how much or how little democracy beyond the state they wish to attempt. For their part, consequentialists are required by their own assumptions to support moving democracy up and down between frameworks beyond and within the state depending on whatever arrangements are most likely to produce those consequences – peace, prosperity, rights protections and so on – that they believe justify democracy in the first place.

Indicators based on a democratic minimum

If, as argued so far, 'public control with political equality' is a necessary condition for either intrinsic or consequential justifications for democracy, its corollaries can be treated as a minimum set of requirements any political system must meet if it is to be classified as democratic. With a view to proposing indicators that correspond to what Bohman (2007b) calls a 'democratic minimum', this section accordingly asks what further conditions are either directly entailed by 'public control with political equality' or follow from it on assumptions that would be hard to dispute.

Rights

As Habermas has convincingly argued, it makes no sense to see either democracy or rights as prior. Rather, the only possibility is that we commit ourselves to both 'rights' and 'democracy' through the very act of committing ourselves to the other. Why is this? A right is a demand for the greatest possible measure of some freedom compatible with others enjoying the same freedom. Rights thus imply '"coercible laws" to render rights compatible' (Habermas 1996: 129). That implies 'legitimate law-making' (ibid.: 111); and that, in turn, implies laws that citizens can see themselves as authoring as equals, that is, democratically. Likewise, viewing the 'circuit' the other way round, 'the principle of democracy can only emerge at the heart of a system of rights', most obviously those rights of free speech and association individuals need to form majorities as free and equal citizens. Thus I propose the following as my first indicator:

> Indicator 1. How far, how equally and how securely do citizens enjoy rights of free speech, association and assembly?

Free and fair voting

Voting may not, as Dewey put it, be enough for democracy. But it is also difficult to imagine democracy without it. Most forms of direct and representative democracy end up by needing to make at least some provision for voting; and even deliberative democracy may require systems of voting for *pro tem* decisions pending the emergence of discursively ideal conditions (Habermas 1996: 177). Moreover, for whatever reason, democracy needs some means of voting although the principle of 'public control with political equality' puts limits on which systems for aggregating votes can be classified as democratic. Public control requires that those who are to be rewarded or sanctioned should not be in a position to administer systems of voting to their own advantage. Political equality requires that all citizens should have the same number of votes and each vote should count equally. Thus the following indicator is proposed here:

> Indicator 2. How far and how equally can citizens exercise public control through free and fair voting?

Representative institutions

The third assumption made here is the familiar one that in contemporary societies citizens will need to be able to exercise day-to-day public control through representatives. On the one hand, this may be the more or less unavoidable consequence of the spatial and temporal limits that modern mass societies put on opportunities for citizens to deliberate and decide all laws for themselves. Before proposing an indicator, it is worth considering John Stuart Mill's classic account of representative government:

> It is an open question what actual functions, what precise part in the machinery of government, shall be directly and personally discharged by the

> representative body. Great varieties in this respect are compatible with the
> essence of representative government, provided the functions are such as
> secure to the representative body the control of everything in the last resort.
>
> (Mill 1861: 228–9)

In other words, the exercise of political and administrative power by all public bodies should be within the 'ultimate controlling powers' of a 'representative body . . . elected by the people themselves'. That said, controlling power can be given to representative bodies in more than one way: through opportunities to appoint and dismiss from office; through powers over budgets; and through agenda-setting and veto powers in the passing of legislation. It is also important to note that 'ultimate controlling powers' do not imply that representatives need assume governing functions themselves.

> Indicator 3. How far can representatives elected by the people exercise ultimate controlling power over all public bodies?

Political parties

It might seem odd to include bodies as unloved as political parties among minimum conditions for democracy. Yet, the role of a well-functioning party system may be vital. First, there has to be some mechanism for considering all issues in relation to all others if public control is to be complete to the point of covering one of the most important roles of the political system, namely that of making trade-offs in the allocation of values and resources across the whole range of public policy, and not just in the handling of one issue. A system that cannot meet this basic requirement will also have no means of exercising public control over negative externalities. One way of delivering such 'holistic public control' is to have parties that compete across a range of issues, and which can be judged on their overall governing performance both *ex ante* (on the basis of their commitments to a manifesto) and *ex post* (on the basis of their record).

Second, well-formed party systems help solve co-ordination problems in mass democracies. By directly or indirectly offering the same menu of choice across the political system, they can allow any two voters to co-ordinate their decisions to sanction or reward incumbent power-holders by simply voting for the same party, even though, of course, most voters are unknown to one another. Third, parties can simplify choice in ways that allow citizens to participate in complex democratic systems with only minimal information. Meaningful choice may require no more than an understanding of the relative position of parties along a key dimension of choice, such as left–right; or no more than an opportunity to renew or recall existing patterns of power-holding by voting for parties of government or opposition. Fourth, parties can help solve some of the inter-temporal problems of democratic politics. Individual power-holders may come and go, but in systems of 'party responsible government' parties can be rewarded or sanctioned sometimes long after the event. This gives them an incentive to 'protect their brands'.

Given that the unifying theme of the foregoing points is that a well-formed party system can structure voter choice in ways that help citizens exercise public control, the indicator proposed here is:

> Indicator 4. How far do political parties structure voter choice in ways that help citizens exercise public control as equals?

Civil society

It is often observed that liberal democracy presupposes a delicate balance. On the one hand, it requires that the political system should not be able to dominate the very society of individuals by which it is supposed to be controlled. Yet, that civil society must, in turn, be regulated by the political system so that no source of private power can interfere with procedures needed to secure public control with political equality (Bauman 1999: 154–5). These difficulties are especially acute in relation to the formation and exchange of political opinions among the people themselves. Even individual preference formation may be social in nature to the extent that it best occurs through political discussion supported by a rich associational life, rather than as a prelude to those things. For its part, norm formation is inherently social and intersubjective. If, moreover, opinion formation is to be spontaneous, it should not just be confined to the polity but should also occur through 'adequate non-institutionalised forms of public communication anchored in voluntary associations of civic society and in liberal patterns of political culture' (Habermas 1996: 358). Against the background of these possibilities and difficulties, the following indicator is proposed here:

> Indicator 5. How plural, how independent and how robust is the range of social groups, organised interests and communications media that seeks to influence the polity? How equal is their access to public institutions and how equally accessible are they themselves to individual citizens?

Public sphere

As seen, John Dewey famously observed voting is unlikely to be enough on its own to make democracy an acceptable form of political rule (Dewey 1927). Being out-voted by others, and being compelled, as a result, to abide by unwanted laws, is a harsh discipline that is only likely to be acceptable to those who first have an opportunity to state their point of view, and have it considered open-mindedly. Perhaps John Stuart Mill provides the classic statement of this position in his argument that representative bodies should provide a 'Congress of Opinions' where all points of view should present themselves 'in the light of day' and those who are over-ruled should 'feel satisfied that [their opinion has been] heard, and set aside not by a mere act of will, but for what are thought to be superior reasons' (Mill 1861: 239–40). John Rawls (1993) has likewise argued that democracy's commitment to political equality ideally requires that decisions should be shaped by the quality of justifications reasoned out in public, and not by distributions of private power or resources. In view of these various insights, the following indicator is proposed here:

> Indicator 6. How far are the decisions of the polity deliberated within a public sphere that allows all points of view to be considered, justified and decided in relation to all others, free of inequalities in power and resources?

Civic capabilities

If there are limits to participatory democracy, there are also limits to representative democracy. Indeed, representation presupposes some minimum level of participation in voting and will-formation themselves. This rules out any possibility of democracy being a costless form of government, without burdens of citizenship or a need to invest in the capabilities of representatives and citizens alike (March and Olsen 1995). Since citizens must enjoy whatever capabilities are necessary to exercise their rights of public control through representatives – and, ideally, they should enjoy those capabilities equally – the following indicator is proposed here:

> Indicator 7. How far and how equally do citizens enjoy civic capabilities needed for them to exercise public control over the polity?

Rule of law

The relationship between law and democracy often appears perplexing. In a democracy, citizens must be able to see themselves as authoring their own laws as equals. Yet there would also appear to be some need for laws that can be made by judges and/or enshrined in constitutions against the will of day-to-day majorities of the people or their representatives. It is thus easy to see law as in some sense autonomous of and prior to democracy to the extent that it must set limits to the operation of the latter by upholding a deeper 'social contract' in which individuals can only be assumed to have rationally consented to a system as potentially coercive as majority rule on the understanding that the law can protect each person's rights against majority will-formation itself.

If, however, we see popular sovereignty as consisting not in the will of this or that majority but in the process by which majorities are formed (Habermas 1996: 170, 185–6), we can, as it were, simultaneously prick any claims that law can be superior to democracy and see all the more clearly why it is of the foremost importance to it. Thus Habermas argues that far from law being an external constraint on democracy, it is in performing or carrying out the conditions for authoring our own laws as equals that we commit ourselves to at least the following roles for law: first, 'comprehensive legal protection for individuals guaranteed by an independent judiciary'; second, 'principles requiring that administration be subject to law and to judicial review'; and third, 'the separation of state and society' (ibid.: 169). In sum then, the following indicator is proposed here:

Indicator 8. How far does the polity rest on a rule of law that itself encompasses no more and no less than those conditions required for citizens to author their own laws as equals?

Polity and political community

Few of us are likely to accept what we perceive to be ruled 'by someone else's democracy'. Not only, though, does a democracy require citizens to identify with it and feel it is theirs, it may also require some determinacy in the definition of its membership: in who is an 'insider' and who not. Voting systems that require careful and uncontested calculations of majorities are especially dependent on this requirement. Representative democracy presupposes some agreed means of establishing congruence between representatives and represented, if it is to be clear which votes should contribute to the elections of which representatives, and which representatives should participate in the making of which binding decisions. But even more deliberative forms of democracy presuppose some understanding of who is and who is not to be included in the conversation on a basis of equality.

On top of all this, we will later encounter the argument that the self-determining ideals of democracy must extend to the design of democracy and presumably, therefore, to the definition of the demos themselves. Thus putting the various elements of this section together, the following indicator is proposed here:

Indicator 9. How far is the polity accepted as a unit whose citizens can (themselves and through their representatives) make decisions that are morally and legally binding on one another? And how far can citizens acting as equals exercise public control over the design of the polity itself?

Beyond the democratic minimum

The last section proposed nine indicators which, I believe, more or less correspond to a minimum any political system must satisfy if it is to be classified as democratic. Yet, the indicators still fall a long way short of a fully specified set of standards of democratic performance. By that I do *not* mean that there are likely to be difficulties testing them. Indeed, I will go on to make a case for defining indicators of democratic performance independently of how readily they can be tested. Rather, the under-specification of the indicators is philosophical before it is methodological. The problem is that democratic theory itself implies that any attempt to base indicators on a 'democratic minimum' is likely to tell us only a part of what we need to find out if we are to make a satisfactory assessment of democratic rule in a particular time or place.

First, it is possible to have varying value preferences for how public control with political equality should be delivered. Perhaps the foremost example here is the argument between those who believe that there is inherent value in civic participation (since the citizen only develops and becomes a citizen through participation) and those who believe, to the contrary, that representation is to be preferred (since it frees citizens to pursue other values and get on with the rest of their lives). But we might also add that different people seem to have different value preferences for how choice, competition, consensus, aggregation and deliberation should be balanced and combined in the delivery of public control with political equality.

Second, it is likewise possible to have different preferences for how democracy should relate to other values and identities that are not themselves explicitly democratic. Minority protections, certain individual rights including rights to administrative fairness, and even certain technical aspects of governing performance (such as how to achieve certain outcomes that are 'time-inconsistent' with the electoral cycle) are all values that different people believe should, to different degrees, be ring-fenced from the normal operation of the democratic process.

Third, as long as we accept that somewhat different justifications of democracy are possible, we have also to accept that there is room for putting different relative weight on those justifications, and that too has implications for standards of how democracy ought to be practised in any one place at any one time. While it makes little sense to suggest that values of autonomy have nothing to do with justifications for democracy, it is up to any one historically situated group of individuals, precisely because they are assumed to be autonomous, to decide how far they *also* value democracy for its consequences, and, if so, which consequences. It is at this point that 'doing what the people want' can quite plausibly be brought back in as a secondary standard of democratic performance. Too contingent, and too context-bound to be part of a universal definition of democracy, it can quite plausibly feature sufficiently among reasons why a particular people value democracy to be adopted as a subsidiary standard of democratic performance (after those that follow directly from a need for public control with political equality) for that people.

Yet it is not just on account of local variations in value preference that indicators based on a democratic minimum will always need further specification in context. A further consideration is that empirical judgements – which will always be contextual in nature – need to be integrated to, and not separated from, the process of deciding what is a good form of democracy. Why is this? One answer is provided by Albert Weale's observation that 'ought implies can' in the framing of any non-utopian political theory (Weale 1999: 8–9). Another answer is to be found in Hilary Putnam's deconstruction of the fact-value distinction that has blighted so much of our thinking about social life. Among Putnam's arguments for holding that we will 'misunderstand the nature of fact as badly as we misunderstand the nature of value' if we do not recognise the degree to which they are 'mutually entangled' (Putnam 2002: 46) is a pragmatic view of how we arrive at values. Far from it being the case that values are somehow 'mysteriously embedded' in individual minds prior to encounters with the empirical world, 'we make ways of dealing with the problematical situations' that the latter throws at us and then 'discover which ones' we think 'are better and which are worse'. In other words, we discover our values through 'learning and experience'; and all forms of 'inquiry' work through revisable 'value *pre*suppositions' as much as they work through revisable 'factual presuppositions' (ibid.: 97–8).

Thus indicators based on a democratic minimum will be doubly indeterminate. On the one hand, publics can have varying value preferences for how the democratic minimum should be realised, for how it should be combined with other values, and even for how it should be justified. On the other, each of those value preferences must depend, in some part, on empirical assumptions that are themselves contingent and changeable.

However, democratic theory also implies that any indeterminacies in how any one polity should meet the democratic minimum can only be cleared up within the democratic process itself; and, even then, they can only be made temporarily determinate. By their nature, norms are socially or 'inter-subjectively' defined (Schmalz-Bruns 2005). The value of a norm to me depends in part on its value to others. What is inter-subjectively defined can, however, be inter-subjectively redefined. Modern – that is, post-traditional – society involves precisely an understanding of norms as requiring continuous reflection on their continuing validity and optimal specification.

To this general recursiveness of norms, democratic theory adds its own reasons why it must be open to democratic publics to make their own normative choices and empirical judgements on a 'real-time' basis. If we hold with James Bohman that the conditions of democracy must themselves be democratically determined, it has to remain open to any demos to define and redefine as often as it wants any standards beyond those required for a democratic minimum, to change its value preferences between alternative ways of doing democracy, and even to revisit its own self-definition as a demos.

Where from here? Democratic auditing based on the RECON models

The last section argued that indicators based on a democratic minimum cannot be fully determinate. There is room for both reasonable and recursive disagreement on what should count as satisfaction of that minimum. This section illustrates the difficulty with the help of three models of EU democracy developed by the RECON project of which this research is a part.

First, a few words are needed on the contentious question of whether it makes much sense to talk of 'models of democracy'. Following David Held (1996) and, before him, Crawford Brough Macpherson (1977: 4), the value of distinguishing models of democracy lies in this: understandings of democracy are many and varied, but one thing they have in common is that each makes a number of closely interdependent assumptions about ethics, norms, institutions, human nature, economic and social relations, and so on (Held 1996: 8). Only by making those assumptions explicit and by exploring the often tight interdependencies between them can we adequately understand each type of democracy and identify what choices of value and what empirical judgements are involved in preferring one to another.

As summarised elsewhere in the book, the models are as follows. Model 1 (Delegated democracy) assumes democratic control of the Union through the democratic institutions of each member state. Model 2 (Federal democracy) assumes 'a democratic constitutional state, based on direct legitimation' at the Union level. Model 3 (Cosmopolitan democracy) assumes that the Union can be democratic without itself being a state (in contrast to Model 2) or without depending on the democratic institutions of its member states (in contrast to Model 1) (Eriksen and Fossum 2007a: 15–26).

Without attempting to be exhaustive, the following paragraphs distinguish the contrasting implications of each model for public control, for political equality and for their corollaries. These conclusions are then set out in a table that demonstrates just how far each model implies quite different tests of how far our indicators of democratic performance are satisfied in the case of the EU.

Public control

Under Model 1, member states contract with one another to delegate powers to the Union. This model requires that the Union is so configured that citizens of each member state can use national democratic institutions to secure *continued* public control of delegations of power to the EU. Procedures for treaty change, for appointing to key Union office, for allocating resources to Union budgets, for retaining national veto rights over Union legislation and for supervising execution of existing measures (such as comitology) would need to be sufficient for majorities of voters or representatives in each member state to have 'the control of everything in the last resort' (Mill 1861: 239–40). While it would be consistent with Model 1 for member states to set up constraining mechanisms at Union level (Eriksen and Fossum 2007a) – such as a European Parliament (EP), a European Court of Justice (ECJ), and an Ombudsman – the only test of such devices is how far they help national democratic institutions in *their* controlling powers by, for example, providing information that is helpful to national parliaments in their scrutiny.

In marked contrast, Model 2 requires that public control of the Union powers should be exercised by pan-European majorities of all EU citizens or their representatives acting as equals. Model 2 assumes the Union is or should be a federal order, which has a *demos* of its own and in favour of which member states alienate – rather than delegate – selected powers.

The core assumption of Model 3 is that European citizens should be able to see themselves as authoring all laws made by the EU (ibid.: 22) even where the Union operates from beyond the state without itself possessing the characteristics of a state; or, indeed, anything approaching an agreed *demos*. By considering what democracy would have to be like under such conditions, Model 3 presupposes conditions for public control that both overlap with, and depart from, the other two models.

The Union would have to reproduce those features of the democratic state needed to meet the central assumption of Model 3 that, whatever the form of the Union's polity, all its citizens should be equally able to see themselves as authoring their own laws through representatives. Thus, however appealing it may be for the non-stateness of the Union's polity to take a loosely networked form that is often based on direct deliberation between stakeholders (Sabel and Zeitlin 2007), all proposals for new laws would still need to be publicly controlled in at least one conventional sense: they would need to pass at some point (Habermas 1996) through representative structures proceduralised for political equality and 'holistic' public control.

Political equality

Although we have begun to touch on them, it is worth spelling out the markedly different assumptions the models make about political equality. Model 1 implies that individual citizens should count equally when the domestic arena is used to control delegations of power to Union institutions, but all national democracies should count equally in the European arena. Since delegated democracy aims to align the Union with continued control by national democracies, it presupposes each of the latter should be equally capable of exercising ultimate controlling powers over the Union. Only if each national democracy formally or informally retains means of reasserting control would it be justifiable under Model 1 for it to delegate powers to the Union that can be exercised by procedures that attribute more votes to some member states than others.

In contrast, Model 2 implies that it is individual citizens, and not just national democracies, who should count equally in procedures designed to ensure representation and control at the Union level. Thus, for example, Model 2 would require either linear or degressive proportionality in the allocation of Council votes and EP seats: once each member state has received the same minimum level of representation needed to make some provision for the representation of cultural-territorial units and not just persons, extra votes and seats should be allocated in some regular and principled relationship to the total adult citizenry of the Union residing in that member state.

Proponents of Model 3, on the other hand, are more likely to assume that political equality should be delivered at least as much through discursive standards as through formal and procedural rights. This is, in turn, a condition that can only be met through procedures for justification rather than aggregation. While, then, adherents of Model 3 would obviously regard equal votes as being essential, they would be likely to do so from a position that regards voting itself as no more than the fairest way of making *pro tem* decisions pending the emergence of discursively ideal conditions in which the real hopes for political equality exist.

Corollaries of public control with political equality

Turning from public control and political equality themselves to their enabling conditions, the three models are, once again, contrasting in their implications. While, as seen, Model 1 implies that Union institutions must be configured to allow for control by national democracies, it also presupposes that all the enabling conditions for democracy – rights, civil society, public sphere, civic capabilities and political community – can and should be delivered through the domestic arena.

In contrast, the core assumption of Model 2 – that only majorities of all Union citizens acting as equals can democratically control the exercise of powers assigned to the Union – implies that rights protections, a public sphere, a functioning civil society and an agreed *demos* will all need to be secured to some measure at the Union level. The following paragraphs elaborate.

If majorities of all EU citizens are to make decisions binding on all, it surely follows that all Union citizens are entitled to some guarantee that the majorities binding on them have been formed with the help of 'fundamental freedoms' of speech, assembly and action' that are adequately secured throughout the territory of the Union? Thus even if the political rights necessary for democratic majority formation in Union institutions originate in the member states, there would be a strong case under Model 2 for agreement at the Union level on minimum standards and guarantees for those rights.

The assumption of Model 2 that pan-European majorities will use the powers of the Union to regulate aspects of their lives in common also implies the need for an EU public sphere. Even if the latter were to operate through a mutual opening of national public spheres, the key point is this: rights and duties to equal consideration would no longer stop (if they ever really did) at the boundary of each national public sphere. Each member of each domestic public sphere would owe all other Union citizens all those obligations – to mutual justification of arguments, to public reason, to non-coercive will-formation and so on – that are necessary for legitimate majority formation.

Model 2 likewise presupposes a sufficiently developed 'political community' at the Union level. It is an open question whether that could be as 'thin' as a shared understanding of those norms of mutual recognition and respect that are needed for individuals to communicate and decide together, or whether 'political community' at the Union level would have to be 'thickened up' at least as far as a 'constitutional patriotism'. Likewise it is an open question whether procedures for majority formation can be varied to lighten the demands of political community formation, perhaps with the help of decision rules that aim at the largest and not the smallest possible majority, or which follow the adage 'the majority should get its way, but only with difficulty' (Lijphart 1984). But whatever combination is adopted from the many possible ways of constructing political community and the many possible ways of designing decision rules, Model 2 presupposes some level of agreement that all Union citizens can bind one another through majorities of voters and of representatives.

Model 3, for its part, is doubly challenging of conventional understandings of how to meet the enabling conditions for democracy. Since Model 3 is premised on a non-state polity, Union law, including that enjoining all actors to comply fully with the controlling functions of the representative system, cannot in and of itself enjoy the coercive force of the state. Thus, Model 3 must assume that compliance is in large part motivated more by processes of will-formation than means of enforcement (Eriksen and Fossum 2007a: 20). As if that is not challenge enough, standards of public control are owed – as are all rights under the cosmopolitan assumptions of Model 3 – to all those affected by Union policy and law, and not just to those who enjoy formal status as citizens of the Union. Whereas Models 1 and 2 are free to reproduce the assumption of state-based conceptions of democracy that there is a distinction to be made between 'insider' and 'outsider' rights albeit within different containers (member states in the case of Model 1 and a European federal state in that of Model 2), Model 3 understands democratic rights as being owed to all addressees of a law and not just those who happen to be the same unit of governance. 'Insiders' cannot expunge the rights of 'outsiders' to at least some consideration in their own internal decision-making.

Pulling the various strands together, Table 3.1 summarises how adherents of the three models might test the indicators of a 'democratic minimum' proposed earlier in the chapter. The table is necessarily crude and provisional. It is intended to provoke, rather than close, debate on comparative institutional means of realising and recognising the three models. These qualifications aside, it confirms that any one of the models could indeed make broad indicators based on a democratic minimum more determinate. Yet they do so in such markedly different ways.

Are, however, the indicators derived from the three models operationalisable? Two studies conducted within the RECON project suggest they are. The first study used audit tests to appraise variations in voter turnout to the 2004 European elections. It concluded that tests derived from Models 1 and 3 explain more variation in participation than those derived from Model 2. In particular, voter turnout would not seem to be much affected by the extent of voter identification with the EU, or, in other words, by the degree of *demos*-formation at the Union level (Model 2). In contrast, voter participation is affected by the instrumental calculations voters make of the costs and benefits of European integration to their own member state (Model 1). Yet it is also higher among those who attach high importance to cosmopolitan considerations of human rights (Model 3) (Tamvaki 2009).

A second study has developed indicators of the quality of deliberation in the EP. Among the indicators used in this study is one that investigates how far representatives justify their positions by appealing to interests, values and rights. A second indicator then investigates how far Members of European Parliaments (MEPs) justify their views by appealing to national, European or international reference groups. Various interaction terms between these two indicators correspond to differences between the RECON models. Rights-based justifications that are also international in their reach correspond to Model 3. Appeals to interests, values or rights that are shared between European citizens are closest to Model 2, and their national equivalents are closest to Model 1. Using these indicators, the study coded 883 speeches of the 2004–2009 Parliament across six different debates designed to test for variations in institutional factors, issue polarisation and the personal characteristics of MEPs. While the study demonstrated an instrumental or utilitarian bias in the structure of justification, it showed too that appeals to shared values, identities and rights also have an important place in supranational parliamentary debate. In addition, it is comparatively rare for MEPs to make any kind of justification that is specific to single member states (Lord and Tamvaki 2011). Thus first-order deliberation would appear to be possible in a parliament whose elections purportedly remain second-order; or, to put the point more philosophically, public reason in a representative body at the European level can have a European public as its public, even where representatives themselves are elected in elections that vary in their focus on Europe.

Conclusion

This chapter has argued that indicators of democratic performance need to be specified in two stages: first, by considering conditions that any democracy should be expected to meet; and, second, by identifying local variations in value preferences and conditions of feasibility. Far from implying anything goes, the two steps are, in combination, quite demanding. Section 2 suggested that there are at least nine corollaries of public control with political equality that all polities should have some means of satisfying. Section 4 then argued that any further assumptions about local variations in value preferences and in conditions of feasibility need to be set out systematically in models of democracy.

The chapter then went on to apply this approach to the EU. If we assume that the RECON models demonstrate just how much room there is for reasonable disagreement on what empirical conditions should count as satisfaction of indicators based on a democratic minimum, it is presumably only by simultaneously testing the democratic performance of the Union against all the tests set out in Table 3.1 that we can avoid presupposing the superiority of any of the value positions that is in dispute in choosing between alternative approaches to the democratic control of the Union. The need to avoid this error will be more acute if we assume that surveys of democratic performance should not just appraise polities against fixed standards. For all the reasons set out earlier, evaluations of democratic performance may themselves have a role in deciding ongoing standards and broader questions of democratic design.

TABLE 3.1 Model-specific ways of meeting the RECON indicators of democratic performance

Indicator	Model 1	Model 2	Model 3
How far, how equally and how securely do citizens enjoy rights of free speech, association and assembly?	National freedoms of speech, association and assembly are available to domestic publics in their control of powers delegated to the EU.	Union-wide guarantees of freedoms of speech, association and assembly in each member state.	EU treats freedoms of speech, association and assembly as cosmopolitan rights to which even those addressees of its laws who are not its own citizens are entitled.

How far and how equally can citizens exercise public control through free and fair voting?	Free and fair elections to national executive and legislative offices that control delegations of power to the Union.	Free and fair elections to executive and legislative office at the Union level.	Free and fair elections to all representative bodies that together exercise controlling powers over the Union (see next point).
How far can representatives elected by the people exercise ultimate controlling power over all public bodies on a day-to-day basis?	Effective national parliamentary scrutiny and control of powers delegated to the Union.	A European Parliament scrutinises and controls the powers of other Union institutions.	Combinations of national and European parliamentary control reproduce aspects of the democratic state (holistic public control and political equality) even in a non-state polity.
How far do political parties structure voter choice in ways that help citizens exercise public control as equals?	National party competition allows citizens to exercise control over delegations of power to the Union.	Parties structure voter choice so that elections to European Union (EU) office can be used to exercise control over Union decisions.	Networks of party actors at the national, European and international levels support an inter-parliamentary co-operation with a cosmopolitan reach.
How plural and how independent is the range of social groups, organised interests and communications media that seeks to influence the polity?	Range and independence of the national civil society actors who seek to influence Union policy, and the equality of their access.	Range and independence of civil society actors organised to influence majority formation at EU level and equality of their access.	National, European and international networks of all civil society actors allow all affected by Union policies to participate equally and critically in their formulation.
How far are decisions deliberated within a public sphere that allows all matters to be justified and decided, free of inequalities in power and resources?	Each member state is a well-formed public sphere where all points of view have equal access to national procedures for controlling delegations of power to the EU.	The EU is itself a public sphere in which all views on the exercise of its powers are considered and justified in relation to one another on a basis of equality.	The exercise of EU powers is guided by a commitment to ideals of a cosmopolitan public sphere in which equal consideration is given even to policy addressees who are not EU citizens.

TABLE 3.1 *Continued*

Indicator	Model 1	Model 2	Model 3
How far and how equally do citizens enjoy civic capabilities needed for them to exercise public control over the polity?	Citizens are able to make informed and deliberated choices in selecting representatives who exercise national procedures for controlling delegations of power to the EU.	Citizens are able to make informed and deliberated choices in elections to executive and legislative office at the Union level.	As well as allowing its own citizens to make informed choices, the EU puts no unreasonable obstacles on capabilities that addressees of its laws who are not Union citizens need for the exercise of their rights to fair consideration in the making of EU decisions.
How far does the polity rest on a rule of law that itself encompasses no more and no less than those conditions required for citizens to author their own laws as equals?	National procedures for controlling delegations of power to the EU are covered by rule of law principles in all member states.	The EU develops its own democratic rule of law controlled by majorities formed at the European level.	Soft law is sufficient to ensure compliance with all conditions necessary for all the Union's policy addressees to see themselves as equal authors of those laws.
How far is the polity accepted as a unit whose members can make decisions binding on all? How far can citizens exercise equal control over the design of the polity itself?	National control over delegations of power to the Union ground public acceptance of the EU polity itself. National procedures for bargaining and ratifying Treaty change allow citizens of all member states to exercise public control over the design of the EU polity as equals.	Majorities of voters and their representatives are widely accepted as having the right to make legally binding decisions in the exercise of powers assigned to the EU. Those majorities can also control the further development of the EU polity as equals in so far as changes affect powers already assigned to the Union.	The EU polity is accepted as a legitimate source of law-making by all addressees of those laws (and not just by citizens of the Union) who are also able to control as equals further developments in how the Union polity will apply to them.

Notes

1   The Economist Intelligence Unit's *Index of Democracy 2007*. Available at: http://www.economist.com/media/pdf/democracy_index_2007_v3.pdf

4

DEMOCRACY AND CONSTITUTION-MAKING IN THE EUROPEAN UNION

John Erik Fossum and Agustín José Menéndez

Introduction

Is the European Union (EU) fit for a full-blown constitution, for a fundamental law that may be similar to, but not identical with, that of nation states? The answer of course ultimately hinges on whether the EU is able to survive through the current crisis. At the time of writing, the jury is still out. But, whatever the fate of the EU, the question is still of interest because, as we shall see, the European experience brings up deeper issues of fundamental importance to constitutionalism and democracy.

The protracted, disparate and rather confusing debate on the future of Europe, which started in earnest in 1979, has produced few answers, many positions and quite a bit of confusion. As noted in Chapter 1, some claim that the EU is unfit for a constitution; others argue that it is a failed constitutional project; and yet others hold that it has had a constitution for decades already. There is currently profound ambiguity as to the status of the Lisbon Treaty.

Two key questions require systematic attention: What type of political entity or polity is the EU? Is the EU a type of entity that is suitable for a democratic constitution? A satisfactory answer must cover both questions properly. This includes finding an answer to the democratic challenge. What compounds the issue is that it is not only a matter of empirical analysis to establish what the EU is. To know what to look for we need a satisfactory set of polity and constitutional benchmarks, including a new constitutional theory. The answer can therefore only be provided through applying the proper polity-constitutional template or conception of constitution to the empirical assessment of the EU.

The question that animates this chapter is: What constitution for what kind of Union? To address this, we need to start by devising a conceptual 'map' that establishes the main positions in the debate on the EU's constitutional–democratic character, and that spells out how each position understands the constitutional-democratic status of the EU. Once the map is in place, we proceed to check it against the terrain: each of the main positions in the conceptual map will be briefly assessed against the Union's character and development. This approach will shed light on the overarching question that this chapter began with, namely that of what constitution for what Union.

Our conceptual map seeks to configure the relations among three core concepts: polity, constitution and democracy. This can usefully be done by spelling out how each of the three 'Reconstituting democracy in Europe' (RECON) models that were introduced in Chapter 2 conceptualises the EU's constitutional dimension. This choice of course has implications for what we cover from the constitutional debate (which is not always attuned to the link between constitution and democracy). Given that our concern is with democracy, we have devised the 'map' to cover what RECON sees as the main angles in the debate on the democratic character and quality of the constitutional arrangement in the EU. This cannot simply be a matter of fleshing out the constitutional dimension in the models: the models may likely have to be further spelt out, or even modified, in order to capture properly the constitutional dimension in the EU. This applies foremost to the third regional-democratic conception of the EU, which brings up both conceptual and theoretical challenges, notably whether the dominant state-based vocabulary, standards and normative-theoretical conception of constitution can adequately capture the constitutional-democratic character of the EU. A state-based constitution has long been seen as the only proper manifestation of democratic constitutionalism (assuming a necessary connection between constitution and nation state). Can a polity that is not a nation state have a democratic constitution? The question is highly relevant: it cuts to the heart of the widely held *sui generis* conception of the EU, which sees it not only as a distinct entity, but as one of a *distinct kind*.

But whereas the EU is clearly distinct, it is nevertheless also made up of member states that are constitutional democracies. The European polity has developed in a setting of *already existing constitutional democracies*. The EU may then perhaps most fruitfully be seen as a constitutional union of constitutional states. This gives a special twist to the question of uniqueness: What is the nature of the 'meta' constitution through which constitutional polities that continue to desire to be democratic may unite? The question requires special attention to the specifics of the European context. It also requires a new constitutional theory. We present the theory of constitutional synthesis as the best way of capturing the nature and development of the EU's constitutional construct. This theory departs from both main traditions of constitutional thought, the evolutionary and the revolutionary.[1] The question that requires special attention now is whether the EU is in the process of veering off from the synthetic constitutional path and, if so, what the constitutional-democratic fallout of that will be.

In the following pages, we spell out each EU democratic polity model with emphasis on how it conceives of the constitutional dimension, how well each polity model corresponds to the EU, and what this entails in empirical and theoretical terms. In presenting the third regional-democratic model, we show how the theory of constitutional synthesis enriches the model and renders it more capable of capturing properly the EU's distinct constitutional features and challenges. The final part holds the conclusion.

Model 1: Audit democracy

This model understands the EU as a functional organisation that is only mandated to act within a delimited range of fields. The Union is set up as a supplement to the member states, and is intended to compensate for the nation states' declining capacity to handle problems independently in a globalising context.

This has direct implications for how democracy is institutionally and constitutionally configured. In the model it is the member states that authorise EU action. This is a form of authorisation that is both highly contingent and also highly confined. The member states delimit the EU's range of operations through the provisions set out in the treaties, as well as through a set of institutions that permit each and every one of them to exercise veto-power, either individually or aggregatively. The model also presumes that the Union is structured so as to effectively bar the EU from claiming its own democratic legitimacy. This means that the only legitimacy that the structure at the EU level can draw on relates to its ability to produce substantive outcomes, that is, output legitimacy (Scharpf 1999; Wallace 1993: 100).

Constitutionally speaking, the model's point of departure is the assumption that the member states have never authorised a European democratic constitution: they have established a limited structure that is devised so as to ensure that the Union's legitimacy remains derived from the democratic character of the member states; and they have also consistently taken active measures to retain core decision-making power within the Union's institutional structure. This does not rule out the label 'supranational institutions' at the Union level, but these cannot be autonomous; on the contrary, they are best understood as agents that are set up to serve the member states. They are thus subservient to the members and help to ensure that the Union carries out its tasks in a manner that is consistent with and respectful of the democratic arrangements in the member states; hence the onus on audit democracy (see Chapter 2).

This conception of the Union is associated with an instrumental, functional approach to the EU's legal order. The model therefore posits that what is understood as EU constitutional law has treaty-type character and corresponds to intergovernmental principles. But for the Union to serve as an effective problem-solver, its legal order has to be grounded on a set of legal norms of material constitutional nature,[2] which ensures a modicum of autonomy to its legal order. This entails that the Union has a material constitution, which regulates the production of legal norms and sorts out conflicts between norms within specifically delineated realms of action. This material constitution is, however, enshrined in an international treaty, because the structure does not need and would not be authorised to establish a formal, procedurally approved constitution. Underpinning this is the notion that the EU's institutional structure is unfit for a democratic constitution.

How well does this model reflect the Union's present legal-constitutional character and status? If we go back to origins, we see that the EU's main architects, notably Monnet and Spinelli, were both federalists: they envisaged a Union that would become far more than a support structure for the member states. Their vision of developing an EU that is more than and different from an international organisation has become manifest, as is shown in all the chapters of this book. But this is not the same as saying that the EU has become a federal state, which will be discussed further later.

The EU's legal structure is supranational and builds on the precepts of higher law-constitutionalism, through the combined doctrines of direct effect and supremacy of Union law.[3] This entails that the European Court of Justice is not a mere agent of the member states, but is better understood as one of the trustees of the European constitutional order. At the same time, the *procedure* for effecting treaty change through specially convened Intergovernmental Conferences (IGCs) is, formally speaking, intergovernmental.[4] Each member state is equipped with the power of veto, and is sovereign in determining the national ratification procedure. The IGC procedure has however (up to the Lisbon Treaty process) been rendered more transparent and come to include more democratic features.[5]

The most important point that distinguishes the EU from the main tenets of this model is that the EU embodies a distinct form of democratic constitutionalism. As we shall see, the Treaty is itself part of a constitutional system that structures relations between the EU institutions and the member states. This constitutional system sets the EU apart from international organisations and makes it different from a mere support structure for the member states. Union law embodies fundamental rights as a founding principle, as is reflected in the Charter of Fundamental Rights for the EU. The citizens of the member states hold European citizenship rights and are referred to as European citizens. Further, democratically speaking, when comparing it with an international organisation, the EU is marked by a democratic *surplus* (Eriksen and Fossum 2000a; Menéndez 2009). The institution of direct elections to the European Parliament (EP) in 1979 meant that from then on there was a directly elected body at the EU level. The EU thus has a democratic institution capable of appealing directly to a European democratic constituency. The EP has over time greatly increased its influence over the EU-level legislative process.[6] Its ability to authorise the composition of, and to hold to account, the main executive body, the Commission, has also gradually increased.[7] This structure has approximated to a parliamentary system, but executive-legislative relations are still structured along distinctive lines that deviate somewhat from parliamentary principles.[8]

The present-day EU contains a material constitution with basic rights protection, and an institutional arrangement with clear representative qualities. In addition, there are provisions in place to ensure transparency and popular consultation, and the EU's social constituency is made up of much more than functional groups – it includes a range of civil and political organisations.[9] In other words, the EU presents itself as a polity with a far more committing relationship to its social contingent than would be the case with any intergovernmental organisation.

This brief analysis has shown that the EU deviates from the audit democracy model in three core respects: the EU's constitutional structure is steeped in a distinct democratic constitutionalism that encompasses the EU level; the EU citizens elect a representative body at the EU level; and the EU is institutionally configured as a political system that is more than and also different from an instrument of the member states.

Does this mean that the EU is well on its way towards statehood? Has the EU, despite the many claims to its *sui generis* character, simply uplifted a state-based constitutional structure to the EU level?

Model 2: Federal multinational democracy

This model conceives of the EU as an emerging state. It posits that the ensuing structure will be a democratic constitutional state, based on direct legitimation and with its own set of coercive means. The model is of course only a template that helps us to spell out what an EU that is organised along federal state lines will look like. The main criterion in choosing a given model is not its empirical accuracy as such, but rather a broader conception of relevance: in this case that it has figured centrally in the European debate and that a state-based federation offers the most plausible representation of democratic constitutionalism. The model is also useful in that it helps us to establish *whether* the EU is on the road to independent statehood, or whether it is moving in another, non-state, direction.

The model assumes that an EU structured as a federal state will be steeped in the basic norms and principles of democratic constitutionalism and a democratic conception of legitimacy. The federal state model requires the Union to have a constitution that symbolises and reflects the existence of a European community of values. The structure would have to be grounded on a European sense of constitutional patriotism (Habermas 1994, 1996, 1998b). It would be a 'rooted' constitution: the legal embodiment of a community of values, the set of values that all Europeans share, and that ties them together.

At the same time, as noted in Chapter 2, the basic federal state model must be modified for it to sit with a distinct feature of the present-day EU, which cannot be eliminated without taking drastic measures, namely the fact that the EU is made up of a multitude of nations and national identities. The very relevance of the federal model for the EU hinges on the possibility of accommodating the federal model to this multinational fact, and the fact that nation-building at the EU level would be taking place *together with* nation-building/sustenance at the member state (and partly even regional, as sub-state) level.

The model of the multinational federal state requires constitutional recognition of this multinational fact, but *within* the norm-set of democratic constitutionalism. This means that such a multinational federal state would contain standard democratic state attributes such as basic rights, a set of representative arrangements to ensure opinion and will-formation (citizens must be able to understand themselves as the authors of the laws they are subject to), a set of coercive measures to ensure norm compliance, measures to inculcate and socialise citizens into 'Europeans', regulatory and redistributive measures, and a common European foreign and security policy.

The model places a heavy onus on the process of forging a democratic constitution because a democratic constitution must have popular authorisation. The constitution-making process also contributes to the clarification of the political system's value basis. Constitution-making establishes a set of common traditions and memories that can be seen as constitutive for Europe. If there is no common pre-political identity, it has to be created. Constitution-making is clearly a forward-looking creative act to establish a set of institutions that shape the ensuing community. But it always takes place in a given setting and can therefore also be a matter of reinvigorating those aspects of the past that lend themselves to democratic communal co-existence.

How well does this model reflect the Union's present legal-constitutional character and constitutional status? The EU is not a state; therefore, an important issue is to establish whether or how far it has proceeded down the statist route. Further, it is clear that the EU's material constitution has not been properly democratically authorised, and it does not qualify as a democratic constitution proper. The model makes clear that, in constitutional terms, the basic challenge facing the EU is to transform its material constitution into the democratic constitution of a sovereign European federal state.

The most explicit route to the democratic constitution is through the constitutional moment (Ackerman 1991, 1998).[10] Popular mobilisation provides the rationale for an explicit constitutional initiative that gets developed into a constitutional proposal and is adopted provided it receives popular sanction. The Laeken constitution-making process (2001–2005) has frequently been touted as the constitutional moment for Europe.[11] The rejection of the Constitutional Treaty (CTE) in the two referenda in France and the Netherlands has in turn been interpreted as evidence to the effect that the EU is unfit for a democratic constitution. In other words, what this appears to suggest was that the federal model was tried through initiating a constitutional moment, but it failed and therefore the federal state model was rejected.

The question is, however, whether the Laeken constitutional process was driven by this model (and whether the EU is oriented at this model) in the first place. For one, it is clear that Laeken does *not* qualify as a constitutional moment (Castiglione 2004; Fossum and Menéndez 2005; Walker 2004). There was no prior popular mobilisation or an explicitly articulated demand for a European constitution. Further, there was no explicit constitutional signal. The Laeken Declaration, which was issued by the body in charge of treaty-making/change, the European Council, did not contain an explicit constitutional authorisation: instead, it brought in the question of a possible constitution for the EU almost as an afterthought. It was the European Convention that took upon itself the task of forging a constitution for

Europe.[12] But the Convention was not in charge of the process: it was a preparatory body whose work would be approved or rejected by the European Council and subsequent ratifications. The Convention's work was heavily influenced by, and its proposal was modified by, the European Council, and it was eventually rejected in the popular referenda in France and the Netherlands in May–June 2005.

But even if the CTE had been accepted, it is important to underline that the Laeken process was not about the forging of a sovereign European federal state. The CTE was no doubt more explicit in the use of state-type language than had been the case with previous treaties, but the symbolism was not matched by substantive changes to equip the Union with the basic vestiges of statehood. There was also more continuity with the past treaties than the title suggests. The CTE ended up as a large and seamless web that failed to single out those parts that were constitutional proper.[13] Instead, the entire 300 pages plus were presented as the CTE, which saddled it with a form of constitutional overdraft that could in turn undermine its constitutional thrust by failing to single out the realm proper of 'higher law' (Fossum 2005b; Menéndez 2005). The very title of the CTE illustrates the ambiguous character of this construct: 'Treaty establishing a Constitution for Europe'. The title appears to signal intent: the equipping of the Union with the vocation to establish a proper constitution for Europe. The standard (state-based) way of construing this would be to see the CTE as paving the way for a proper constitutional moment for Europe that would in turn instantiate democratic statehood. But the process of European integration is not really about state formation, which should make us reconsider what the title alludes to. With a different understanding of the EU's constitutional structure and how it came about, the title could be understood as referring to the *making explicit* and to the lending of constitutional credence to a constitutional process that had proceeded for quite some time instead of establishing a future constitution. We need to render clear what kind of process this is and how it figures in relation to the next, the most radical, democratic polity model.

Model 3: Regional-Europe democracy

This model posits that democracy can be properly institutionalised and constitutionalised beyond the nation state. More specifically, it assumes that it is possible to establish a viable democratic constitutionalism for the supranational EU. The model differs from the two previous ones in that it is foremost an intellectual construct. The two previous models are two different formalised versions of state-based democracy, whereas this model has no precedent or organisational template that it can readily draw on.

The model takes as its point of departure the set of principles (basic human rights, democracy and rule of law) that animate the democratic constitutional state. These must then be adapted to the non-state supranational context for them to work at the regional – European – level. The ensuing democratic polity model, as depicted in Chapter 2, envisages the EU as a political community that is based on the citizens' mutual acknowledgment of their rights and duties. The supranational structure performs the functions of authorised jurisdictions. It is a system of *govern-ment*, but with weaker coercive measures and confined to a far narrower functional remit than is the case with the sovereign state. In its internal make-up, it is a fed-erally structured system of non-state-based government.[14] This presupposes that the Union's democratic legitimacy must be based on the democratic credentials of its decision-making procedures and on the protection of fundamental rights. The Union's democratic legitimacy is thus to be understood as based on citizens who are capable of seeing themselves, not only as the addressees, but also as the authors, of the law. This system of government is premised on a very thin sense of allegiance, based on a post-conventional form of consciousness. The model presup-poses a public sphere steeped in and upheld by the essential conditions of freedom, inclusion, equality, participation and open agenda. Its support resides in a reflexive notion of constitutional patriotism,[15] which posits a set of legally entrenched fun-damental rights and democratic procedures, embedded in a particular socio-cultural context, but where the ensuing political affect and identification are constantly subjected to trial by discussion. This model propounds a rights-based, procedural notion of legitimation.

The model, as outlined in Chapter 2, is actually far more explicit on the antici-pated institutional character of the polity than it is in terms of spelling out the anticipated character of the constitution. The latter has not been specified very much in procedural and substantive terms. This means that the model in Chapter 2 is not well enough spelt out to give us proper answers to the constitutional puzzles we outlined in Chapter 1 and at the beginning of this chapter.

The analytical challenge is to ensure that this model is able to capture the demo-cratic character and potential of the European constitutional experience, a highly volatile process with no historical precedent and lacking an explicitly articulated normative design on the part of the key actors/architects. We have therefore dis-cerned a constitutional theory from the European constitutional experience.[16] Before spelling this out, it is useful to highlight certain distinct features of the EU's constitutional arrangement and experience that must factor in such a theory.

The EU was forged in a historical situation with a certain 'cosmopolitan opening',[17] reinforced through national constitutional provisions that embedded the national constitution in a broader international legal framework with a clear cosmopolitan orientation.[18] Five out of the original six member states had constitutional provisions that not only authorised, but also mandated, the active participation of national institutions in the creation of a supranational legal order, as the only way to fully realise the principles that underlie the national constitution. The distinguishing post-war feature was that these states recognised that they could only retain democracy through a form of binding co-operation that would also have direct constitutional-democratic implications. These are some of the key traits that distinguish the European effort to establish a supranational European constitu-tion – that simultaneously incorporates established constitutional democracies but without abrogating their constitutional identities as national constitutions. These and other features, we have argued, can be systematised into a distinct theoretical approach to constitution-making, which, if successful, could form a viable alternative to the evolutionary and revolutionary approaches to constitution-making.

Constitutional synthesis

Constitutional synthesis represents a new theoretical approach to constitution-making.[19] It refers to how a new constitutional order can be created out of a set of already existing (and persisting) constitutional arrangements. The process is powered by a regulatory ideal, that of a common constitutional law, which forms the *leitmotif* for a process of constitutional synthesis: of an 'ever closer' putting in common of national constitutional norms (normative synthesis), and of the development of a supranational institutional structure (institutional development).

In the following, we will spell out the main features of this approach as the most apt way of theorising European constitution-making. It provides us with a clearer sense of how the EU has over time established an institutional-constitutional structure that has clear affinities with the third regional-democratic model. It will shed added light on how, and the extent to which, the present-day EU still falls well short of this model in democratic constitutional terms. We will demonstrate that through the lessons we discern from the EU experience.

Constitutional synthesis entails that the constitutions of the participating states take on a new *seconded* role as a part of the emerging collective constitutional law of the new polity. Each national constitution then starts living a 'double constitutional life': each continues as a national constitutional arrangement, while it also simultaneously forms a part of the collective – European – constitution. Constitutional synthesis therefore presumes a substantive identity between national constitutional norms and Community constitutional norms. In this scheme, European integration presupposes the creation of a new legal order, but not the creation of a new set of constitutional norms; a key source of the legitimacy of the new legal order is indeed the transfer of national constitutional norms to the new legal order.

A further distinguishing mark of constitutional synthesis is a distinct sequence and process dynamic in the development of the new constitutional order. The 'synthetic founding moment' is one where a rudimentary supranational institutional structure is set up. The details and reach of this are worked out over time, as the process of synthesis proceeds and comes to cover a broader range of policy areas. Constitutional synthesis combines normative synthesis and institutional development and consolidation, two processes with different inner logics: the former exerting a centripetal pull towards homogeneity, the latter with far stronger built-in centrifugal elements. This complex structure is one where there is one supranational law but several institutions that apply the supranational law in an authoritative manner. The peculiar combination of a single law and a pluralistic institutional structure stems from the fact that there is no ultimate hierarchical structuring of supranational and national institutions. The peculiar combination is, if anything, compounded by the pluralistic proclivities of institutional consolidation at the supranational level. The ensuing structure will therefore likely be far more fragile and susceptible to upsets, whether brought on from external environmental shocks or upsets, or from built-in tensions. Such a complex and compound process has a certain built-in propensity for self-subversion.

This constitutional theory provides us with a number of relevant lessons that help to clarify where the EU stands in relation to the regional-democratic polity model. The first lesson is that the process of constitutional synthesis relies on those very principles, the core constitutional-democratic ones that animate the modern democratic *Rechtsstaat*. Constitutional synthesis comes with a mandate to establish a system of government whose legitimacy would naturally be based on compliance with the core principles that animate the democratic constitutional states that came together to form it. In the EU these principles had to be configured to support the establishment of a system of supranational *government* at the EU level, a system of authorised rule that relies on member states for their effectuation. The theory of constitutional synthesis offers the best way of accounting for how this process has been taking place (it is far from complete and might even unravel). This process offers no automatic assurance of state formation. That is not to deny that constitutional synthesis could over time produce a state at the European level, but that would then effectively also end the process of synthesis.

The second lesson refers to a distinct take on the manner in which the system of European government is authorised. The regional-democratic model as presented in Chapter 2 emphasises the development of democratic institutions at the EU level – as part of a broader process of establishing a democratic infrastructure which European citizens orientate themselves at and identify with. Constitutional synthesis shows how this has come about, and, in doing so, it also underlines an important distinguishing trait of this process: the supranational structure (that is established at the EU level) comes equipped with a *conditional* constitutional-democratic licence from the member states. This democratic licence necessarily has to be *conditional* (and based on the need for compliance with democratic norms). The licence of course covers the development of an own set of democratic institutions that will be capable of establishing and sustaining a European democratic constituency, and it provides specific requirements for how European-level integration can redeem this in constitutional-democratic terms over time.

The development and gradual strengthening of the EP show how this process has manifested itself in elements of responsible government at the EU level. The supranational system of government at the EU level has moved closer to parliamentarianism, but it nevertheless still falls well short of that. This supranational structure contains important institutional and procedural vestiges to sustain the conditional character of the democratic licence – in such a manner as to limit the EU level's independence. This includes explicit national democratic controls/safeguards that are baked into the decision-making procedures at the EU level. As one illustration, consider how the democratic authorisation of the EU executive continues to take place. The main EU executive is located in the Commission. The Commission president and its members are composed from national lists of candidates proposed to the European Council and elected by the EP.[20] This cumbersome procedure reflects how the selection of the Union's main executive agent first activates the agents of the national constituencies before the proposal is put to the body in charge of representing the European constituency. This joint yet sequential activation of constituencies at the member state and at the EU level is a clear illustration of how the continued presence of the conditional democratic licence delimits EU-level parliamentarianism. In federal states, sub-units would have no direct say in the process of selecting the central executive.[21]

The contingent democratic licence also continues to structure and to give a distinct twist to inter-parliamentary relations in the EU.[22] Many of these features can be traced back to how the logic of constitutional synthesis has put its mark on the EU's democratisation process. As noted in Chapter 5, this process has not proceeded along the standard federal state lines, but has taken on the shape of a multilevel parliamentary field (Crum and Fossum 2009).[23] With the Lisbon Treaty's protocols on national parliaments and subsidiarity,[24] national parliaments are directly involved in the decision-making process at the EU level.[25] These developments raise distinctly new challenges pertaining to democratic authorisation and accountability.

A distinguishing mark of the theory of constitutional synthesis is that the notion of democratic conditionality applies foremostly to the supranational level, but the theory also has bearings on the entire multilevel system. It unleashes both vertical and horizontal processes. In the EU the most obvious is of course the vertical dimension – through the strengthening of the democratic institutions at the EU level. But there is also a horizontal dimension, which refers to the need to sustain workable constitutional democracy in the member states.[26] This process requires mutual monitoring and oversight, across member states and across levels of government.

Consider how the theory of constitutional synthesis understands the process of adding new member states. This is a process that adds an important 'diagonal' component; it shows that constitutional synthesis has a distinct take on how to ensure the democratic dimension in the process of adding new member states (what in the EU is misleadingly called enlargement, but should be understood as reconstitution-alisation [Eriksen *et al.* 2005]). The theory takes as its point of departure that EU enlargement is based on democratic conditionality, to ensure that only constitutional democracies become members. This process of harmonisation must be, and actually also is, initiated well before an applicant joins the EU. The institutions at the EU level are operating the democratic entrance criteria. This process necessarily feeds back on the EU, which, in monitoring the applicant's democratic credentials, knows that its own democratic credibility is also a part of the equation. The theory posits that the EU cannot serve as a credible democratic monitor unless it fulfils the conditions in the democratic licence afforded it by the member states. Similarly, the member states must retain workable democracy to sustain credible democratic conditionality (in relation to the EU level and to the applicant[s]). It is presumed that, over time, as the process of constitutional synthesis proceeds, the institutions at the EU level equip themselves with stronger democratic credentials.

In principle, then, the process of adding new members is structured so as to help reinforce both the vertical and the horizontal democratisation characteristics of constitutional synthesis. *Whether*, or better the extent to which, this is borne out in practice is a more difficult question. What is clear is that, from a democratic perspective, the process is sustainable only so long as (a) the institutions at the EU level can effectively ensure democracy at the EU level; and (b) the member states (new and old) are able to provide mutually reinforcing support for democracy.[27] It should be obvious that the theory of constitutional synthesis presupposes that this mutually reinforcing process does not stop at the point of entry; it must be a continuous process that operates on all levels simultaneously.

Reality is more complex and falls well short of this ideal: both new and old member states have at times violated basic civil and political rights, including mobility rights, and have taken measures to roll back democratic arrangements and/or sought to quell opposition. These are important horizontal limits to synthesis, which, if powerful enough, will undercut the entire process. The financial crisis has also brought up a vertical problem with EU-level institutions (and the International Monetary Fund) intervening in member states' internal democratic processes.[28]

Nevertheless, it is worth pointing out that the *theory* of constitutional synthesis comes with a rather complete conception of how the process of constitutionally ensured democratisation in the EU could unfold. The conditional character of the democratic licence afforded the EU injects a strong justification requirement on the EU, which must in an ongoing manner justify that integration is compatible with the core tenets of constitutional democracy. The same applies to member states, which cannot credibly seek to enforce the democratic licence unless they can demonstrate that they are in line with democratic norms. These comments show how the theory of constitutional synthesis fills in the regional-democratic model; adapts it somewhat through the onus on the contingent character of the democratic licence; makes the model more sensitive to the interaction between the EU level and the member states; and underlines that the process of EU democratisation is one that encompasses all levels and locates them in a broad and encompassing structure of mutually reinforcing normative-democratic expectations.

But the third lesson underlines that today's reality appears to be *moving away from* what this theory presupposes. The EU is marked by *stymied* synthesis and heightened uncertainty as to the future viability of synthesis (even if the EU is able to weather the present crisis). We see this in a number of features and developments, including the rejection of constitutional status to the Lisbon Treaty; in the removal (from the CTE) of the reference to the primacy of Community law (now listed as Declaration 17); in the lower symbolic status assigned to the European Charter (incorporated through mere reference); and in a number of institutional and other features and developments.

One example is that the EU of today falls well short of being a uniform system of supranational government. It is better understood as organised along two sets of closely imbricated institutional structures that may be seen as associated with two different conceptions of integration (supranational and inter/transgovernmental). We can summarise these in, on the one hand, the supranational Community, and, on the other hand, the so-called intergovernmental but more fittingly labelled *transgovernmental* (Wallace 2005) component, mainly pertaining to the Common Foreign and Security Policy (CFSP)/Common Defence and Security Policy (CDSP), although core elements of this Council-led institutional procedure are also applied to what remains of Pillar III (Justice and Home Affairs [JHA]). What is notable regarding the second procedure is that this has changed from a mere intergovernmental to a more institutionalised transgovernmental system (Smith 2004), with decision-making increasingly lifted to the European level,[29] but where this transgovernmental component is still based on national democratic authorisation, because the EP has obtained only some limited powers of scrutiny. The effect is that far from all the tasks that are carried out at the EU level are properly democratically authorised. This applies to the limited role of the supranational system of democratic government; it also applies to clear operational limits to democratic authorisation through the national channel. There is also in the EU a structural discrepancy between market-making and market-correcting institutions and procedures (Menéndez 2009; Scharpf 2010), a structural discrepancy that effectively weakens the substantive identity between national constitutional norms and Community constitutional norms. A similar argument applies to a Monetary Union upheld by an independent central bank but without a stabilising Fiscal Union. These instances of stymied synthesis are if anything amplified by the EU's turn towards 'governance' through 'soft law' and a managerial approach to politics. A further manifestation of this increased discrepancy stems from the increased role of *vertical* conflicts that can undermine the logic of synthesis. These are cases in which EU law 'emancipates' itself through diverging from the constitutional traditions common to the member states.

One of the clearest examples that the EU may be veering off the synthetic constitutional path is procedural, and pertains to the highly secretive and narrowly intergovernmental procedure that was used in forging the Lisbon Treaty. This shows that the gradual opening and democratisation of the treaty amendment process that preceded Lisbon (and is a mark of constitutional synthesis) was at Lisbon completely reversed with a return to a narrowly defined and conducted intergovernmental procedure. The result is a significant discrepancy between the substance of the treaty and the procedure of forging it. An undemocratic and elite-driven procedure cannot but undermine the democratic credentials of the EU's constitutional construct.

The European Council's denial of constitutional status to the Lisbon Treaty simply underlines the fact that the Lisbon Treaty has increased ambiguity and uncertainty as to the constitutional character of EU law. This may signal an end to the EU's synthetic-constitutional vocation; deprive EU-level democracy of its symbolic constitutional association; and ultimately empty out EU democracy.

Conclusion

This chapter has focused on the question of what constitution for what kind of Union. It was shown that this question still continues to haunt the EU after several decades of almost continuous constitutional reform (what could be referred to as the unfinished constitutional season of the EU). High levels of political contestation are mixed in with considerable conceptual confusion to render the debate very complex and multifaceted. This chapter sought to address the question through devising a conceptual 'map' and briefly assessing the EU terrain against this map. It was found that the EU did not resemble very much either of the first two different state-based models. This opened the door to consider it against the third, the most radical democratic polity model with a clear cosmopolitan bent. The model is an intellectual construct without any real-life examples to draw on. It was therefore necessary to spell it out in more detail for it to work in the constitutional realm. In order to do so, we had to take the EU's constitutional development properly into account. But this forced us to consider the distinct features of the EU's constitutional experience, thus prompting us to devise a distinctly new theory of supranational constitution-making (which is more in line with how we conceptualise the third model in Chapter 2 than it is with standard notions of transnational multilevel governance). The characteristic mix of the regulatory ideal of a single legal order and a pluralistic institutional structure renders both EU politics and law genuinely pluralistic. This considerable degree of complexity and sophistication was essential to gain the democratic licence to integrate, but becomes a liability as integration proceeds.

This chapter has shown how this theory could be used to 'fill in' the regional-democratic model with constitutional substance. It was found that the EU's development has approximated to this model, but also that there are clear signs that the constitutional synthetic dimension has reached the point at which it cannot any longer foster integration without revealing the problematic legitimacy basis of the European constitutional settlement as it has evolved. The effect is to heighten uncertainty as to the legitimacy of the EU's democratic arrangements and its legal order, which will be increasingly understood as imposed upon citizens instead of being the result of a democratic choice to integrate.

This is the constitutional democratic backdrop against which we need to understand the present crisis facing the EU. The asymmetric economic and monetary union that constitutes the fundamental constitutional structure of the Eurozone is a clear manifestation of a growing distortion in the pattern of synthetic constitutional transformation. While asymmetric monetary and economic union allowed member states to constitute tightly structured webs of mutual interdependence without deciding on the ultimate principles and institutional structure of fiscal and wage policies, such arrangements introduced an element of normative inconsistency and in the long run weakened the institutional capacities of public institutions, while reinforcing the structural power of big capitalist firms. The net effect of monetary integration and capital liberalisation has been both to undercut the degree of public control over the use of capital and to undermine the traditional arrangements that limited the degree of states' exposure to financial risk. If to that we add the fact that the Eurozone was never close to a perfect currency area, the present crisis was more or less foreordained. Uncertainty only concerned when and which member states would melt down.

This results in a lose-lose situation for the Union. Trapped in the 'governance' mind-frame and its attendant managerial conception of politics, the EU seems condemned to play a central role that comes close to odious in fronting demands for cutbacks and for reinforcing the need to honour debts.

This is a point in time when democratic legitimacy and constitutional commitment figure as the greatest and most precious of all assets. Recent developments show an EU whose constitutional-democratic asset base appears to be drawn down and undercut – a perilous moment for Europe indeed.

Notes

1 On the evolutionary tradition, see, for instance, Bagehot 1865; Dicey 1866. On the revolutionary tradition, see, for instance, Ackerman 1991, 1998; Arendt 1970.
2 The *formal constitution* represents the set of legal norms contained in a document (or compilation of documents) that in social practice is referred to as the constitution. The material conception of the constitution is based on a different consideration of what figures as prevalent social practice in a given society. Instead of considering the relevance of the social practice that is already labelled under the heading of a constitution, it starts from the other end and focuses on what social practices regard as being the basic norms of a given society. The normative conception of the constitution is composed of those legal norms that present certain normative properties, notably democracy and basic rights (Fossum and Menéndez 2011; Menéndez 2004).
3 The doctrine of direct effect of Community law had a clear and open constitutional import because it affirmed that the Community, not a national norm, was to determine the effect of Community norms *in all national legal systems*.
4 It is imbued with strong vestiges of international diplomacy (cf. Curtin 1993; Fossum and Menéndez 2005).
5 There are clear points of resemblance with the Canadian constitutional procedure (Fossum 2007a; Fossum and Menéndez 2011).
6 Hix *et al.* (2007: 3) claimed that 'In a rather short space of time, a matter of decades rather than centuries, the European Parliament has evolved from an unelected consultative body to one of the most powerful elected assemblies in the world.' The EP has developed a lot, but this particular claim overstates its case. See Eriksen and Fossum forthcoming.
7 The introduction of the co-decision procedure (in the Lisbon Treaty labelled as the ordinary legislative procedure, cf. Article 294) is a case in point.
8 Within the so-called community method, the independent European Commission has the exclusive right to present legislative and policy proposals; these are adopted by the EP and the Council; and the European Court of Justice maintains the institutional balance (Majone 2005: 44). This structure falls short of parliamentarianism, for several reasons. The first is that the EP election procedure offers no clear safeguard for European citizens' voting preferences through parliamentary elections to carry direct implications for the composition of European government. The second is that European political parties (with the partial exception of the Greens), are still organisationally tied to the nation state level and have not developed Europe-wide party organisations: 'European parties play virtually no role in European Parliament *electoral* politics' (Hix *et al.* 2005:

50). The party constellations formed in the EP after elections are very weakly anchored in the member states' party systems. The third reason is that the Council has executive functions (with the Council Secretariat even playing the role of agenda-setter in the CFSP and ESDP [cf. Curtin 2009] [the latter changes to CDSP in the Lisbon Treaty]), which the EP cannot effectively control. See also Chapter 5 on the distinct structure of EU representation.

9 Fossum 2005a; Liebert and Trenz 2010; see also Chapter 7.

10 Applied to the EU, see Fossum and Menéndez 2005, 2011.

11 The European Convention president Valéry Giscard d'Estaing (2003) noted that 'the European Union now stands at a crossroads, not wholly unlike that of Philadelphia 1787.' ('The Henry Kissinger Lecture', at the Library of Congress, Washington, 11 February. Available at: http://www.loc.gov/loc/kluge/fellowships/lectures-destaing.html

12 Peter Norman (2003), who followed the entire Convention process, tellingly labelled his account as 'The Accidental Constitution – The Story of the European Convention'.

13 The detailed provisions in Part III, for instance, retained key vestiges of the pillar structure, notably the second pillar, despite its removal from Part I.

14 Note that a federal entity need not be a state (cf. Elazar 1987).

15 Markell (2000) has discerned a more critical, less identitarian mode of constitutional patriotism in Habermas' political writings. See also Fossum 2008. For the standard formulation of Habermas' conception of constitutional patriotism, see Habermas 1994, 1996a, 1998b.

16 This is precisely what we do in Fossum and Menéndez 2011.

17 The EU, as Jürgen Habermas (1998b) has noted, is a case of learning from disaster. See also Chapter 10 and Fossum 2011a.

18 Article 79 (3) of the German Basic Law's *eternity clause* deems amendments that might negatively affect human dignity or the principle of democracy to be unconstitutional. The Court has recently noted that the Basic Law's eternity guarantee:

> . . . makes clear . . . that the Constitution of the Germans, in correspondence with the international development which has taken place in particular since the existence of the United Nations, has a universal foundation which is not supposed to be amendable by positive law. (The Federal Constitutional Court 'Judgement [GCC]', 2 BvE 2/08 vom 30.6.2009, para 218. Available at: http://www.bverfg.de/entscheidungen/es20090630_2bve000208en.html)

19 The following account of constitutional synthesis draws directly on Fossum and Menéndez 2011.

20

> Taking into account the elections to the European Parliament and after having held the appropriate consultations, the European Council, acting by a qualified majority, shall propose to the European Parliament a candidate for President of the Commission. This candidate shall be elected by the European Parliament by a majority of its component members. If he does not obtain the required majority, the European Council, acting by a qualified majority, shall within one month propose a new candidate who shall be elected by the European Parliament following the same procedure. (Lisbon Treaty, Article 17.7, Consolidated versions of the Treaty on European Union and the Treaty on the Functioning of the European Union, *Official Journal of the European Union*, 2008/c 115/01)

21 This strong element of such sub-unit influence is even more pronounced in those issue areas where the Commission shares executive functions with the Council (in core aspects of common foreign and security policy/European security and defence policy), and where the EP plays a limited (at most a scrutiny) role. The question here is whether these issue areas are sufficiently democratically controlled in the first place. See Chapter 8 in this volume.

22 This structure, as we note in Chapter 5, raises distinct authorisation and accountability problems.
23 A distinguishing mark of this field is that the parliaments are linked together through such mechanisms as the Conference of Parliamentary Committees for Union Affairs (COSAC) and various EU legal provisions.
24 Lisbon Treaty, Article 12 and Protocols 1 and 2.
25 We also see elements of the parliamentary field logic in the manner in which the European semester procedure is structured (but where the supranational dimension is less pronounced because of the weak role of the EP).
26 Member states that violate basic rights or undercut their democratic arrangements can no longer credibly effectuate the conditional democratic licence. When such violations are grave enough, the process of constitutional synthesis will break down.
27 This point effectively provides a democratic guideline to the speed and scope of EU enlargement: only at such a rate and at such a scope as to ensure sustainable democracy.
28 *Financial Times* journalist Leigh Phillips quoted the Commission's economy spokesman Amadeu Altafaj-Tardio as telling the Irish before the last election that:

> The citizens of Ireland have an important date with democracy tomorrow. . . . They'll have an important job to do because they will be applying the programme which was negotiated with the EU, the IMF and the European Central Bank and their international partners. ('The Junta of Experts Tells Us: "Vote how you Like, but Policies Cannot Change"', *EUobserver*, 17 June 2011, available at: http://euobserver.com/7/32501).

Another example is the requirement that Greek parties should form a coalition government to deal with the debt crisis.
29 It is more than a simple aggregation of disparate national voices; it works to facilitate common national positions; it has a legal basis in the treaties; and there is a gradual strengthening of Brussels-based institutional capacity, so-called 'Brusselising' (Allen 1998; Christiansen and Vanhoonacker 2008; Duke and Vanhoonacker 2006a; Smith 2004).

5

THE EU POLITY AND ITS
PATTERN OF REPRESENTATION

The multilevel parliamentary field

John Erik Fossum and Ben Crum

Introduction

It is widely held that the European Union (EU) harbours a democratic deficit. Most of the democratic deficit proponents understand it as a representative-democratic shortfall. There are two readings of how this shortfall manifests itself in the multi-level configuration of the EU. One understands the EU as undercutting national representative systems of government, the very harbingers of popular sovereignty (e.g., Grimm 1995; Graf Kielmansegg 1996). The other recognises that, whereas new institutions of democratic representation have been established at the European level, most importantly associated with the European Parliament (EP), this has not been enough to offset European integration's weakening of national (and regional) representative systems (e.g., Føllesdal and Hix 2006).

But there are also those who challenge the very notion that the EU has a democratic deficit. This amounts to a second strand of debate, which argues that couching the debate on the EU's democratic character and quality as an EU-level representative defect is akin to barking up the wrong tree. Giandomenico Majone (1998, 2005) argues that the Union's distinctive confederal character and relatively limited scope of competences render Union-level representative democracy unnecessary. Many analysts concur because they hold that international arrangements cannot be evaluated by traditional standards of representative democracy. International systems are still premised on national democratic systems. Hence, they can be evaluated by means of less demanding standards of legitimacy or accountability (Dahl 1999; Keohane 2002; Moravcsik 2002).

Yet another strand of debate argues that, instead of insisting on specific terms of representation, we must re-consider democracy itself, along transnational deliberative democracy lines. James Bohman argues that, in today's interdependent world, '[t]he main issue is not the real or supposed democratic deficit, but the democratic criterion itself . . .' (Bohman 2007b: 10).[1] The upshot is that we need to rethink the meaning of democracy, in particular the presumption that democracy requires a single *demos*. Bohman's alternative, transnational conception of democracy is based on *multiple demoi*. To Bohman, deliberative democracy, when properly institutionalised within a decentred reflexive system, can serve as a democratically viable near-substitute for representative democracy. The EU offers the closest approximation to such a system.

Other deliberative theorists, notably the proponents of deliberative democratic supranationalism (Eriksen 2005, 2009a; Eriksen and Fossum 2004, 2007a), disagree, not so much with Bohman's diagnosis, but rather with his cure. The EU's deliberative traits cannot make up for its representative defects. Thus, in line with the first position listed earlier, the EU must address these representative defects. At the same time, Bohman is correct in noting that majoritarian representative arrangements are difficult to transpose to the EU without significant frictions, for several reasons that will be spelt out later. However, many of the EU's deliberative traits serve rather narrow groups of stakeholders and elites, rather than citizens in general; hence they cannot make up for the Union's democratically deficient representative arrangements.

This brief overview of the main positions in the democratic deficit debate reveals that the debate is not simply one of how best to transpose a familiar (state-based) representative-democratic system to the EU level. As underlined in Chapters 1 and 2, the debate is far more profound: it pits different conceptions of democracy against each other. These conceptions of democracy differ in what they see the key challenge to consist in; they reside in qualitatively different conceptions of what the EU is (and should be); and they refer back to different normative standards. Accordingly, we cannot disentangle the debate, and get a proper handle on the different positions, without clarifying what these underlying conceptions of the EU are.

What is of particular relevance to this chapter is that each such conception comes with its own distinct understanding of the character and the structure of democratic representation in the EU. Therefore, in order to understand the character and quality of EU democracy, we need to outline the three democratic polity models and consider them against the character of the representative structure that the EU already has. This is because, as we will show, this representative structure holds a number of distinct – unique – traits. Insofar as these unique traits really distinguish the EU from other representative systems, it makes sense to accord them proper weight in the broader undertaking of clarifying the character of the EU as a political system. In modern democracies, representative arrangements are central components in the definition and delineation of the democratic constituency and how this manifests itself in the very character of the polity. Accordingly, there is a need to clarify the EU's distinct representative traits, and, further, to outline and discuss each model once these elements have been properly taken into consideration.

In the extension of this, the main question that we address in this chapter is: Which conception of the EU *qua polity* fits best with what we know about the representative structure? We start from the notion that it makes sense to conceive of the present-day EU's representative structure as a 'Multilevel Parliamentary Field' (Crum and Fossum 2009). The label 'parliamentary field' has been chosen to highlight the central role of representative bodies in the EU. These bodies, we argue, make up a particular field configuration that forms part of a much broader system of representative arrangements in the EU (cf. Lord and Pollak 2010; Pollak *et al.* 2009).

On this basis, we proceed with the question: What does the EU's Multilevel Parliamentary Field suggest about the character of the EU polity? When we hold this concept up against the three models that were developed in Chapter 2, is the nature of the EU's representative structure best understood in terms appropriate to a special purpose kind of international organisation, an entity that is set up to serve the member states through performing functions that have been delegated to it (Model 1)? Or does the EU's representative structure better fit an understanding of the EU as a federal state in the making (Model 2)? Or does it indeed point to an EU that is a subset of a new emerging global-cosmopolitan system best understood as a regional-European system of *government* (which does not necessarily amount to a state) (Model 3)? These three conceptions have been spelled out in Chapter 2 to capture the most important polity options and axes of debate on the EU's democratic character. As will become clear later, they vary greatly in terms of how accommodating they are to the notion of the Multilevel Parliamentary Field. So to the extent that the field brings to light certain distinctive features of the nature of democratic representation in the EU – most notably its dispersed character across different parliamentary sites at different levels – and these features only figure within a certain polity configuration, the field can usefully serve to discriminate between the different models.

Given that in this chapter we are concerned with the 'fit' between what we know about the structure of representation in the EU and the type of political entity it constitutes, our approach appears to have a certain 'bottom-up' orientation, in that we actively use what we know about the character of the representative-democratic system to clarify the character of the EU polity. But we do not simply approach this task from a 'bottom-up' perspective. We spell out the models in Chapter 2 in a more *recursive* manner, that is, we specify the distinctive features of the representative configuration that the EU has developed (the EU Multilevel Parliamentary Field) as part of the delineation of the democratic polity models. Thus, in the following pages, we first outline the main features of the Multilevel Parliamentary Field and justify why it is relevant to the study of the EU. Second, we flesh out the three EU polity models. Here we discuss how compatible each is to the Multilevel Parliamentary Field, and how the field itself shapes the third model. The third and last part holds the conclusion, including a brief summary of theoretical implications.

Representation EU-style: the Multilevel Parliamentary Field

A distinctive feature of the European integration process is that it takes place in *a setting of already existing representative democracies*. The integration process unfolds amidst these existing arrangements; the forging of the EU takes place *by and through* them: each member state is directly involved in the process; it can veto any treaty amendment it does not agree with; the EU is based on consensual decision-making; and the EU itself has very weak sanctioning mechanisms. Whereas the representative structure in the EU is two-pronged – from the EP to a European constituency, and from each national parliament to its respective national constituency – this system deviates in important respects from the two channels of representation that we normally associate with multilevel federal systems: a House of Representatives that represents the people directly, and a Senate or *Bundesrat* that represents them through their states. This serves to underline that, even if we side with the majority of researchers who claim that the EU needs a viable representative-democratic system, we cannot directly transpose a statist or a state-derived mode of thinking representative government to the EU, without first modifying it.

The concept of the Multilevel Parliamentary Field provides an apt alternative. It depicts a system whereby parliamentary-representative institutions make up an organisational field, that is, a set of 'institutions that, in the aggregate, constitute a recognised area of institutional life', with some element of connectedness and structural equivalence (Powell and DiMaggio 1991). What keeps the components of the field together is not a single hierarchical organisational structure but rather patterns of interaction combined with a shared function and the role perception that comes with it: that of representing people's interests in EU decision-making.[2] Thus, the field can encompass a wide range of parliamentary institutions at different levels within the EU. The characteristic features of the EU's parliamentary field are discerned through the character and density of inter-parliamentary interaction[3]; the character of the field's constitutive units (parliaments); and the manner in which these two dimensions interact to give overall shape to the field. Both main features are distinct: the EU is marked by a whole web of arrangements that link parliaments – at national and EU level – together; at the same time, national parliaments and national representative systems vary greatly across the EU.

An organisational field is an apt analytical device to capture these traits because it does not have to be made up of organisations that are mirror images of each other. Pierre Bourdieu (1980), the grandfather of the field notion, suggests that, whereas each field has its own distinct norms and structure, it is also clear that the actors within a given field share certain dispositions that incline them to act in certain ways. All parliamentarians are socialised into the norm-set, the role conceptions, and the ways of understanding their own and other's behaviour that are characteristic of parliamentary-representative bodies. This is not something that emerges through relatively sporadic networked interaction; it is a phenomenon and a process that runs much deeper, and is much more entrenched: in language codes and the standard repertoire of organisational forms that we attribute to modern societies; in normative conceptions; in legal provisions; in cultural expectations; and in organisational forms. Students of organisational fields then also underline how organisational fields are sites of isomorphic pressure that operate through coercion, mimesis and normative pressure.[4] But we cannot *a priori* assume that isomorphism will be the dominant tendency; notably within the complex and dynamic European setting, there are also strong fissiparous and centrifugal forces.

The EU's organisational complexity is one central feature that renders it distinct from the main existing organisational configurations in place when thinking about representative arrangements in complex and composite political entities, namely parliamentary network (cf. Slaughter 2004: 104–30) and two-channelled federal system of representation. All EU member states are representative democracies, and they are integrated in the EU polity. This helps to ensure that the EU's Multilevel Parliamentary Field has a greater level of coherence than a parliamentary network, in legal-organisational structures to some extent, but certainly in the norms and orientations that permeate the field. The notion of the Multilevel Parliamentary Field recognises the normative character of parliaments as the main sites for democratic representation, but it also accommodates to the fact that there are qualitative differences between these parliaments, notably the distinctive role held by the EP.

The Multilevel Parliamentary Field also holds traits that set it apart from mainstream federal representative-organisational models, because the field neither presupposes institutional symmetry among representative bodies, nor that they must fit into a clearly laid-out (hierarchical) organisational structure. The Multilevel Parliamentary Field allows for greater variation among the component units and patterns of formal and informal parliamentary interaction (horizontally and vertically), and hence is compatible with less hierarchical and more loosely coupled patterns of interaction than those of federal states. Still, such coupling is premised on a set of basic values and a shared democratic practice.

The upshot is that the EU contains a distinct pattern of representation that we need to take into consideration when discussing the nature and quality of the EU as a democratic polity.

The Multilevel Parliamentary Field and EU polity models

The EU is a highly contested entity. To take adequate heed of this fact, we discuss how well the conception of the EU representative structure in terms of a Multilevel Parliamentary Field sits with the three conceptions of the EU polity outlined in Chapter 2, and what the field does to the model(s). The first position focuses on the EU as a system of audit democracy (Eriksen and Fossum 2002, 2007a). In this view, the member states continue to be the strongholds of representative democracy; the EU level undertakes tasks that the member states have conferred upon it but subject to member state oversight and control; and the EU level maintains democratic audit mechanisms as an additional safeguard. The second position focuses on the EU as a federal state in the making (cf. Morgan 2005), made up of representative democratic arrangements at both main levels of government: EU and member state, and with a division of powers and competences between them akin to that of federal states. The third position focuses on the EU as a fledgling regional-cosmopolitan – non-state – entity, made up of representative governing arrangements at multiple levels (Eriksen and Fossum 2007a). By including configurations that are modified versions of nation state-based democracy *and* a configuration that is a clear departure from the nation state, the analysis below can also shed light on whether the multilevel configuration that makes up the EU is *based on* and actively propounds nation state-based presuppositions; or whether it has developed new and non–nation state-based standards.

Each position involves a distinct model of EU representative democracy, including the proper repository of (parliamentary) sovereignty; the appropriate distribution of authority (or hierarchy) between the institutions; their interaction; and the acceptable level of internal diversity. We discuss the models in relation to the main tasks that parliaments undertake, which (as seen from a deliberative democratic perspective) are: legislation/budgeting; control/accountability; and deliberative forum.

Legislative/budgeting refers to parliaments' effective role in the process of decision-making; and their ability to formulate, pursue and control the political agenda, issues and spending priorities. Control/accountability speaks to representative bodies' ability to hold the executive to account, and the character, range and effectiveness of mechanisms for audit, monitoring and control. Deliberative forum refers to parliaments as deliberative bodies and forums for public debate: bodies that adopt issues, frame issues, structure debates and provide justifications to the public for legislative and other action.

The model of audit democracy

The first model can be labelled as 'audit democracy' and envisages the EU as a functional regime set up to address the kinds of problems that the member states cannot resolve when acting independently. This model presumes that the member states delegate competences to the Union, which contains bodies that ensure (mainly through some form of audit) that the powers thus delegated do not undermine the member states' representative-democratic institutions. The delegation of competence to the institutions at the Union level entails a form of self-binding on the part of the member states; the presumption is that such delegation comes with controls imposed by the member states, in order to safeguard that they remain the source of the EU's democratic legitimacy.

For the EU to comply with the democratic tenets of the nation state model, the Union's structure must be set up in such a manner as to ensure that the member states retain core decision-making powers within the Union's institutional structure. The audit democracy model concedes that this national democratic authorisation draws on some form of a Union-wide representative body, like the EP. However, it would serve the task of democratic audit,[5] and not that of a fully-fledged representative democratic system. The representative body would, together with transnational and/or supranational institutions (such as a court and an executive), be set up to help member states supervise and control the Union's actions. These would be specifically mandated to hold intergovernmental decision-making bodies to account.

The audit democracy model is based on the notion that the representative-democratic dimension of the EU integration process foremost exhibits a *path-dependent* pattern of change, where no real substantive change has taken place at the national parliamentary level. Insofar as there is a change, it is associated with the EP developing democratic audit functions at the European level. The European-level representatives undertake audit functions; such a delimited type of activity certainly does not involve the construction of an EU-level democratic constituency.

The extent to which this structure can be conceived of as a Multilevel Parliamentary Field hinges on the one hand on the EP's role as an audit body, that is, its role as a further parliamentary check on national executives, in conjunction with national parliaments, and on the other on inter-parliamentary interaction. The presumption embedded in the notion of audit democracy is that the EP will, through standing committees and special enquiries, through debates and hearings and so forth, shed light on the nooks and crannies of the EU system, and thereby aid the national parliaments in their efforts to hold their executives accountable when they operate at the EU level. The main function of this system at the EU level would be that of deliberative audit; hence, the EP would be barred from undertaking several of the main tasks that parliaments normally undertake. Little would be expected of it in terms of legislation/budgeting and also its control/accountability function would be limited to soft controls without any substantial sanctions put at its disposal. In contrast, national parliaments would retain all of their traditional roles. They would be expected to monitor and control EU decision-making through their governments and also ultimately control EU legislation (albeit indirectly) through the confidence that they bestow upon their governments.

It is difficult to understand this system of deliberative audit as a Multilevel Parliamentary Field, for several reasons. First, because each member state would retain its own controlling power of the central institutions and not be very dependent on any other parliament; thus there would be little horizontal inter-parliamentary interaction. Second, the system of delegated powers is designed to deter the central audit body, the EP, from taking on a greater legislative and decision-making role; thus there are clear vertical restrictions. Third, because the deliberative audit function does not require very strong institutional measures, which underlines the weakness of the vertical control dimension. As a consequence, the Multilevel Parliamentary Field has little purchase on the audit democracy model. Indeed, on balance, the audit democracy model is far more compatible with a weakly integrated parliamentary *network*.

Having said that, we now need to consider model fit: how well does the audit democracy model capture the character and workings of the present-day EU as a political system? We may start by noting that the early, pre-1979 (when direct elections were introduced) EP bears clear resemblance to this deliberative audit version, because the EP was composed of representatives from the national parliaments. This ensured direct contacts across levels. Since the EP was not directly elected and consisted of national parliamentarians, this system was more akin to a structure of EU-level audit than to a system of EU-level representative democracy.

But clearly the present-day EU has moved beyond the audit democracy model: the EP is directly elected and can claim a direct popular mandate, and it is a decision-making body in a host of EU issue areas; as such it is not different from national parliaments (cf. Hix *et al.* 2005). Having said that, we should add that the EU also holds traits that give the audit democracy model some empirical credence. One is the EU's poly-centric, and thus highly uneven, representative character (with the EP having different degrees of control/presence in different functional realms, and national parliaments also exhibiting great structural and operational variation). In some of the issue areas that have been uploaded to the EU level, the EP has only scrutiny, not decision-making, power. There is also, therefore, an important trend towards 'integration without parliamentarisation' – in those domains where decision-making remains dominated by an intergovernmental approach (Curtin 2007). The question is therefore whether this development at all corresponds with what we should expect from an audit-based Multilevel Parliamentary Field, or whether it is instead a mere instance of executive empowerment or predominance, at the behest of representative bodies.

One recent development that at least on the face of it appears to sit quite well with the audit democracy model is the development of measures to reassert national parliamentary controls. These are foremost the provisions on national parliaments and subsidiarity in the Lisbon Treaty (2007) that underline the need to consult and inform national parliaments. Articles 1–8 of the Protocol on National Parliaments provide specific guidelines for the how and the what, of the Union's duties to inform and keep national parliaments abreast with the Union's legislative proposals. Articles 9–10 are specifically designed to ensure inter-parliamentary co-operation. As a complement to the Protocol on Subsidiarity attached to the Lisbon Treaty, Article 3 in the Protocol on National Parliaments contains specific provisions on subsidiarity. These can be seen to strengthen the *horizontal* patterns of interaction because they permit national parliaments – when operating together – to challenge the Union's actions and range of activities. At the same time, these provisions can also be construed as means for encouraging deliberative exchanges on the confines of Union action. What is thus set up is a joint monitoring system, which involves parliaments across levels. But this is *not* the kind of monitoring system that we should expect from a system of audit democracy because the provisions have been set up to reinstate an element of national parliament control over actions at the EU level, in a context where the EP already operates as a legislator and not as a mere auditor.

To sum up, then, it is clear that the audit democracy model presupposes a weak mode of inter-parliamentary interaction that does not amount to a Multilevel Parliamentary Field. The audit democracy model operates with very weak vertical linkages between the national and supranational levels because the model assigns such a limited role to the EP; the horizontal (based on national parliamentary inter-action) dimension is also weak because lines of accountability still work mainly from individual country national executives to their respective national parliaments. What we have shown is that the EU has in several important respects *moved beyond* the model of audit democracy, and the EP's development is the clearest example of this. At the same time, we also noted that the EP is *not* a full-fledged representative body on a par with a national parliament. The notion of audit democracy has merit in helping to understand these *deviations*. But the main conclusion is nevertheless that the EU's representative structure is more institutionalised and forms a denser field than the model of audit democracy can accommodate.

The model of EU federal democracy

The second model, federal state-based democracy, posits the Union as a political community based on institutions that are capable of sustaining an identity-building process and a European demos based on common values. The federal democracy model highlights democratic will-formation through the voter-party-legislature chain, which is stabilised through a common identity and culture. Its vision of democracy is premised on an EU with a commitment to direct legitimacy founded on basic rights, representation and procedures for will-formation, including a European-wide discourse. It assumes that the basic structural and substantive constitutional principles of Union law, as well as coercive measures required for efficient and consistent norm enforcement and policy implementation, will be institutionalised at both core levels of government (member state and European).

The federal democracy model thus posits a high degree of institutional *congruence* across levels, through the EP gradually becoming a fully fledged supranational parliament. In other words, this model highlights parliaments across Europe as conventional strong publics: deliberative and decision-making bodies. For this model to have any real bearing on the EU, there will have to be strong forces working towards isomorphism along the *vertical* dimension, that is, to render the EP a fully fledged parliament and to situate it in the role of senior representative body in the EU federation. Further, for this development to qualify as properly *federal*, the isomorphic pressures have to work towards considerable convergence also along *horizontal* lines (i.e., that the national parliaments will become increasingly structurally and operationally similar). The further presumption is that such isomorphic pressures would operate equally along all three main parliamentary functions, namely legislation/budgeting, control/accountability and deliberative forum.

A successful federalisation process thus presupposes (a) that national parliaments willingly rescind power and prerogatives to representative institutions at the European level; (b) that this comes with strong vertical isomorphic pressure from national parliaments to ensure that the institutions at the EU level will have the same democratic credentials as themselves; (c) that national parliaments seek guarantees that the institutions at the EU level do not threaten their fundamental role; and (d) that the parliaments at the EU and national levels agree on a federal division of powers and competences that renders each level supreme within its sphere of competence. The federal model presupposes the construction of a European-wide constituency, and a division of powers and competences between levels that clarifies in what sense and how the citizens are represented by European-level institutions and by member state institutions, respectively.

As we have underlined in previous work (Crum and Fossum 2009), the model of federal state-based democracy is not very compatible with the present Multi-level Parliamentary Field in the EU. The federal model is based on two lines of parliamentary accountability, each of which refers back to a clearly delineated and integrated constituency. However, having said that, one could consider that in the European setting a Multilevel Parliamentary Field might be a useful mechanism in *working towards* a federal system. Precisely because the EU is forged in a system of already established representative-democratic systems, the present-day EU's Multilevel Parliamentary Field offers a means for conveying isomorphic pressure on the EU level and across widely different national representative systems. The pressures within the field could then help to shape the necessary symmetry among the national parliamentary arrangements that a federal system requires. Once the federal system is properly entrenched, the field would be reconfigured into a two-channel arrangement, and this then *replaces* the field.

Such isomorphic federalisation pressures exist in the EU because the process takes place in a context made up of already established constitutional democracies, all of which have systems of representative government that are in terms of fundamentals more similar to each other than they are different. But for this to become a *European* process proper, the values and forms of representative government would have to be properly 'uploaded' to the European level in a single, integrative model.

Berthold Rittberger (2005) has shown that, slowly but steadily, national governments have exerted isomorphic pressure on the EP to model itself on national parliaments throughout the EU.[6] In the European setting of forging a representative system on top of established representative systems, isomorphic pressures can draw on well-entrenched norms that are already embraced by the actors involved. The primary actors in the integration process – governments – are themselves institutional carriers of, and must answer to, their own (and other) democratic constituencies. These norm-sets highlight the centrality of parliament as the institutional embodiment of democratic government.

Nevertheless, there are several questions pertaining to how well this federal model can be transposed to the contemporary EU. First is the question of the appropriate version of federalism: Insofar as there is a development in the direction of the federal model, which *version of federalism* – uni-polar or bi-polar – does the EU most closely resemble?[7, 8] Institutionally speaking, the EU is much closer to the uni-polar than it is to the bi-polar version of federalism, but falls well short of both. Consider how the two channels of parliamentary representation are organised and operate. At the EU level, national governments, through the Council formations, have a direct hand in all EU matters. In much legislation (where the co-decision procedure (now labelled the ordinary legislative procedure) applies), the EP acts as a co-legislator. Thus, the two bodies (EP and Council) have to hammer out decisions between them. Within this modified uni-polar structure, national parliaments work through their national governments. At the same time, national parliaments enjoy powers over the full range of tasks that the government subject to their oversight undertakes.

However, in practice, the representative system in the EU operates through two incompletely, or at least distinctly, institutionalised federal-type channels: it is predominantly uni-polar (focused on one level) within the realm of Community action, where issues are hammered out at the EU level by the EP and the Council. At the same time, the initial Maastricht rationale to establish two intergovernmental 'pillars' was to serve as curtailments on further integration, so that the member states would retain competence within these areas. But what is important to keep in mind is that, over time, more and more issues have been 'lifted' up to the EU level. Many of these are now dealt with under the system of uni-polar decision-making associated with the Community method. Yet, a host of critical issues, notably pertaining to security and foreign policy, has become the preserve of an intergovernmental decisional network, which is basically outside the purview of the EP but is subject to the Council (see Chapter 8 in this volume for more details). Thus, ironically, some of the bi-polar logic has been retained but without including the EP and the Commission, which are shut out from decision-making over issues that are increasingly handled at the EU level through the Council structure. This has given a particular twist to the way in which the vertical and horizontal coordination takes place across and within the levels of the EU system of governance. One obvious effect is to have made it more important for national parliaments to involve themselves in EU matters. We thus end up with a unique way of constructing a bi-polar federal system as far as intergovernmentally run EU affairs are concerned. The upshot is that the EU is basically run by a uni-polar logic in the Community domain, and an incomplete and very awkward 'bi-polar' logic in those competences that are subject to more intergovernmental methods.

Thus, we see that the EU system contains elements of the federal model. But it should also be added that there are several traits of the EU that set it apart from all federal state-based systems. First is the distinct lack of parliamentary congruence in the EU. National governments have direct influence and/or final say on the entire range of political issues, whether these are defined as European or as national. But this does *not* translate directly into national *parliamentary* control because much of this is situated in the Council where individual states may be outvoted and decision-making transparency is limited. Second, the absence of parliamentary congruence in the EU is reinforced by the fact that, whereas each national parliament has its own government to control, the EP has no proper government to hold accountable. In fact, most executive responsibility for EU policies goes back to the national governments. Third, the EU is a modified poly-centric, not a classic mono-centric, system of government. A poly-centric system is:

> an arrangement for making binding decisions over a multiplicity of actors that delegates authority of functional tasks to a set of dispersed and relatively

autonomous agencies that are not controlled – *de jure* or *de facto* – by a single collective institution.

(Schmitter and Kim 2005: 6)

Essentially then there is no single institution, and not even a single level, within the EU that can be seen as the centre wherein sovereignty is embodied. Indeed in many respects, the national governments operate as distinct political (sub)centres for their citizens even if they have come to pool and delegate important powers to the European level. Fourth, the EU is marked by an almost unprecedented cultural pluralism and institutional heterogeneity. This lack of institutional symmetry makes it extremely difficult to work out and to operate any division of powers and competences in a manner consistent with federal principles. Fifth, the EU system, as we showed in the discussion of the deliberative audit model, contains procedures and arrangements for linking parliaments across levels that are far more extensive than in any other federal system.

To sum up, then, it is clear that the gradual strengthening of the EP as a decision-making body is informed by a uni-polar version of the federal model, which is quite similar to how the German federal system works. But in the EU, when this process really took off, from the Treaty of Maastricht onwards, important provisions were put in place to prevent the Union from intervening in what were seen as core national prerogatives. The last decade has seen a significant hollowing-out of these constraints, either through their transfer to the first pillar or through the Council taking over the role as national chaperon, as more and more of the issues have been lifted up to European level.

The upshot is that the EU's development has traits of both models – audit and federal democracy. But the latter development presupposes very strong isomorphic pressures, which the present-day EU does not contain. The EU is not a state. It is barred from taking on the hierarchical arrangements and the degree of territorial control that are characteristics of a state. Further, there are significant constraints on the process of transfer of functions to the EU level. The EU therefore falls well short of the model of state-based federal democracy. There is nothing to suggest that whatever we see of federalisation in the EU has replaced the distinct field-type traits of the EU, an entity that fails to attain statehood proper. Hence, we need to consider if non-state-based models are more apt to capture the EU, and what kind of parliamentary field such a structure would yield.

The regional-cosmopolitan model

The regional-cosmopolitan model envisages democracy beyond the template of the nation state. The model we discern here posits the EU as the trans- and supranational level of government in Europe, and as one of the regional subsets of a larger *cosmopolitan* order. This implies that the Union will be a post-national *government*, a system whose internal standards are projected onto its external affairs; and further, that it will be a system of government that subjects its actions to higher-ranking principles – to 'the cosmopolitan law of the people'.

This regional-cosmopolitan model highlights democratic opinion and will-formation through a regional-European representative system that, as a subsystem of a wider cosmopolitan order, operates within a *limited remit* of governmental functions. Its diversity, complex composition, and thinly based allegiance posit public deliberation as playing a greater role than formalised structures of representation, although such are necessary and must be established at all relevant levels of government.

The regional-cosmopolitan model posits that the European integration process transforms parliaments. First, in line with Bohman's notion of transnational democracy, any given parliament is no longer the main institutional manifestation of a given, sovereign, democratic *demos*, but is rather one among a chain of strong publics who *together* seek to accommodate the interests and concerns of a multitude of interdependent *demoi* (Bohman 2007b). These demoi are nevertheless territorially delimited; they co-exist within a delimited political entity that is able and willing to uphold a set of borders to the outside world. But these borders are far more permeable than state-based borders.

Second, within this structure, parliaments in the EU operate together in an interactive field to forge legislation and to check executive power. Third, this field is not confined to the parliaments that inhabit the given polity (EU); it links up with parliamentary bodies outside the EU as well. This is necessary to handle a level of interdependence that not only ties the EU together but also links the EU to the outside world.

Thus, from these three points it should be clear that our regional-cosmopolitan model has affinities with Bohman's transnational democracy version. But our model also differs from Bohman's because we see parliaments as components of systems of *government*, not mere systems of governance, which Bohman portrays these as. In other words, in our view, parliaments are not simply institutionalised publics; they are also able to entrench will-formation in legislation and hold the executives to account.

The regional-cosmopolitan democracy model is entirely compatible with the notion of the Multilevel Parliamentary Field. Schematically speaking, such a model will have the following characteristic features. First, it will be made up of systems of governments, which differ from both states and networked systems of governance. This is entrenched as a field through formal structures of interaction, consultation, and co-operation, with different degrees of density at different levels but where all parliaments are able to entrench will-formation and hold the executives to account. Second, at each level of the field we find a distinct functional delimitation. With this we mean that in contrast to the sovereign state, which is formally equipped to handle all issues and concerns on its territory, the regional-cosmopolitan model shares with federal systems the trait that no single entity is permitted to handle all types of issues, but rather has a set of issues over which it wields supreme power, while the rest are dealt with at lower or higher levels.

This division stems from how the vertical dimension operates, which is to uphold a division of tasks across at least three core levels (national, regional-European and global). In contrast to the audit democracy model, the regional-cosmopolitan model posits the presence of parliaments as strong publics, and as effective legislators, at all three main levels. The system is set up with a division of tasks between levels, where each level has some functions over which it is supreme. At the same time, there is far more diversity among parliaments than in the federal model. The regional-cosmopolitan model recognises, on the one hand, differences in the parliamentary structures as an expression of democratic autonomy while underlining, on the other hand, the need for parliaments to be linked together and to operate in relation to each other (horizontally and vertically). Close co-operation across these institutions makes up for and reduces the difficulties that institutional difference and diversity produce.

The regional-cosmopolitan model contains considerably weaker isomorphic pressures than the federal model. One reason is because the model presupposes a stronger civil society and deliberative component as part of action co-ordination than is the case in the other two models (audit democracy and federal democracy). Another reason is because, in a regional-cosmopolitan system, all representative bodies will be functionally delimited even if these limits themselves are open to deliberation. Functional delimitation is devised precisely to avoid conflicts, turf-battles, etc.

Thus, it is quite clear that among the three EU democratic polity models presented here, it is the regional-cosmopolitan model where the Multilevel Parliamentary Field seems to be most at home and where its distinctive features come out most clearly. What is also clear is that, whereas in Europe we have already seen for decades a process of entrenching representative government in the EU, this process has thus far *not* been a simple matter of uploading a state-based institutional arrangement to the EU level. The EU's development has been more uneven and contested; it also contains a sufficient number of distinct features to warrant discussing it under this different – non-statal – frame.

This has implications for how we understand and theorise democracy. The Multilevel Parliamentary Field notion is of particular value to heighten our understanding of how recent advances in the theory of representation have direct bearings on the EU. One such pertains to new insights into *how* the representatives construct the represented, and to the existence of a *dynamic* interaction between the representative and the represented. Representative theory, as Michael Saward (2006) has noted, has generally taken the constituency of the represented *as a given*. As a consequence, analysts have focused on how well the representatives reflect the represented, without questioning who and what may be represented politically. As an alternative, Saward introduces the notion of 'the representative claim':

> Seeing representation in terms of *claims to be representative* by a variety of political actors, rather than . . . seeing it as an achieved, or potentially achievable, state of affairs as a result of election. We need to move away from the

idea that representation is first and foremost a given, factual product of elections, rather than a precarious and curious sort of claim about a dynamic relationship.

(Saward 2006: 298)

The regional-cosmopolitan model and its Multilevel Parliamentary Field is that polity model that provides the greatest scope for the dynamic interaction between representatives and represented, reflected in the representative claim. This model is therefore also able to capture the EU's many representative ambiguities. It shows that the dynamic interaction of representatives and represented unfolds not simply between levels (which the other polity models suggest), but within a more complex *field*, marked by complex vertical and horizontal patterns of interaction. In this sense the construction of the European constituency warrants special attention: it takes place amidst a wide range of differently constituted national constituencies, which highlights also that the process of reconstituting national constituencies is complex and multifaceted.

The EU context is, as noted earlier, marked by the forging of a representative-democratic system on top of already existing representative democracies. This process is not simply one of hammering out distinct constituencies; the opposite may far more often be the case. We see a highly dynamic process of integration along both vertical and horizontal lines, which still manifests itself in underdeveloped representative channels. This is for instance reflected in the characterisation of EP elections as 'second order elections' (Marsh 1998; Reif and Schmitt 1980), which implies that the European constituency is activated but the processes are structured so as to encourage the citizens in each member state to use the European-level elections to send signals to their national leaders; hence the elections lose much of their *European* orientation. From our perspective this assessment incorporates one important dimension but to some extent also misses parts of the larger picture, namely the dynamic interaction between representatives and represented; how representatives frame the European elections (and fail to do so) and how voters pick up on this. In a context of increasingly overlapping and imbricated constituencies, it is not simply a matter of the European serving as a proxy for the national. Rather, there is a broader, more comprehensive, process unfolding here: because the European integration process takes place in a setting of existing representative systems, it is also a process wherein a broad range of representatives from European, national and regional levels seek to construct – both in substantive and symbolic terms – their respective constituencies, that is, *whom* they represent, and *in what sense* they represent them. This process is not only a matter for the institutions at the EU level, with the representatives in the EP and the Council of the Union defining whose Europe they represent and in what sense they represent this Europe; it is also a matter of national (and regional) parliamentarians defining whose nations (or regions) they represent and in what sense they represent these nations (or regions) within a tightly interlinked European setting. The process is therefore a complex blend of construction (EU) and *re*construction of (national and regional) constituencies. Precisely because the field notion is so strongly focused on interaction, it can capture the overall character and effects of these processes of construction and reconstruction.

The Multilevel Parliamentary Field, understood as a collection of (competing/ overlapping, etc.) representative claims, therefore helps to make sense of some of the distinctive features of the EU. One such, as noted, is European integration's interweaving of levels (European and national), which heightens uncertainty as to the nature and the character of the relevant democratic constituency – the repre-sented – that each representative body speaks to. In Europe, national parliaments do not only handle national issues; they also address issues that are to be decided at the European level. What then is the relevant constituency – is it the national *or* is it the European? This is suggestive of a broader tendency, where issues that are formally dealt with at the European level are framed as national concerns and vice versa. But simply to portray these events as second-order affairs is also to downplay the dynamic character of the process of construction and reconstruc-tion of constituency. What we see are ongoing dynamic processes of construction and reconstruction of *European* and national constituencies. In this connection it could be argued that the greater the ambiguity pertaining to constituency, the more merit there is in assessing representative arrangements through the notion of the 'field', because the field is not premised on a given constituency and is thus able to grasp the nature of and the interaction among these processes of construction and reconstruction of constituency.

It should also be added that the cosmopolitan component of this polity model adds to the complexity in these processes of construction and reconstruction because it makes the question of constituency *scope* an ever-present critical concern: the construction of the European constituency takes place within a broader global set-ting, which brings up the issue of bounds: when and under what circumstances can the constituency be confined to Europe, and when is it global? When and under what circumstances can representatives appeal to Europeans as Europeans only? In what sense does European-ness manifest itself in representative claims across Europe? There is no reason to assume that this will be the same across Europe; thus how it manifests itself within each national constituency is an important question.

Conclusion

This chapter had as its point of departure how multifaceted the discussion of the EU's democratic deficit has become. The fact that the positions in this debate differ greatly on what are the appropriate democratic standards and, further, that they operate with widely divergent conceptions of what the EU is and should be, shows that there is a clear need for an analytical framework that can breach these divisions. This framework, we have underlined, needs to take proper heed of the present-day EU's representative character, namely that it has taken on the shape of a Multilevel Parliamentary Field. The Multilevel Parliamentary Field offers a more apt description of the system in place in the EU today than can otherwise be found in the literature. Most students of representative democracy in the EU operate with a conception of the EU's representative system that mostly approaches the different representative sites in the EU in isolation rather than by highlighting how they interact within a single, multilevel polity. We have shown that the EU holds a sufficient number of distinct features to force us to rethink this notion.

In this chapter our purpose was to clarify what kind of polity the EU is by focusing on the character of its emerging representative structure. We started by arguing that the distinctive character of EU representative democracy is well captured by the notion of a Multilevel Parliamentary Field. Thus, a proper conception of the EU needs to be compatible with the Multilevel Parliamentary Field. We analysed three different models of European democracy and found that the third model, the regional-cosmopolitan, offers the best reflection of the Multilevel Parliamentary Field. It is also the model that best reflects the character of the contemporary EU *qua* polity.

Representative democracy has generally been understood and studied within a state-based frame. To properly capture it within such a complex non-state-type entity such as the EU represents a major intellectual challenge. The challenge is threefold. The first is to envisage a polity that is regional-cosmopolitan in character. What kind of entity will this be, that can sustain a cosmopolitan vocation yet also serve democracy? We have suggested that it can be a multilevel structure based on authorised jurisdictions. This can also be cast as a system of government, but with the important proviso that government need not add up to state (see also Chapter 2 in this volume).

The second is to understand representation within such a system. How does representation work within a parliamentary field? We have drawn on Saward's notion of representative claim because it provides us with an approach to representation that is compatible with the idea of a field. But forging this link between representative claim and field also means that we must rethink representation. This involves a potentially very significant departure from orthodoxy. We need to consider the dynamic relationship between representative and represented, not simply as a dynamic that unfolds within one constituency, but rather as a set of parallel processes that unfolds within a multitude of overlapping constituencies that are also being reconstructed in the process.

The third and final challenge is democracy. Relevant questions pertain to democratic quality and democratic accountability. A field will necessarily foster multiple, overlapping accounts; can such a field preserve accountability or will it undermine it by diffusing it across a multitude of actors? Or does the sheer multitude of imbricated parliamentary actors foster more effective demands for justification and more active control points on experts, executives and technocrats?

We have sought to demonstrate that, contrary to Bohman and the transnationalists, there is no need to abandon representative democracy when discussing EU democracy. At the same time, we have shown that the EU holds so many distinct features that we cannot directly transpose state-based representative arrangements to the EU. We can only establish these through means of an appropriate analytical framework. Up until now no such framework has existed. The relevant framework, we have proposed, is the Multilevel Parliamentary Field, coupled with the representative claim. This framework comes with its own theoretical and empirical agenda, which requires further elaboration.

Notes

1 Proponents of directly deliberative polyarchy (Cohen and Sabel 1997, 2003, 2005) also embrace a transnational notion of democracy but are less comprehensive than Bohman on the need to revise existing conceptions.
2 Our conception of organisational field therefore differs somewhat from that of Powell and DiMaggio (1991). To them 'recognised area of life' has generally been defined in sectoral terms, often understood as a (professional) sector.
3 Formal procedures that facilitate such inter-parliamentary interaction include: mechanisms for consultation and sounding-out across levels; procedures for establishing whose responsibility an issue is (cf. subsidiarity provisions); institutionalised meeting-places, exchanges of information, personnel and resources; and procedures for the conveyance of best practices. A prominent example is the Conference of European Affairs Committees (COSAC). National parliaments have established offices in Brussels to monitor the work of the EP and have taken measures to involve MEPs in their work. In turn, the EP has also developed various means to engage national parliaments (Neunreither 1994: 310).
4 According to Powell and DiMaggio (1991) *isomorphism* relates to 'formal and informal pressures exerted upon organisations by other organisations upon which they are dependent and by cultural expectations in the society within which organisations function'. Actors also opt for isomorphic change without coercive pressures being exerted. In attempts to reduce uncertainty about their own situation, actors often imitate and mimic established practices and organisational structures, which they perceive as efficient and legitimate. This practice can be referred to as *mimetic isomorphism*. There is of course economy in emulating established practices; when the dominant organisational arrangements within a given organisational field are known, new and newly emerged organisations that enter the field tend to mimic the established ones that dominate the field. Finally, isomorphism can also be said to emanate from the professional standards that govern an organisational field. Such standards shape which practices and behaviours are considered acceptable and legitimate within a particular field. Professional associations and guilds yield incentives for *normative isomorphism* among actors within a field.
5 This term denotes a type of institutionalised discourse – strong publics – that promotes democracy through its monitoring and stock-taking role more than through its decision-making role (Eriksen and Fossum 2002; Fossum 2004).
6 Rittberger uses this notion of isomorphism he uses to discuss the degree of 'resonance between internalised norms and ideas and a social situation which upsets the *match* (or resonance) between "a situation and the demands of a position"' (Rittberger 2005: 18).
7 The uni-polar, or compact or co-operative model of federalism is based on a functional notion of federalism. It sees the federal compact as embedded in a set of central institutions, which have binding force on the parties to the federal compact in those issue areas that are regulated by the compact. The central institutions are based on a mix of two principles of representation: representation by population and representation by territory. The people are represented in the central institutions through directly elected representatives; they are also represented in the central institutions through representatives from each member state/entity. The closest contemporary variant of this is the German version of federalism (Jeffery and Savigear 1991; Scharpf 1988, 1994).
8 In the bi-polar model, the parliament or representative assembly at the federal level has as its constituency the entire polity, but only where this pertains to those issue areas that are under federal jurisdiction. Each parliament at the state or provincial level has the

state or province as its constituency, and again only pertaining to those issue areas that are under state or provincial jurisdiction. Federalism is premised on a clearly delineated division of powers and competences between levels, so that it is possible to discern clear jurisdictional bounds. For its operation, this model is based on institutional symmetry: the institutional structure of the government at the federal level is duplicated at the provincial/state level. This is often thought of as jurisdictional federalism, and the most salient contemporary examples are the USA (not based on parliamentary rule, though), Canada, Australia and India (all parliamentary federations).

6

GENDER, JUSTICE AND DEMOCRACY IN THE EUROPEAN UNION

Yvonne Galligan

Introduction

The central concern of this book is to explore what democracy looks like in today's European Union (EU). The multilevelled arrangements that characterise EU governance call for a reflective, theoretically driven understanding of how democracy works, or does not work, in this complex setting. To aid this analytical task, this book presents three models designed to elicit a clearer understanding of the democratic character and quality of the EU polity: audit democracy, federal multinational democracy and regional-cosmopolitan democracy. This chapter takes these three models and considers what form of democracy each one delivers from a gender justice perspective. It approaches the question of democracy in the EU through reflecting on the incorporation of gender as an essential aspect of decision-making in this multilevelled polity. As the EU is an essentially contested entity, adopting a gender perspective on the EU models illuminates the principles and institutional arrangements on which this system could, or should, be based. Because there is no consensus around which principles and institutional arrangements deliver the most appropriate democracy in an EU setting, a gender view on these issues adds important insights to this debate. The models permit us to consider the gendered implications of different democratic arrangements, along with the present status of gender democracy in Europe.

This chapter utilises the concept of gender democracy to describe, in ideal terms, what is required to effect a gender-equal, gender-sensitive democracy, and then asks a key question: What does gender democracy entail within the complex, multilevel European political order? This necessitates a focus on process as much as on the outcomes of processes, and so is closely aligned with proceduralist conceptions of democracy. The three models that encapsulate different aspects of the European democratic polity are then examined to see how they contribute to the analysis of gender democracy.[1] Given the centrality of the concept of gender democracy to this discussion, the chapter begins by defining it.

Defining gender democracy

There is now a substantial body of literature revealing, through theoretical and empirical investigation, that democracy has a gendered imprint (Craske and Molyneux 2002; Hoskyns 1996; Pateman 1989; Phillips 1993; Siim 2000). This finding carries important consequences for the study of democratic processes, institutions and practices. It questions the construction of the sexless 'majority' in democratic theory and practice, and interrogates the gender-blind representation of interests in empirically grounded studies. Research exploring the gendered nature of democracy is extensive, but fragmented. It generally investigates particular aspects of the democratic process in depth (such as social movement activity, policy-making), but in relative isolation from other elements of a political system. The corpus of work offers well-honed analyses of political behaviour and decision-making focused on institutional arrangements (parties, legislatures, bureaucracies), or on addressing normative elements of democracy (such as feminism, citizenship, power). The comprehensiveness of this body of work is now such that it is possible to think in terms of devising an overarching concept that embraces each of these, and other, dimensions of democratic process and practice, while also giving due weight to the institutional context. This concept is 'gender democracy'. It is a term capturing the notion that democracy is imprinted by gendered assumptions influencing processes and practices that go unquestioned in the course of decision-making in any given political environment. It takes the established democratic ideals of political equality and popular control, and seeks to consider what these mean in practice, and could mean in terms of reform, for democratic decision-making. It gives substance to the normative notion of gender justice through its empirical focus. Indeed, in assessing a democracy for the fairness with which it treats women's expressed interests, gender democracy can illustrate the extent to which a given political process conforms to the gender justice ideal. By examining a decision-making process through the lens of gender democracy, it is possible to uncover the gendered nature of these democratic processes and practices in the specific institutional contexts in which they occur. The concept can be applied to all levels of democratic decision-making. Given its generic construction, it opens the way to valid comparisons across single and multiple levels of governance, institutional realms and policy fields. This contribution is a response to Schmidt's (2006: 220) observation that there have been 'relatively few studies that attempt to theorise across institutions and countries about the impact of EU institutions on national institutions and democracy more generally'.

This chapter considers the gender quality of the multilevelled decision-making processes that these institutions engage in. Conceptually, it perceives democracy in the first instance as 'a right to join together with others as equals to exercise public control over a polity' (Lord 2008: 2) and inscribes the criteria with a gendered sensitivity. Normatively, gender democracy foregrounds the importance of civic engagement and open discussion between citizens and their representatives on matters of public interest. Empirically, it provides an investigative framework for assessing the quality of democratic decision-making that is sensitive to the gendered nature of these processes in an institutional context. In other words, we ask under what circumstances – in terms of institutions and processes – is a democracy responsive to gender issues, inclusive of those who express gender claims, and accountable to women citizens. While it is important to observe that the burgeoning literature on intersectionality suggests that multiple oppressions must be analysed in an integrated way, the case for considering gender differences alone in this particular study remains strong. After all, gender inequality is a fundamental and persistent cause of women's oppression, irrespective of locus and polity. It takes different forms in different global regions, but is an identifiable form of political, economic, social and cultural inequity in every country, whatever the level of democratisation reached by a state and society. Indeed, while it is important to be attentive to the intersection of gender with race, class, religion and other oppressions, putting an emphasis on the gender aspect does not negate other dimensions in the gender democracy framework.

The focal point of analysis in gender democracy is the decision-making process. This can be on an issue identified as important by gender actors, or on an aspect of gender equality put forward by other participants. The parameters around an issue of this kind, and the manner in which the issue is constructed by participants, can include an awareness of the multiplicity of disadvantage. Importantly, though, gender democracy is an empirically grounded concept dealing with actual political debates. How these issues are framed, debated and decided upon, and the positions of the actors involved, is the focus of study – and the actors may, or may not, incorporate an awareness of intersectionality as they present their positions. Gender democracy can incorporate this aspect into the evaluation when there is the evidence to do so, because the evaluation is based on a close study of the content of actors' exchanges in institutional democratic settings.

These are the broad foundations, then, on which the concept of gender democracy rests. But foundations alone are not sufficient to make it a practical instrument for evaluating the gendered nature of democratic rule. Confining the concept to relatively abstract dimensions runs the risk of making it an empty vessel into which any aspect of democratic theory and practice can be placed, thereby losing the explanatory power it has to offer. The task now is to imagine what gender democracy looks like – what are the principles of gender democracy that makes it recognisable and distinct from other conceptualisations of democratic rule?

From a feminist perspective, the criterion of political equality is a necessary condition for the achievement of democracy. Indeed, at the moment of birth of modern democracy – the 1789 French Revolution – the feminist Olympe de Gouges chafed at the exclusion of women from the new democratic project in her country. To this day, feminist thought continues to confront the embedded masculinism of democracy. In her path-breaking essay on feminism and democracy, Carol

Pateman (1989: 210–20), mounts a cogent and influential criticism of the gendered nature of liberal democracy that accords women political equality with men while upholding the social and sexual domination of men over women. Anne Phillips (1991) too, argues that political equality has embedded within it a gender-neutral understanding of the individual and citizen. This logically leads to the male continuing to be privileged over the female in democratic theory and practice, hence the exclusion of women from democratic politics. Iris Marion Young (2000: 141–2) develops this idea further, observing that, when the experiences and interests of dominant groups (such as men) become universalised and established as a norm, subordinate groups (such as women) experience a particular range of disadvantages in trying to claim their 'equal' place in society. For one, their interests and experiences are silenced. Second, should women seek equal legitimacy for their claims, they are forced to express these in the language and norm perspectives of the dominant group, men. Following Young, it can then be argued that the universalising of men's interests and experiences, which results in the constitution of their world view as representative of the perspectives of women and men alike, is a gendered political and cultural domination. This strand of analysis has permeated feminist political theory and political science. It has exerted an important influence on feminist legal theory, constitutional, and human rights analyses. It has also provided a theoretical foundation for feminist political action. However, it is one thing to point out how and when the principle of political equality is contravened on gender grounds. While doing so is important in its own right, spelling out an ideal democratic system in which political equality is fully realised for women with men is a more challenging task.

One way forward is to adopt Nancy Fraser's (2007: 27–9) emphasis on 'participatory parity' as an ideal of justice requiring social arrangements that permit all adults to participate as peers in social life. This entails a redistribution of the material resources of a society so as to enable all to participate independently and express their unique 'voice'. It also requires that the cultural context is equally respectful of all participants, and that difference is recognised and valued (Fraser and Honneth 2003: 36–7). Fraser's third condition for participatory parity – one that is central to any assessment of gender democracy – is the possibility to participate in, and influence, decision-making processes.[2] In Fraser's view, the political sphere is the arena in which struggles over justice claims of redistribution and recognition are carried out. It is the sphere in which questions of who is included and excluded from those entitled to make justice claims are decided. It is also the context in which the rules and procedures for resolving competing justice claims are established (Fraser 2005a: 74; Holst 2008: 8). Thus, when women are deprived of the possibility of participating as peers with men in politics, this represents a distinctive type of injustice which, although related to economic and cultural injustice, cannot be reduced to either of them.

This discussion provides us with some of the requirements that need to be in place for the ideal gender democracy. An equal empowerment of women with men along two major dimensions – material and resource equity – is necessary so as to enable them to join as equals in exerting popular rule of the polity, which in turn requires validation and respect for gender-based differences. The fulfilment of these conditions addresses Pateman's concern about the subordination of women in liberal democracy, and the risk of their exclusion as highlighted by Phillips. It takes account of Young's concerns for the silencing of marginalised groups among women, as well as between women and men. It places Fraser's criterion of participatory parity within a democratic context, and, when applied to gender-based issues, deepens the foundational principles of democracy.

In researching gender democracy, we have sought to scrutinise political equality along with popular control as essential criteria for effective responsible government (Lord 2008: 3; Phillips 1995: 28). Along with Beetham, we view the principle of political equality as 'a key index of democratic attainment' (1999: 569). This is because a successful democracy is deemed to rest on the ability of citizens to reason with one another and, in that regard, women's exclusion from these public reasoning processes has been a consistently negative feature of most democratic polities. Indeed, critical theorists such as Seyla Benhabib (1994) and Lynn Sanders (1997) point out that, when put into practice, the deliberative emphasis on reasoning, with its intimation of impartial, objective and emotionally distant exchanges, excludes women on the double from participating in public debates – one because of the dominance of the male gender, the other because of the 'rational' tenor of the discussion that supposedly leads to a consensus on the resolution of a common problem. Reilly (2007), too, is sceptical of the practice (though not the promise) of political and human rights discourses based on reality. Furthermore, empirical studies show that the outcome of deliberations is clearly influenced by the gender composition of the groups involved as well as by the institutional rules governing decision-making (Mendelberg and Karpowitz 2006). In this regard, the historical marginalisation of women and other under-represented groups is explained by Fraser as follows:

> [D]iscursive interaction within the bourgeois public sphere was governed by protocols of style and decorum that were themselves correlates and markers of status inequality. These functioned informally to marginalise women, people of color and members of the plebeian classes and to prevent them from participating as peers. Here we are talking about informal impediments of participatory parity that can persist even after everyone is formally and legally licensed to participate.
>
> *(Fraser 1997: 70)*

The second principle underpinning gender democracy is that of popular control. While the majority of feminist research places the spotlight on political equality, Anne Phillips (1995: 24–9) is particularly concerned with popular control as expressed in the term 'government of the people'. For Phillips, this element addresses the extent to which decision-making processes incorporate, and are influenced by, women's perspectives. She argues that a politics of presence, as expressed in equal numerical representation of women and men, is not sufficient to ensure gender democracy. Nor is she convinced that policies designed to represent women's interests can suffice to ensure gender justice. What is additionally required, she argues, is the incorporation of women's interests, views and perspectives into the decision-making process so as to produce gender-just outcomes. In other words, a politics of presence requires that representatives are accountable to women for the decisions they take in women's name.

These two principles, political equality and popular control, have a number of overlapping dimensions that are revealed when examined through the lens of gender democracy. They share the elements of inclusion, accountability and recognition, from which democratic legitimacy is derived. For those who study gender politics, ideas about inclusion encompass formal and symbolic (i.e., numerical) and substantive (i.e., policy) representation. Accountability refers to the accountability of elected representatives through regular elections as well as through other mechanisms of public control, such as public debates, town hall meetings, media investigations and quasi-judicial forms of public investigation into representatives' actions and behaviour. The aspect of accountability also carries within it an expectation that civil society representatives involved in public decision-making will be accountable to the particular public on whose behalf they speak, such as organised interests (labour, employer, other sectional groups) and civil society organisations (equality-seeking and human rights groups, minority and other articulated interests). Under the banner of accountability, gender scholars also expect there to be some transparency about the decision-making process. Without this element of transparency, the notion of representation as a substantive element is diminished because closed, opaque decision-making perpetuates women's disadvantage in, and exclusion from, public affairs. The issue of recognition is a touchstone for feminist politics, because it brings the status accorded to gender justice in a political debate to the fore. It is, as Lynn Sanders notes, more than formal equality between women and men in access to, and engagement in, decision-making. In her words, '[Deliberation] requires not only equality in resources and the guarantee of equal opportunity to articulate persuasive arguments, but also equality in "epistemological authority", in the capacity to evoke acknowledgment of one's argument' (Sanders 1997: 348). Thus the egalitarian nature of the communicative exchanges between participants, and the extent to which there is a willingness on the part of men to listen, recognise, respect and be responsive to women's testimonies, voices and claims shows the extent to which the decision-making process is marked by the gendered sharing of power.

Our investigations, then, seek to evaluate the gender quality of democracy along the criteria of inclusion, accountability and recognition, informed by feminist scholarship. We consider that this melding of critical perspectives allows us to take the concept of gender democracy and invest it with substantive meaning and analytical power. Our empirical research on gender democracy is challenged by the multilayering of democracy in the compound EU polity. As Lord and Harris (2006: 124) point out, democracy in an EU context is as much about democracy beyond the state as it is about democracy within the state. It is a matter of 'joint supply'. In order to make a coherent contribution to the debate on the nature of democracy in this 'amalgam of the national and the supranational' (Schmidt 2006: 222), we need, at least at this stage, to keep a relatively narrow empirical focus while considering the gendered interplay of institutions and processes at EU- and member-state level, and between them.

However, these three criteria need further elaboration in order for them to be applied with some rigour in an empirical context. This specification of the criteria comes in the form of indicators that, when applied in a particular context, illuminate the gendered imprint of democratic institutions and practices (Galligan and Clavero 2009: 140–9). The advantage of these indicators is that they are not bound by territory, an important consideration when assessing a complex multilevelled governance polity such as the EU. This enables us to identify and compare the nature and extent of gender democracy across different units of governance. For the purposes of this discussion, the indicators listed in Table 6.1 are aggregates of the more detailed and focused indicators employed in the empirical research. Combining the empirical indicators makes it possible to map the three foundational principles of gender democracy – inclusion, accountability and recognition – onto the three models of democracy so as to indicate what gender democracy would look like under the political conditions generated by these ideational models.[3] Thus, the extent to which women enjoy with men the right to free and fair voting, for example, can be compared across member states, local and regional polities, as well as for the EU. Given the historic exclusion of women from political life, it is not surprising that the bulk of our indicators focus on inclusion (INC), while two address accountability (ACC) and another two tap into the recognition (REC) criteria (Table 6.1). The

TABLE 6.1 Indicators of gender democracy and the RECON models

Indicator	Type	Model 1	Model 2	Model 3
To what extent do women enjoy with men the right to participate in free and fair voting?	INC	Women's right to participate as individual citizens in free and fair elections to the national legislative assembly of member states is upheld through law and supported through specific policies and actions.	Women's right to participate as individual citizens in free and fair elections to the EU executive and legislative offices is upheld through law and supported through specific policies and actions.	Women's right to participate as individual residents, irrespective of country of origin, in free and fair elections to all representative bodies exercising controlling powers over the Union is upheld through Union law based on provisions in EU-regional and global human rights treaties, and supported through specific policies and actions.
To what extent do women enjoy equal representation with men in	INC	There are mechanisms in place in each member state to provide for	There are mechanisms in place to provide for women's equal representation with	There are mechanisms in place to provide for women's equal representation with men in all

TABLE 6.1 *Continued*

Indicator	Type	Model 1	Model 2	Model 3
legislative and executive bodies?		women's equal representation with men in legislative and executive institutions that control delegations of power to the Union.	men in legislative and executive office at the Union level.	representative bodies exercising controlling powers over the Union, and in Union initiatives/ activities and representative delegations at global level. These mechanisms are the product of the critical engagement of regional–global feminism with the institutional loci and international laws of cosmopolitan governance.
To what extent do women enjoy the right, and capacity, to partake in the public sphere on a basis of equality?	INC	Each member state is a well-formed public sphere that attends to gender inequalities in civic and public engagement.	The EU is a public sphere in which gender inequalities in engagement are actively addressed.	The exercise of EU powers is guided by a commitment to ideals of a cosmopolitan public sphere in which women's participation on the basis of their equal moral worth and their active agency is a prerequisite for deliberation, and provided for in a manner that achieves this requirement.
To what extent can women's representatives (civil and political) and the affected female public participate in shaping law and policy proposals affecting their interests?	INC	Female citizens and their representatives contribute to the policy-making process in each member state through conventional channels, on a basis of equality.	Women's representatives and the affected female public contribute to policy formulation in the EU on all federal matters, on a basis of equality.	The affected female public and representatives can network across national and EU democratic institutions to influence EU policies affecting their interests; in addition, the affected female public can mobilise global support networks, and activate international human rights treaties to advocate their causes in regional and global settings.

Are there institutionalised deliberative sites available for the consideration of women's interests prior to taking decisions on gender-relevant issues?	INC	Each member state has a parliamentary forum that reflects on gender equality matters with the assistance of the affected female public (individual and organised), and forms a considered view arising from these deliberations with the power to influence institutional decision-making.	The federal EU has a parliamentary forum that reflects on gender equality matters with the assistance of the affected female public (individual and organised), and forms a considered view arising from these deliberations with the power to influence institutional decision-making in the fields in which it has competence.	The cosmopolitan EU has a parliamentary forum that reflects on gender equality matters with the assistance of the affected female public (individual and organised), and forms a considered view arising from these deliberations with the power to influence institutional decision-making. This parliamentary forum is linked to global institutional settings – economic and political – where deliberation incorporates feminist challenges to the systemic and intersecting oppressions of patriarchal, racial, colonial and economic power relations.
To what extent can female members of the public hold parties and legislative bodies to account for upholding gender equality?	ACC	Member state governments, legislatures and parties indicate their commitment to gender equality in manifestos, action plans, laws, treaties and other binding and account-giving documents (such as open sessions, publicly available minutes, broadcasts of hearings) on which their performance can be judged.	The federal EU indicates its commitment to upholding gender equality through manifestos, action plans, laws, treaties and other binding and account-giving documents (such as open sessions, publicly available minutes, broadcasts of hearings) on which their performance can be judged.	Combinations of national, European and international political actors indicate commitment to upholding gender equality through manifestos, action plans, laws, treaties and other binding and account-giving documents (such as open sessions, publicly available minutes, broadcasts of hearings) on which their performance can be judged.
To what extent can female members of the public hold	ACC	Women's representatives and other equality-seeking	Women's representatives and other equality-seeking	Women's representatives and other equality-seeking spokespersons

TABLE 6.1 *Continued*

Indicator	Type	Model 1	Model 2	Model 3
informal (as distinct from elected) representatives to account in articulating gender equality claims?		spokespersons in member states communicate their aims, strategies and objectives in public documents, and through other communicative media in a reciprocal dialogue process.	spokespersons in the federal EU public sphere communicate their aims, strategies and objectives in public documents, and through other communicative media in a reciprocal dialogue process.	in the cosmopolitan EU communicate their aims, strategies and objectives in public documents, and through other communicative media in a reciprocal dialogue process. This accountability is facilitated through the use of regional–global forums as sites around which cosmopolitan solidarity is enacted.
To what extent are positions on gender equality equality, as expressed by the affected female public and women's representatives, accorded recognition and respect, and given due consideration during political deliberation?	REC	Member states' political spheres are attentive to equality issues and to those presenting these issues, giving them equal regard and due consideration with other interests and responding in a reason-giving manner.	The EU political sphere is attentive to equality issues, and to those presenting these issues, giving them equal regard and due consideration with other interests and responding in a reason-giving manner.	The EU cosmopolitan political order, given its concern to promote a rights-based global framework, is attentive to equality issues, and to those presenting these issues. It recognises and respects the intersectional nature of gender equality issues, giving them equal regard and due consideration with other interests and responding in a reason-giving manner.
How far are the positions of women's representatives, and others, articulated in terms of the 'public good' as distinct from sectional interest?	REC	Participants in equality debates in member states express their positions in terms of enhancement of 'public good' and justify them in relation to one another on a basis of equality.	Participants in equality debates in the EU express their positions in terms of enhancement of 'public good' and justify them in relation to one another on a basis of equality.	Participants in equality debates in the cosmopolitan public sphere (with intermingled regional–global aspects) express their positions in terms of enhancement of the 'public good' as a global construct and justify them in relation to one another on a basis of equality.

table maps how the indicators can manifest themselves in each of the three models, and the next section discusses this in more detail.

The RECON models and gender democracy

The models of democracy constructed by Eriksen and Fossum (2009: 7–41) are designed to be heuristic devices rather than a categorisation of democracy's real-world attributes. They are intended to be aids for investigating the real world and imagining how democracy in an EU context would work in the three models. We treat gender democracy in the same way; as an ideational construct that enables one to imagine the gendered quality of EU democracy in these ideal-type settings. In each model, the gender democracy aspect will be different. In the next sections, these models are taken in turn and the interplay between gender democracy and the ideal type discussed.

Model 1: Delegated democracy

In this model, democracy is directly associated with the nation state, with the features of inclusion, accountability and recognition emphasised in the national context. Within this model, the EU is an intergovernmental forum, a *functional regime* where state governments agree on ways of pooling their sovereignty so as to solve common problems (e.g., the movement of people, economic competition, communication, environmental degradation) and delegate the EU institutions to address these issues on their behalf (ibid.: 16–22). As the authors point out, this delegated authority can take a number of institutional forms – as intergovernmental bodies and/or as an EU-wide representative body. However, as they go on to show, these transnational or supranational institutions would only have powers in relation to the competencies that member states had delegated to them to address. They would have no constitutional powers to make laws for the Union, nor could they extend the competencies of the EU beyond those agreed to by the member states. In all important areas of government, such as foreign policy and revenue-raising, along with redistribution of collective goods, the powers of the EU would be limited. In addition, member states could individually exercise a veto power over collective action proposals. Herein lies the problem for EU democracy: it is not democratic in the 'demos' meaning of the word. The member states, not citizens, would be the sole sources of legitimacy and the EU would act as a contractual order between states, implementing a juridical arrangement entered into by member states for the pursuit of agreed and specified common interests or the solution of common problems.

In this model, gender democracy is also centred in the nation state. Gender democracy requires the articulation of gender interests and the making of claims on the basis of gender justice, both of which are often focused on the redistributive aspect of democratic governance, as well as on the recognition and political participation dimensions. In this model of delegated democracy, gender claims cannot be made in forums beyond the state, because the legitimacy for democratic action resides in the individual states. The inclusion dimension of gender democracy can, in some contexts, be delivered more effectively through the nation state than through other arrangements. Expanding the representativeness of parliament through gender quotas to reflect women's share of the demos is one example. At best, gender claims on democratic processes and arrangements can only be considered at EU level if there is consensus among the member states that a particular aspect of gender relations (such as equal pay) is a common problem requiring a common solution. But the EU would not have the capability to make a binding order on member states in solving this gender-based inequality, because some member states could veto the EU-proposed solution. Thus, the restricted, audit-type EU democracy resulting from the functional delegation of powers limits the space in which an EU-wide public control can be exercised.

The allocation of binding decision-making to member states has implications for the realisation of gender democracy in individual nation states too, because the particular forms in which inclusion, accountability and recognition are expressed are unique to each national context. Public control by equals is interwoven with gendered norms and assumptions specific to each state, and thus gender democracy has different gradations across the member states. Some nations, then, will perform better than others in terms of their delivery of gender democracy. It is even conceivable that a truly gender-democratic nation state could outperform the two other democratic models in this regard. Uploading member state democracies to a supranational level would not deliver the requisite conditions for gender democracy, because it would not require a co-ordination of democratic legitimacy or a greater pooling of sovereignty – both necessary for the conditions of representativeness, accountability and recognition to be fulfilled at this level of governance.

Nonetheless, there is scope, albeit limited, for incorporating a measure of gender democracy into the model. Given its features of 'audit democracy' (Eriksen and Fossum 2010: 4), it is possible to envisage this model as containing elements of a gender democracy audit. This would require the EU's institutional arrangements to have the capacity to evaluate whether or not the issues addressed at EU level contained a gender dimension. If this was the case, then member states would need to be made aware of this and decide if it were appropriate for this gender dimension to be addressed at the EU level. The reality is, of course, that the 'audit democracy' model, given its reliance on the goodwill towards the issue of gender equity by individual member states, could be thinner in its incorporation of gender democracy than the actual working of the EU. The EU's treaty and legal framework, and the fully fledged representative nature of the European Parliament (EP) (including the influential activities of the Parliament's Women's Rights and Equality Committee), indicate that the EU has taken on a commitment to gender democracy that exceeds those provided for in the 'gender audit democracy' model. This point is all the more evident when one considers that gender issues of a cross-border nature, such as equal pay, gender-based violence, and trafficking in women and girls, come within the remit of EU action and, through EU links to the international human rights order, are reinforced as issues of policy concern. An audit model of democracy, grounded as it is in EU institutions that are accountable to national democratic systems, would not have the ability to take EU action on such transnational issues independent of unanimous member state agreement.

Model 2: Federal multinational democracy

The democratic arrangements consequent on a multinational federal European state give explicit significance to the demos, because 'the EU will be distinguished by a commitment to direct legitimacy founded on basic rights, representation and procedures for opinion and will-formation, including a European-wide discourse' (Eriksen and Fossum 2009: 22). This model envisages that people in the member states could retain their distinctive national identities and at the same time consciously develop a European identity that is important for collective action at the European level. Statehood in this model is conceived as a 'nested' arrangement, with the EU legally recognised as a state in the same way as individual member states, with clear jurisdictional powers accorded to each entity.

At first sight, this arrangement seems to offer much to gender democracy, because the core requirements of the gender democracy concept – inclusion, accountability and recognition – are applicable to both the EU and member state democratic will-formation processes. In addition, the democratic constitutional state based on direct legitimation, on which this model rests, provides gender democracy with a legally binding framework containing enforceable gendered provisions. In terms of collective action, the federal model provides an important alternative to the nation state that was not available in the audit democracy model, which is the possibility of appealing to a legitimate authority outside national boundaries. There is, then, the possibility of an inclusive debate among all citizens of the EU so long as the three criteria of gender democracy are respected. As a multilevelled set of political arrangements for delivering gender justice in democratic practices, the federal model has distinct advantages.

When applied to gender democracy, the model offers a substantial constitutional commitment to equality between women and men, predicated on a sense of a collective obligation to this issue. Inscribing gender equality as a feature of a European identity would presuppose that nation-building at member state level would incorporate this dimension too. In practical terms, it would allow for institutional arrangements that included women equally with men in the executive and legislative bodies of the federal European state and the constituent states. It would also offer women citizens multilevelled opportunities for influencing policy-making and agenda-setting. Furthermore, given the explicit constitutional and institutional facilitation of gender equality this model of gender democracy promises, the incorporation of gender interests, issues and concerns becomes an integral feature of democracy in the multinational federal European state.

Currently, though not constituted as a federal entity, the EU offers a developed form of supranational democracy with a gender imprint. Through the Lisbon

Treaty, the EU has accorded gender equality the status of a 'fundamental value' and equal opportunities between women and men have received a new impetus with the according of co-decision powers between the Council and the EP (Clavero and Galligan 2010). Furthermore, the Charter of Fundamental Rights, which confers EU citizens and residents with specified political, social and economic rights, was given treaty status in 2009. This basic legal framework provides a bedrock of social guarantees on the equal status of women with men, and underpins extensive policy development in matters of gender relations. However, it is important to note that the EU's 'constitutional' advocacy of gender equality is a conditional one. Family law, social security and social protection will remain areas for unanimous decision in the Council when the new qualified majority rules come into effect in November 2014 (Bisio and Cataldi 2008: 8). Thus, policy areas of special importance for gender equity will be subject to stricter decision-making rules than other policy areas.

Nonetheless, the EU forms an important arena for the realisation of gender equity, particularly in the field of employment and economic equality. It is gradually stretching its remit to issues of gender equality in political and social arenas, including representational equality and gender-based violence (European Commission 2010). In the process, it is using constitutional, legislative and persuasive power, backed up by jurisprudence to give effect to gender equity principles and commitments. It thus has elements of federalist political arrangements that work to enhance gender equity in the EU. The conditional and varied collective commitment to gender equality among member states, however, tempers the extent to which gender equality is perceived as a common vulnerability and therefore a common point of action. This is seen in the varied implementation of gender directives, the binding laws emanating from the EU (Falkner *et al.* 2008). Ultimately, it is not the model *per se* that is problematical. The main problem is the EU's inability to give effective expression to the model's potential. This difficulty should not be underestimated, for, as Eriksen and Fossum (2009: 23) point out, there is strong opposition to a federal 'super state'. However, this is a problem of perception, for the multinational federal European state model is more complex and interdependent than the popular view allows.

Model 3: Regional-European democracy

There is a growing discussion on the EU's emerging cosmopolitan features in the context of an ever-growing globalising public and political sphere. The effect of this globalising order is to reduce nation state sovereignty and diminish the range of issues over which citizens and their elected representatives can exert control (Eriksen and Fossum 2009: 26–7). In effect, the locus of political power does not reside solely in the nation state (and its subsidiary units), but is dispersed more diffusely, and sectorally, across combinations of states at a regional (such as EU) or global (such as G7) level. Over half a century of progressive integration, the sharing and pooling of sovereignty between member states and the EU as a supranational political entity has created multiple points of entry to democratic decision-making processes. These points exist in institutional arrangements beyond the state, enabling transnational networks of citizens to access decision-making forums that can, in turn, influence state-based policies and actions. Indeed, the experience of gender politics illustrates the utility of being able to appeal to a legitimate authority beyond the nation state in the pursuit of equality claims (Abels and Mushaben 2011; Kantola 2010). This route has given expression to the cosmopolitan system of democracy envisaged in Model 3, in which a non-state polity can embody a system of government when it performs the functions of 'authorised jurisdictions' (Eriksen and Fossum 2010: 5).

There is much in this model that speaks to gender democracy as an ideational construct. The importance of public debate as a legitimising feature chimes with the emphasis on the inclusion and influence of women's voices and perspectives advocated by gender democracy. The multilevelled decision-making component provides multiple access points for an autonomous, transnational civil society, of which women's organisations are an integral part. Through this multilevelled functional governance, gender equality advocates can bring decision-makers to account for their positions on gender concerns. Furthermore, there is an emphasis on consensus and the attention to deliberative quality that sets this model apart from the two previously discussed. Underpinned by a transnational commitment to the protection of fundamental rights, the model speaks to the cosmopolitan reach of gender equality norms, their application as overarching principles of governance, and the prospect of emancipatory feminist politics. Unlike the state-based models, this regional-cosmopolitan system of democracy rests on a more fluid set of political relationships coexisting with – and recognising – multiple identities that include (but are not exclusive to) national identities. It is open to the recognition of intersectional discriminations that arise from overlapping inequalities in power relations between men and women, including those inequalities consequential on the effects of patriarchal, economic, racist and colonial power dynamics.

The EU as a regional democracy contains opportunities for the development of gender democracy not afforded through the two earlier models. The ability to influence the composition of the EP is extended under this model in specific and important ways. Residency, as distinct from citizenship, is the basis on which the right to choose elected representatives is conferred. It draws on human rights justifications, expressed through European law and facilitated through concrete actions that empower the demos to exercise the franchise. This commitment fosters the inclusion of ethnic minority women, for example, whose enfranchisement can be problematic.[4] As the political rights of the demos are based on human rights, of which equality is a core norm, the enactment of laws to ensure gender equality in the Union's decision-making bodies is less of an issue than in the other two models. Through the representative capacity of the EP, for example, it offers opportunities to reflect the diverse concerns and interests of women in Europe, alongside those of men. This parliamentary body has the power to influence the decision-making process in a manner responsive to women's claims. In terms of accountability, the transparency of decision-making procedures has been enhanced over the decades, and attention is paid to reason-giving, its recording, and making the reason-giving process accessible to third parties, at a minimum. A second aspect of accountability for gender democracy is the inclusion of voices and interests directly affected by the problem, concern or issue under consideration. Through the use of hegemonic gender discourses, it empowers some (experts, bureaucrats) at the expense of others, thereby inscribing the exclusion of diverse gender concerns from the elite-agreed agenda. In this aspect, networking across national boundaries, identities and cultures is a challenge for the female members of the demos, but for which there are existing models and practices in the European Women's Lobby, KARAT Coalition, and coalition-building on gender issues with sectoral interest representatives such as trade unions, national equality bodies and gender advocates within, and affiliated to, the European institutions. Polycentric and multilevelled networks of gender equality activists and supporters exist in recognisable form at present. To foster a regional-cosmopolitan democracy, these networks, and the civic space they inhabit, require support and meaningful inclusion in decision-making. Their contribution to this public dialogue is to articulate a transformative, critical perspective on gender power relations. In return, the representatives of such gender-focused networks must be accountable to their own publics if gender equality deliberations are not to be confined to experts, technocrats and professional lobbyists, to the exclusion of groups expressing other identities carried by women (Beveridge 2010).

However, an empowered and gender-aware demos will make little headway if the sovereignty of female citizens is marginalised in deliberative procedures. Hence the real test of the cosmopolitan ambition of a regional-European democracy is the extent to which it listens, and is responsive to, the voiced concerns and interests of women. This can be facilitated by an open communication between all those interested and affected by a particular issue. Indeed, a transparent communicative process, in which all involved share their positions and justify their claims in terms of the public, regional-global good as distinct from sectional interest, represents the ideal public sphere in action. However, care needs to be taken to avoid the 'rationality' trap discussed earlier. For a regional European democracy to be a gender democracy, it would enable and empower women to participate as peers with men. It would also leaven the emphasis on impartial debate and argumentation with recognition of the importance of context, particularity, emotion and story-telling in the construction of political consensus. The validation of different styles of communication, then, is as important as descriptive participation in the creation of a cosmopolitan gender democracy.

At this point in time, practices in the EU democratic decision-making processes tend towards the marginalisation of women's perspectives and privilege those advocating neo-liberal economic interests with a restricted understanding of women's contribution to this set of priorities. This highlights the imbalance between the economic project of the EU and its social agenda – the latter consistently relegated to a secondary status. Furthermore, the embeddedness of patriarchal power relations in EU politics and policy is seldom problematised, because most critical feminist voices work within the neo-liberal paradigm, with its attendant hidden discriminations that characterise EU policy-making. Nowhere is this more apparent than in the handling of gender claims that have the potential to challenge this overarching value. Care work, for example, an issue that has the potential to challenge the patriarchal gender order, is subsumed into the EU employment agenda and constructed only as a problem for women's participation in the workforce. This rationalisation downgrades the vital social contribution of care-giving to the public good, and marginalises care-givers in the context of an economic definition of equality. It also hides cultural forms of patriarchy to which all women, and in particular, women from ethnic minorities residing in the EU are subject. The sharing of care work between men and women, and its potential for contributing to gender equality in the public and personal spheres, is not on the EU agenda despite a decade of policies seeking to support 'the reconciliation of work and family life'. Other issue areas of vital importance in supporting women's full human rights – such as reproductive rights, gender-based violence and freedom from cultural/ religious impositions – are far from being central to the EU agenda at the present time. Yet, the essential elements of a cosmopolitan order are in place: a human rights framework, a directly-elected body, recognised deliberative forums, and a stated commitment to gender equality. So too is broad consensus at elite level and in the public mind that a gendered identity co-exists in the EU alongside national, cultural and other identities. In addition, as an actor on the global stage, the EU has played a progressive role in developing women's human rights through its contribution to United Nations-led action plans for women, and in acknowledging the importance of gender issues in foreign and development aid initiatives. Building a gender-aware reflexive political culture from these foundational elements leading to an emancipatory cosmopolitan democracy should not be an insurmountable challenge.

Conclusion

This chapter has elaborated on gender democracy as an ideational concept resting on three distinctive pillars – inclusion, accountability and recognition. The concept is used to examine the gendered imprint of political decision-making processes and the institutional environment in which these decisions are taken. Gender democracy analyses the nature and extent of political equality in gender politics, and allows for comparisons between, across and beyond national state borders. It is a concept that critically considers the nature of democracy through a gender lens.

Gender democracy, then, is a useful device for assessing the heuristic models of democracy at the heart of the RECON project. When considered in this light, it was found that each model had advantages, depending on the aspect of gender justice being considered. While the audit democracy model was seen to be particularly effective in improving women's representation, and therefore inclusion, in democratic politics, it was less responsive to fostering gender justice on an international stage. This was primarily because of the rigid hold of member states on a European agenda, and the lack of a way to build consensus among member states as to what would properly constitute gender justice in a democratic setting beyond the nation state. It was additionally caused by the fragmentation of the demos along nation state lines, with scarce opportunity to articulate a common gender agenda transcending national borders.

The federal model of democracy held promise in the field of gender-just policies and politics primarily because it allowed for the uploading of specific responsibilities and competencies to a federal state (the EU) with the power to legislate for all members within its jurisdiction. The advantage of this model over the audit democracy arrangement, from the point of view of gender democracy, is that it allows for the possibility of cross-border civic engagement with an institutional focus that lies beyond the state to which it can direct its efforts, engage in dialogue and contribute to the federal decision-making process. There is the potential to make this a viable model for gender democracy through a significant boosting of political commitment to gender equality and social capacity for civic engagement on gender matters. This presupposes that the EU, as a federal entity, would be prepared, given power, to invest in issues that tackle gender power hierarchies.

From the perspective of gender democracy, some features of the regional-cosmopolitan model are already in place. Treaty commitments to gender equality as a political and social, as well as an economic, good exist; multiple issue networks involving the demos, of which women's perspectives are a constitutive part, are a feature of deliberation; and there are multiple public and political forums for engagement on agenda issues. There is, therefore, a nascent cosmopolitan order in the EU with the potential to be supportive of gender democracy. Ultimately, each of the models serves the purpose of gender justice in different ways. They treat the three essential aspects of gender democracy – inclusion, accountability, recognition – according to the logic embedded in each model, and illuminate different facets of gender democracy. All have something to offer a quest for gender democracy, each has a unique context in which gender democracy can be realised. In turn, each offers differing opportunities for addressing the emancipatory political project of gender democracy. In doing so, the three models highlight how the EU could develop democratic legitimacy and deepen democratic practice through being attentive to the principles and values of gender democracy.

Notes

1 This chapter is greatly informed and enriched by the comments of Sara Clavero who also contributed to earlier discussions and publications on gender democracy, including a precursor of this chapter in the RECON report 'Theory in Practice'. Indeed, the concept 'gender democracy' is a product of the fruitful collaboration between Sara Clavero and the author.

2 With thanks to Cathrine Holst for drawing my attention to this point, and for her helpful comments on an earlier draft.

3 I would like to acknowledge the important influence of Christopher Lord's (2009) discussion on a democratic audit for the EU in the development of this table.

4   'Equality between Women and Men', 6th European Ministerial Conference, Stockholm, 8–9 June 2006 [CM 92006 166]. Available at: http://www.coe.int/t/dghl/standardsetting/equality/05conferences/ministerial-conferences/6th-Ministerial%20Conference/MEG-6(2006)28_en.pdf

7

CIVIL SOCIETY, PUBLIC SPHERE AND DEMOCRACY IN THE EU

Ulrike Liebert

Introduction

A decade after the 2001 Laeken Declaration's roadmap for a more democratic and efficient European Union (EU), initial optimism appears to have been replaced with a greater pessimism in EU scholarship.[1] Ideas about strengthening the EU's supranational democratic legitimacy by injecting public deliberation and political participation into the EU constitution have lost out to doubts about the viability of a democratic constitution for the EU (see Graf Kielmansegg 1996; Grimm 1995; Scharpf 1999; see also Chapter 4).[2] Ordinary people allegedly stick to their nation state frames of reference as the main locus of interest, notably pertaining to domestic social welfare benefits, and arguably fail to engage with an international entity as distant and abstract as the EU (Moravcsik 2006; Shapiro and Hacker-Cordón 1999). Taking issue with this liberal intergovernmental account, the 'postfunctionalist' view underscores the politicisation of European integration in elections and referendums and how it contributes to the erosion of the mass public 'permissive consensus', but points to the mobilisation of identities that give rise to a 'constraining dissensus' regarding the jurisdictional architecture of the EU (Hooghe and Marks 2008). By contrast, empirical Europeanisation highlight to the emergence of Europeanised identities and a European public sphere with far reaching effects for the deepening and widening of European integration and, namely, for democracy (Risse 2010: 177ff).

Against the background of this fundamental controversy over the theory and practice of reconstituting democracy in the EU, the present analysis adopts a civil society and public sphere approach to the problem of the EU's democratic legitimacy in order to address two issues: first, assuming that the EU polity requires some form of democratic legitimacy, the main question is 'What democracy for what type of Union?' (see Introduction to this volume by Eriksen and Fossum). In other words, which model of democracy is appropriate and viable in the European context – a Europe of democratic nation states, a European supranational democratic state, or a regional-democratic union with a cosmopolitan imprint? Second, what can we learn from mass media-based, party political and institutionalised European communication about how democracy in the EU evolves? In particular, what does this tell us about where it is heading? Countering unreflected and unfounded optimistic as well as pessimistic stances, the present chapter aims at a more nuanced assessment by exploring how democracy matters in different spheres of European communication. It takes an empirical approach to European communication to shed light on democratic norms in practice. The complex nature of the EU requires a research design that takes the specificities of its setting into account, and namely the centrality of domestic spheres of European mass, political and institutional communication.

The present review of the communicative presuppositions for the three different models of EU democracy is contextualised by two instances of contentious EU politics: on the one hand, it is the process of constitutional treaty reform, from the signing of the Constitutional Treaty at the 2004 Intergovernmental Conference and its ratification failure in 2005 to the 2009 entry into force of the Lisbon Treaty; this protracted and contentious intergovernmental reform was subject to mixed procedures of ratification, parliamentary and by referendum. On the other hand, we have selected the 2009 European elections as an instance of direct elections to a supranational body with political party campaigns in all the member states. We conceive both instances as 'revelatory mechanisms' (Meyer 2007) for studying the democratic quality of European communication in three different domestic arenas, namely mass media, party campaigns and parliaments (see Appendix, Table A7.1). Accordingly, to develop our empirical knowledge, we have compiled systematic empirical evidence on European mass, political and institutional communication in six member states. The selection of different settings – mass media, party campaigns and parliamentary debates – enables us to scrutinise the democratic norms invoked by social, political and institutional actors in different arenas of EU communication practices.

In particular, this exploration serves three aims: (1) to contribute to the conceptual clarification of the meaning and status of democracy in contemporary Europe; (2) to develop an analytical framework for democratic stock-taking in a range of different spheres in European political communication; and (3) by presenting some basic findings from European communication research to illustrate the present EU's dilemma where mass media, party political and institutional discourses about Europe neither within nor across the member states respond to each other sufficiently to foster democratic legitimacy.

The chapter is structured in three parts: the first section develops the analytical framework by spelling out the implications of each of the three models of democracy in Europe for different arenas of civil society and public spheres. In the second part, selected findings are presented for assessing how civil society and public spheres matter for reconstituting democracy in Europe. The third part summarises and discusses these findings asking, in the light of the available empirical evidence, whether they indicate where democracy in the EU should be heading in the future.

Democratic polity models as a framework of analysis

Responding to the key question posed by this book, 'What democracy for what type of Union?', this section complements the institutional and policy analysis in the book through developing an analytical framework for assessing which democratic norms emerge from the evolving practices of civil society and the public sphere in Europe. This framework comprises three elements.

1. A conceptual clarification of what the different models of democracy imply regarding the configurations of civil society and public spheres, conceiving them either in strictly national terms; or as pan-European infrastructures on which the democratic legitimacy of a supranational federal Union is premised; or as mechanisms bent on conferring legitimacy on the European subsystem of a larger cosmopolitan order where citizen sovereignty replaces state sovereignty.
2. An analytical distinction between different forms and arenas of European political communication in order to establish their role in the circuits of public opinion and political will-formation in the EU context.
3. Finally, empirical criteria to operationalise the conceptual and analytical framework so as to render it amenable to empirical assessment of social and media communication practices, thus hoping to contribute to a more nuanced understanding of how civil society and the public sphere matter for democracy in the EU.

Democratic polity models and conceptions of civil society and public spheres

Theorists of democracy generally agree that civil society and public spheres are a 'sine qua non' of democracy: in some form or another they are acknowledged as pivotal sources of empirical legitimation and preconditions for the legitimacy of a democratic polity (see Dahl 1999: 221; Fraser 1992, 2005b; Habermas 1998c; Habermas *et al.* 1974: 54; Gerhards 2002; Eder 2007; Fossum and Schlesinger 2007). Therefore, for the context of the EU, we can assume that the Europeanisation of civil society and public spheres will foster the articulation of and debates among a plurality of voices, shape 'considered' public opinions on matters of EU policy, bring issues of public concern onto the political agenda and put pressure on authoritative decision-makers to respond to public opinion (Habermas 2009a: 158ff.)

Each of the three democracy models that frame the present book moulds a different kind of understanding of the configuration of the EU and the nature of its democratic legitimacy. Accordingly, this has implications for the configurations of civil society and public spheres (Eriksen 2007; Eriksen and Fossum 2009). In the following pages these three conceptions are outlined in more detail.

Model 1: Audit democracy

Under the first model of a Europe of democratic nation states, we place intergovernmental modes of European governing at the centre stage. Here, the member states will be conceived as the masters of the treaties as well as the sovereign principals who may choose to delegate powers to their EU-level agents. Following this conception, we would expect the EU to develop forms of indirect democratic legitimacy that rest on national electoral procedures, on territorial and party political forms of citizens' representation through national parliaments, through governments in international arenas and, occasionally, citizens' direct participation via civil society organisations or national referendums (Closa 2004; Peters 2005; Scharpf 1999). Following this model, civil society and the public sphere are conceived in terms of more or less pluralistic but in any case nationally confined arenas of social, political or mass media communication (Norris 2000; Habermas 2009a; Hallin and Mancini 2004). This conception of the EU depicts media communication on EU issues as typically segmented along national boundaries (Sifft *et al.* 2007).

Model 2: Federal multinational democracy

The second model of a European supranational federal, multinational state posits the EU as claiming direct democratic legitimacy. Following this model, the form of supranational democratic legitimacy of the EU is conceived in terms of participatory governance, with civil society organisations as partners of the EU institutions, on the one hand; and, on the other hand, direct elections to the European Parliament (EP), co-decision-making as the ordinary legislative procedure shared by the EP and the Council and powers conferred to the EP for confirming, controlling and holding accountable the other EU powers, namely the Commission, the Council Presidencies and the Agencies, including the European Central Bank (see Hix 2008; Liebert 2007b; Pinder 1999; Stie 2010). The model of a participatory and representative democratic European polity presupposes pan-European arenas of civil society organisation, party politics and mass communication, enabled by the new electronic media. Within the federal democratic configuration, the role of domestic arenas of European communication – national NGOs, parties, parliaments and mass media – is strictly limited to matters covered by the principle of subsidiarity, including institutional reforms of the EU polity.

Model 3: Regional-democratic union

Finally, under the third model, the EU is a regional association that is different from both an international organisation and a supranational state. It is conceived as a system of government and, moreover, as a government with cosmopolitan imprint. Given its far reaching impacts on citizens' lives, it requires a form of democratic legitimacy (Eriksen and Fossum 2000a, 2007a; Habermas 2009a; cf. Bohman 2007a).[3] In this respect, civil society and the public sphere – conceived as sources of legitimacy – are configured as transnational networks of cross- and subnational civic and public spheres (Eder 2007). Thus, the third model invokes a configuration of European transnational arenas for the pluralistic articulation and communication of economic, social and functional interests and cultural identities and, therefore, as preconditions for their representation in EU decision-making. The European public spheres will be populated by interest groups (Greenwood 2007), pioneered by transnational contentious movements (Della Porta and Tarrow 2005; Imig and Tarrow 2001) or promoted by civil society agents and public spheres at large (Liebert and Trenz 2010). Moreover, transnational civil and public spheres will be expected to promote shared patterns and dynamics of European political communication practices across national boundaries. Finally, in a cosmopolitan democratic perspective, civil society and public spheres represent agents of legitimation: by articulating cosmopolitan and universal norms and values in European civil society and public spheres and representing them in EU decision-making, they can confer democratic legitimacy on the EU.

In sum, to contribute to a more nuanced assessment of how civil society and public spheres matter for the democratic legitimacy of the EU in actual practice, it is neither sufficient to conceive of their role in the liberal democratic terms of preconditions for formal legal procedures of territorial, party political or functional representation. Nor is it enough to conceptualise them as generators of democratic norms and, thus, sources of democratic legitimation. In addition, another key question needs to be addressed: How do civil society and public spheres interact as agents, and to what extent do they matter for EU decision-making? For a systematic assessment of how national, federal as well as regional European conceptions of civil society and public spheres perform in communicatively linking citizens' preferences to EU decision-making, the following proposes a single analytical framework for the three different configurations of European social, mass media and institutional communication.

Analytical framework of European communication

Building on the earlier conceptual clarifications of what it means to configure civil society and public sphere in the perspective of different models of democracy, the present section develops an analytical framework aimed at making democratic stock-taking possible over a range of diverse social, political and institutional realms of European communication.

This framework comprises the three polity models of democracy by reframing them in terms of three different patterns of European political communication: (1) the 'nationally segmented' exclusive national patterns of communication about Europe; (2) the pattern of an encompassing European-wide 'supranational pattern of European communication'; and (3) 'regional cosmopolitan communication' with cross- and subnational patterns of European communication. Each of these three practices involves a different set of arenas and flows of European communication.[4]

Figure 7.1 outlines the three patterns of European communication for the context of the EU.

Analytically, this framework specifies five kinds of 'arenas of European communication' (1–5), each of which is located at one or several different scales (national, European, global). Applied to empirical research, this will help to identify (a) the scope of European communication in different types of arenas, and (b) convergence and divergence of democratic norms and communication practices across different types of public spheres. More specifically, the framework is supposed to help us to answer the following three questions: First, which civil society – including civic, economic and partisan – discourses on Europe are reflected in mass media communication, especially regarding the democratic norms by which the media frame EU politics and policy-making?[5] Second, to what extent do institutional public spheres – for instance, national parliamentary decision-making on EU treaty reform – represent mass media discourses on democracy in the EU? Finally, to what extent do government and parliamentary discourses on the democratic legitimacy of the EU resonate with political party and civil society discourses, for instance, in European election campaigns? By comparing institutionalised to media-based and party political arenas in European communication, we want to better understand whether they interact and how this matters for European democracy. To that end, the next section will present empirical criteria for assessing European communication practices.

MODES OF COMMUNICATION	ARENAS OF COMMUNICATION	THREE PATTERNS OF EUROPEAN POLITICAL COMMUNICATION
Institutionalised discourses and negotiations	(1) EU Council, Commission, Parliament, European Court of Justice, etc. (2) National governments, administration, parliament, courts, etc.	I. NATIONALLY SEGMENTED Structured through (2), in interaction with (3)/(4) and rooted in (5), but only at national scale, no direct impact from (3)/(4) on (1)
Media-based mass communication in dispersed public spheres	Published opinions ⟵ (3) Media system ⟍ State ⟱ ⟰ ⟵ Capital (4) Publics ⟹ Results of opinion polls ⟍ Civil society	II. SUPRANATIONAL Structured through (1), in interaction with (3)/(4) and rooted in (5) at European scale; direct impacts from (3) and (4) on (1)
Communication among the addressees	(5) Social constituencies (citizenry), with arranged or informal relations, social networks and movements	III. REGIONAL-COSMOPOLITAN Structured from below through transnational networks of (4), rooted in (5) at subnational and global scale

FIGURE 7.1   Modes, arenas and patterns of European political communication

Source: Adapted for EU context from Habermas 2009a: 160

Criteria for assessing European communication practices in different arenas

This section operationalises the conceptual and analytical framework developed earlier and links it with empirical analyses. To explore whether, to what extent and how European communication practices reflect any of the three RECON polity models, we want to compare the extensiveness of European communication (Model 1 versus 2); the types of 'discursive frames' for assessing which of the Models 1, 2 and 3 prevail in it; the extent of representation of different social, economic and political discourses (Model 1 versus 2 and 3); and patterns and dynamics of transnational communication (Models 1 and 2 versus 3). A discursive frame is defined as a mode of contextualising issues of European politics in a broader frame of reference, such as images of democracy in Europe, as they are mapped for instance by the RECON models (see earlier). For empirically assessing the democratic frames and practices of European political communication within and across different public arenas, the following four measures are suggested (see Table 7.1):[6]

TABLE 7.1   Democratic frames and practices in European political communication

Arenas of EU political communication	Empirical measures	
National parliamentary EU debates	(a)	extension of plenary debates on EU issues (no. of sessions, length)
	(b)	salience[1] of democratic norms in relation to EU issues; type of dominant democracy frame[2]
	(c)	diversity of voices[3] representing government and opposition parties, economic and civil society actors in parliamentary discourses
	(d)	transnational references to and arguments about views of EU and non-national actors.
Media-based: EU party campaigns EU news coverage	(a)	extent of coverage of specific EU issues (no. of articles, length)
	(b)	salience[1] of democratic frames in media coverage of EU issues; dominant democratic framing[2] in discursive reasoning
	(c)	diversity of voices[3] representing state, economic and civil society actors in media coverage of EU issues
	d)	transnational interactions with non-national actors, media outlets.

Notes:
1 'Salience' measures in comparative terms how extensive the proportion of specific issues or actors in EU-related political communications is.
2 'Dominant democracy frame/framing' refers to the relative proportion of a specific model of democracy in Europe compared with competing ones to which European political discourses can refer for situating and interpreting given EU policy issues.
3 'Diversity of voices' refers to the distribution of different types of actors – state, economic, civil society – and their interests or identities in European political communication.

- quantitative measures for the extent of political communication on EU issues (in terms of number of parliamentary plenary debates, or the news media coverage in the number of news items or articles devoted to that coverage);
- substantive criteria for measuring the salience of democratic frames as schemes for interpreting and arguing about EU issues in public discourses (namely the dominant model of democracy);
- measures to establish the diversity of social, economic and political discourses that are represented by the mass media or by state (parliamentary) institutions in debating EU issues in the public sphere; and
- measures to establish the extent of transnational interaction between national and non-national discourses in European communication.

In sum, to examine how the different models of democracy cohere with the European communication practices, these criteria help to establish degrees of their discursive representation in the member states: how institutionalised communication about the EU represents mass media and civil society discourses, and to what extent the latter are responsive to partisan and institutional discourses in the processes of public opinion and will-formation in EU decision-making.

The answers to these questions depend on the evolving social and political communication practices. The following section summarises systematic empirical findings from exemplary cases of European political communication research.

How civil society and public spheres matter for reconstituting democracy in Europe: Selected findings[7]

Prominent scholars from the field of international communication remind us of the challenges of cross-national comparative media research. They also point to the 'slow pace of media studies' to respond to this challenge by carrying out comparative research at the aggregate level of systems (Hallin and Mancini 2004; Livingstone 2003; Nordenstreng 2010: 1). The following draws on several comparative data sets that were compiled by two cooperative research teams, mostly comparative political scientists or sociologists. To collect systematic comparative data from institutionalised as well as open arenas of European political communication in old and new EU member states, we have developed a method of Atlas.ti-based comparative political discourse analysis that combines quantitative methods of content analysis with qualitative features of discourse analysis. Complementing the analytical framework and normative criteria outlined earlier, we have called this method accordingly 'Comparative Political Discourse Analysis' (ComPDA). We have found ComPDA useful specifically for assessing the patterns of European political discourses in parliamentary arenas, the mass media and party campaign analysis.[8]

In the following, our major research findings are summarised under three headings: (1) National parliamentary discourses on EU treaty ratification; (2) Print media coverage of EU treaty reform, and (3) Print media-based European election campaigns.

National parliamentary discourses on EU treaty ratification[9]

In the EU, national parliaments play a central role in the democratic legitimation of EU constitutional reform. In the most recent Constitutional and Lisbon Treaty reforms, ratification has been subjected to referenda in six member states. Yet, in all 27 member states but one – Ireland – parliaments have remained firmly in control of ratification. Nationally elected representatives have kept the decisive say, yet with considerable variation regarding their views of the EU's democratic legitimacy. Following the deliberative democratic approach to representation (Liebert 2007b; Mansbridge 2003), parliamentary representation is conceived in terms of ongoing processes of communication between representatives and constituents that can take on different forms. The quality of parliamentary EU proceedings can be assessed in terms of procedures and practices facilitating high-quality discursive processes of will-formation and decision-making, in four dimensions (see Table 7.1). To assess parliamentary performance in practice, we draw on a comparative parliamentary discourse analysis of treaty ratification debates from six EU member states.[10]

Our research findings suggest that parliaments in the EU exhibit quite a mixed picture. On the one hand, we find the salience of democratic norms and procedures as topics of parliamentary treaty ratification debates to be quite noteworthy. Among the top ten topics debated most intensively, the mode of treaty ratification ranked highest on the agendas of the British, Polish, French and Hungarian parliamentarians, and much lower in the cases of the Czech Republic and Germany. The Council decision-making procedure was another topic that received much attention, namely the use of qualified majority voting, as well as issues of the EU's decision-making procedures and institutional architecture. A third prominent issue was citizens' rights, the Charter of Fundamental Rights and, in the Hungarian case, minority rights (Appendix, Table A7.9).

On the other hand, the assessment of alternative democracy frames in national parliamentary discourses demonstrates the continued predominance of national models over supranational or cosmopolitan models of democracy in the EU (Appendix, Table A7.12). Only in the French and, to a minor degree, the Hungarian debates, did parliamentary discourses privilege a supranational democratic EU. The conception of a cosmopolitan regional Union gained considerably less visibility. However, at a closer look, references to the three different models in parliamentary discourses vary, depending on which national and EU institutions or policy areas are under debate. Also, right-wing parties share a more uniform position with respect to the 'EU of the nation states' and opposing a 'federal Europe'. First, any governmental and some of the large opposition parties favour more diversity, advocating pragmatically variable models of democracy, depending on policy issue or institutional domains under consideration. Second, the discursive diversity of some parliamentary debates is limited, in particular because of the predominance of the governmental voice. In the German ratification debate, speakers from the Government took the largest share of the floor, while in the Polish Sejm and the British

House of Commons their role was more constrained, leaving the debate of the contentious treaty to other parliamentary groups. Finally, in most cases, parliamentary discourses show less consensus orientation and more polarisation. While less than a quarter of all statements made by MPs in plenary debates are neutral in tone, we find two articulate camps of political party groups with opposed positions on treaty ratification (Appendix, Table A7.9). Although the No-votes are in the clear minority – even in the British case the 348 Yes-votes outnumber the 204 No-votes in the Lisbon ratification by far – the opponents are over-proportionately vocal and they account for a quarter to a third of all statements that express negative positions (Appendix, Table A7.9). Yet, as Aleksandra Maatsch has demonstrated in a cross-national comparison, the intraparliamentary political divisions between Social Democrats and Christian Democrats are stronger than divisions between old and new EU member states: 'Political parties belonging to the same ideological group do not only share the same positions on EU institutional and policy reform but also share very similar discourses for justifying these positions' (Maatsch forthcoming).

In sum, albeit the discursive quality of parliamentary ratification proceedings in three old and three new EU member states varies considerably, the parliamentary discourses share a number of common features, namely the concerns about direct democratic procedures of EU treaty ratification on the one hand coupled with attachments to national democratic frames, except in the French case, on the other. Most importantly, the polarised nature of the debates – in part due to the schedule for parliamentary ratification debates – appears an unfortunate handicap for non-partisan actors, experts or civil society organisations. All cases of parliamentary treaty ratification debates considered here, except the Polish, suffer from the same caveat; they are scheduled after the fact, after national governments and EU elites have typically concluded treaty negotiations 'behind closed doors', and without involving the opposition and minority parties. Lack of parliamentary debates in the early stages of EU treaty reforms will not only inhibit cross-party consensus orientation but also a sufficient extent of media coverage to educate the general public. Both would be required to enable interested citizens to inform themselves and allow for participation in public opinion formation at a relatively early stage of binding intergovernmental decision-making.[11] The ex-post intervention of parliaments forecloses the coupling of parliamentary debates with media-based public opinion formation early enough to give citizens and civil society a chance to meaningfully and constructively engage with important issues of EU treaty reform.[12]

Print media coverage of EU treaty reform

The print media coverage of the EU's constitutional reform process has been studied by a number of researchers and research groups who have produced single case studies (see Evas 2007; Gaisbauer 2010; Kitus 2008; Maatsch 2007; Packham 2007; Rakušanová 2007; Vetters *et al.* 2009; Wyrozumska 2007), paired comparisons (see Seidendorf 2010), as well as a growing amount of comparative analyses (Liebert 2007a; Mokre *et al.*, 2009; Krzyzanowski and Oberhuber 2007). The following assessment draws on two comparative data sets that have been compiled within two research projects.[13] Taken together, the integrated data set surveys print media coverage of the EU's Constitutional Treaty and the Lisbon Reform Treaty in six member states during the period October 2004 to July 2007. It is designed as cross-national comparisons in three old and three 'new' member states (See Appendix, Table A7.1).

Summarising the insights gained from this analysis, several important findings stand out. In three respects, we find the mass media to have benefited democratic legitimation in the EU (see Appendix, Table A7.4; Table A7.7; Table A7.11; Table A7.12). First, the quantitative record is noteworthy regarding the extent of space that the media devote to covering EU treaty reform.[14] In this respect they can be said to have contributed to educating their audience by translating the highly specific and complex contents into frames that are interesting for the readers and thus, arguably, enabling them to make informed choices between political opinions. Second, regarding their discursive performance, media coverage of EU treaty reform politics makes a difference as regards the salience of the democratic frames chosen to interpret these issues.[15] The media more often than not do frame EU issues in a language of democracy that transcends traditional nation state conceptions and reflects, for instance, a supranational federal polity, but pointing much less to a cosmopolitan-regional rights-based community. Also, the news media do not restrict their coverage to national actors but include a higher proportion of European and non-national voices as well. Last, but not least, regarding their transnational communication performance, the media practices can be said to improve the preconditions for democratic legitimation in EU politics by developing transnational political communication about publicly shared concerns in EU politics across national boundaries.[16] In sum, the comparative analysis provides evidence of overlapping transnational public spheres, in terms of cross-border exchanges about issues of EU treaty ratification and reform, thus focusing cross-nationally shared concerns with collective European problems, albeit judged by different normative lenses, and linked to different topics of domestic relevance.[17]

Turning now to more critical notes on print media performance, the following can be observed. First of all, although the media pay considerable attention to European and non-national political and institutional actors – sometimes even more than to national actors – the overall discursive diversity is quite limited. A minority of news outlets devotes coverage to non-political actors, such as economic or civil society organisations.[18] The discursive patterns of media-based EU communication are defined by European institutional and national state actors and political parties, with restricted space for voices from those social constituencies that the media have deemed worthy of coverage. Moreover, news media that employ an argumentative mode are also in a critical minority. The media typically cover news related to EU treaty negotiations, ratification failure and crisis, but they rarely devote space to substantive arguments and discussions (Appendix, Table A7.11).

The scrutiny of mass media-based European political communication about the EU brings strengths and weaknesses of national media performance to the fore. The lack of discursive pluralism and especially the limited access of voices from civil society is certainly a restriction if the media are to play the role of arenas for deliberative European political communication. On the other side, regarding the extent of media coverage of EU Constitutional and Lisbon Treaty reform, the modes of democratic framing and the cross-border coverage clearly transcend the national realm. Transnational observation and discursive interaction with non-national actors increase the leverage of the mass media in building an agenda for transnational democratic discourses in EU politics.

Print media-based European election campaigns

The data sets consulted here for the purpose of the present assessment have been compiled from print media coverage of the 2009 European election campaigns in six EU member states.[19] As established wisdom holds that European elections typically deal with domestic political issues – therefore constituting 'second-order elections' – it comes as a surprise that, as a matter of fact, the EU's Lisbon Treaty, the EP and institutional questions of the Council and the Commission were on top of the 2009 election campaign agenda.[20] Moreover, in our analysis of discursive patterns of media-based election campaigns, we find a strong incidence of argumentative modes referring to European-level problems, ideas and interests.[21] Yet, again, the conspicuous bulk of media attention is devoted to populist, right-wing fringe parties that take a decidedly Eurosceptic stance, namely, for example, the Front National (FN) in France, Jobbik in Hungary, Libertas in Poland and the United Kingdom Independent Party (UKIP) as well as the British National Party (BNP) in Great Britain. While such voices were largely absent in the domestic German discourse, their electoral success drew attention to the phenomenon in Germany too. The Dutch Freedom Party as well as the British Eurosceptic parties were duly covered in German media. European-level actors such as influential (former) Members of European Parliament (MEPs), domestic EU Commissioners or Commission President Baroso were given space in most of the media.

How influential are the media for shaping public opinion and, especially, citizens' predispositions for voting in view of upcoming elections? A comparison of the media contents about European elections to the post-election public opinion survey suggests that media communication is not just cheap talk – it seems to matter. Nevertheless, the media analysis provides additional dues.[22]

First, media discourses reveal one of the most important motives for voters to abstain from elections, one that is frequently overlooked by opinion polls: the intention to punish the elites or to protest against them. This claim was particularly prominent in the French and British media coverage of European elections. The opinion survey establishes instead 'lack of confidence in, or dissatisfaction with, politics in general' as the main reason for electoral abstention. It is, however, possible that this motive is framed in the published debate as the wish to punish elites.[23] Second, as regards the 'feeling that one's vote is inconsequential' and the 'lack of knowledge of the EU and the EP and about the elections', these are issues primarily in the German public debate. Both the German and the Hungarian press complain about the lack of electoral campaigning, which is also among the motives driving abstention established by the Eurobarometer survey. Third, the 'feeling that the EP elections are not important' is indeed a very important issue in the coverage of all cases included in the media study. In Britain this is the dominant perception that the media reproduce. However, in the other five media contexts, the speakers make strong cases *in favour* of the importance of the EP and the elections, thus presuming that voters do indeed have to be persuaded to participate in them. Finally, our comparative media discourse analysis confirms that economic development and unemployment were among the top five issues in the French, German and Hungarian media-based election campaigns – here, the financial crisis was the overall most important issue hitting the election campaigns. In the French context, national economic growth was always connected to the role of the EU on the international scene, while taxation policy was particularly salient in Hungary.[24] Yet apart from economics, the media sample selected for analysis was also concerned with other issues of domestic and European politics – the election campaigns, domestic and European-level party competition and the performance of the national executive. The issue of election turnout was important and debated in all election campaigns.

In sum, published opinion and public opinion reflect each other in important respects. Polling results on the salience of issues are, by nature, biased by the list of answers made available to the respondents by the interviewers. Public debates encompass a much broader range of issues. Still we find that in important respects the patterns of public opinion resonate with the media contents and framing, indicating that public discourses on Europe matter for public opinion formation.

Summary and discussion

The instances of European communication examined here – from the 2005 constitutional ratification failures to the 2009 Lisbon Treaty ratification issues in EP election campaigns – provide us with selected insights into the patterns and dynamics of discursive engagement with contentious issues of EU politics. The research findings presented earlier shall now be confronted with the conventional wisdom on the subject[25] with an aim towards developing a threefold argument.

1.   As to the widespread belief that it was wrong to expect the Europeanisation of national mass public spheres to happen in the near future (Grimm 1995, Graf Kielmansegg 1996, Peters 2005), our empirical evidence from two crucial episodes of the recent development of the EU – the 2004–2007 Constitutional Treaty Ratification and the 2009 European Elections – is testimony to the contrary. We have demonstrated that both events have triggered intense coverage by the national news media. For explaining these dynamics, politicisation appears a crucial part of the story. In the context of EU treaty reform, the contentious nature of these protracted struggles has certainly provoked

deep controversy among state actors, so that controversial EU debates have spilled over from institutional arenas – namely intergovernmental bodies, national governments, parliaments and parties, as well as courts – into media-based political communication and civil society, and has even reached mass publics. Thus, politicisation has proven at least beneficial, if not necessary, to the expansion of European public communication practices. The mass media increasingly tell readers to think about Europe, thereby advancing the Europeanisation of public agenda-setting and, at the same time, setting the initial stage in the formulation of public opinion. The selection and coverage of EU issues – among them the contentious norms and presuppositions for the EU's democratic legitimacy – and their exposing to national audiences makes them potentially part of the public agenda and, eventually, increases their salience in the eyes of the public. In this respect, the mass media's role in European communication increasingly consists 'in telling readers what to think about' (Cohen 1963).

Of course, politicisation of EU issues is by no means sufficient for explaining the Europeanisation of national public spheres. The patterns and dynamics of the European public debates in different national contexts do not depend alone or primarily on politicisation, but are shaped, in the first place, by the institutional media settings and cultures. Variations in the quantity and quality of news media coverage of EU politics is no surprise, given the uneven quality of the democratic systems of the member states, some of them with weakly consolidated democratic institutions and media systems that have not reached full independence from the state or have fallen into new external and internal dependencies.[26] Among other new but also old member states, Hungary is a telling case in point.

2. Another question is what politicisation and contentious Europeanisation of national public agendas have got to do with the democratic legitimacy of the EU. The established wisdom on this matter is that both are at odds if not outright antagonists. For understanding the role of civil and public spheres for the EU's democratic legitimacy, they cannot be reduced to forces for eroding the longstanding 'permissive consensus' in support of a supranational EU, or for driving new patterns of 'constraining dissensus' vis-à-vis EU politics and policy-making, patterns that are motivated less by collective interests and more by identities (Hooghe and Marks 2008). Pointing out the shortcomings of such an approach, Stefano Bartolini has warned us not to have illusions about the 'politicisation' of the EU as 'the right sort of medicine to cure the EU's ills' (Bartolini 2006). But neither should we conclude from these points that the politicisation of public opinion and the mobilisation of European civil society will necessarily lead to problems rather than solutions, as authors adopting a sceptical view generally maintain.

Under the third democratic model, as depicted earlier, that frontloads citizenship vis-à-vis national or supranational statehood, civil society and the public sphere need to be measured against the requirements of democratic legitimacy

for the EU. That is that they provide for citizens and mass publics the preconditions for becoming knowledgeable about and engaging in 'considered' public
opinion formation on issues 'beyond the nation state', and specifically questions
of EU politics and policy-making by which they feel affected. For reconstituting the EU as a democratic regional union without a state, civil society and the
public sphere are indispensible preconditions for political participation and representation, including the responsiveness of political elites to polyethnic publics
as well as the publics' awareness of and responsiveness to EU policy-making.

Our research findings support these notions in three ways. First, issues of
democracy constitute important topics on the public agendas, on EU constitutional ratification as well as in European elections. Second, when framing
the EU as a matter of democracy in public debate, the national media provide
a pluralist arena. Contrary to methodological nationalist assumptions, national
democracy does not serve as the default option, but supranational or transnational democratic models receive coverage as well. Third, not only in media
contents and framing but also in their communication practices can we identify
tendencies of media-based European political communication that transcend
national frameworks of democracy by promoting transnational observation,
translation and discursive exchange. Transnational communication practices
generate networks of cross-border communication flows, extending discursive
acts of communication between speakers and audiences as well as between
speakers from different national communication communities. In sum, the
national media promote the Europeanisation of agenda-building also at this
second level of framing issues (Fortunato 2005: 56). Choosing how to present
an EU issue, by framing the issue content, they construct the media messages
that shape people's perceptions. They tell readers not only about what to think
but how to think about impacts of European integration (ibid.). However,
to cohere with a realistic image of the media society, the notion of European
deliberative politics and policy-making should not be normatively overloaded.
The argument developed here is that an emerging European public sphere can
favour the EU's democratic legitimacy only to the degree that the dominant
democratic frames from the European 'official' discourses resonate with the
ones selected by the domestic arenas that are involved in EU decision-making.
In the case of EU treaty ratification examined here, and comparing national
media and parliamentary discourses, resonance of the dominant democratic
frames has been limited if not absent. Arguably, this can be read as an indi-
cation of 'cheap talk' and that media communication matters little for the
democratic legitimacy of the EU.

3.   The last question to be addressed is whether the expansion of media-based
     European communication and the salience of democracy in public discourses
     about the EU will also contribute to EU legitimacy through representing
     civil society voices in public communication. The answer to this question is
     straightforward. On the one hand, we find evidence about the potential and
     willingness of European civil society to discursively engage with contentious

issues of European integration (Liebert 2010; Liebert and Trenz 2010; Trenz *et al.* 2010). On the other hand, declining European election turnout and rising Euroscepticism among social constituencies seem to tell contrary stories. In a critical examination of the news media, the performance of national and transnational networks of European political communication with respect to EU legitimacy exhibits deficits in regard to inclusive democratic communication practices. Conceiving political communication as a configuration of social practices,[27] media engage in relationships with different types of constituency groups. Presupposing Johan Galtung's three-sided model of society with conflictive relations between the three pillars of the State, Capital and Civil Society, the media 'take a challenging place in a field of conflicts'; floating somewhere between these pillars, they serve as 'vital channels not only for Civil Society in relation to the State and Capital, but also in communication between the State and Capital in order to ensure a common public sphere and dialogue in society' (Galtung 1999; 3f).[28] Analytically, all three pillars can provide contents to the media. Regarding our available evidence on news media coverage of EU treaty ratification and European elections, primarily EU institutions, government and political parties, to a lesser degree economic interest organisations and only very marginally civil society actors have actually generated inputs raising their voices about the critical events of EU politics examined here. European public political communication is certainly freely accessible for lay people as readers, but only in exceptional cases for non-governmental organisations as speakers, as well.

The intention pursued in this section was to review and assess empirical evidence as regards the role of civil society and the public sphere for the democratic legitimacy of the EU. I have suggested that their role is enhanced depending on democratic contents and inclusive practices by the media in covering EU news. On the other hand, it is constrained by the incoherence between political parties' media messages about European elections and the same parties' EU discourses in national parliaments. What the data tell us about the salience of democratic frames in the reconstitution of Europe can be summarised as a mixed message: different models of democracy – and the RECON models in particular – count differently, depending on the kind of public sphere. Media messages, on the one hand, construct an image of a supranational EU that shapes public opinion but not necessarily the public agenda. National parliamentary discourses, on the other hand, reproduce an image of a Union, the legitimacy of which depends on the democratic member states alone.

Illuminating these deficiencies, constraints and incoherencies does not mean to deny national public spheres and civil society the cognitive and practical potential to engage with EU issues in forms that contribute to the democratic legitimacy of EU governance. On the contrary, our findings suggest a segmented mode of European political communication the quality of which hinges to a large extent on how and at which stage the interplay with domestic public forums is built into EU decision-making procedures at both national and supranational levels. Hence, provided that the respective lessons for procedural and institutional aspects of EU reforms are drawn from past communication failures, it would be misleading to assume that politicisation is the wrong sort of medicine for curing the EU's ills.

Conclusion

How can we develop further the research agenda to rethink European democracy from the perspective of civil society and the public sphere? The contemporary intellectual and political controversy over competing norms and forms of democracy in Europe will gain from better understanding its evolving practices. In conclusion, reflecting on the problems of the EU's democratic legitimacy from the angle of civil society and the public sphere is not only normatively desirable but also necessary for better understanding the status of democracy in European integration, despite the occasional stalemates in the EU's democratisation projects.

Last but not least, seeking lessons from past experiences to answer these present and future challenges means trying to understand, and in some depth, why the constitutional treaty ratification in 2005–08 failed or why turnout in European elections continues to decline. In light of the evidence presented here, the questions 'What democracy for what type of Union?' and, more specifically, whether 'politicisation' can be the right sort of medicine for curing the EU's democratic legitimacy deficits can both be answered. This answer is informed by our selective findings that illustrate that the allegedly missing social and communicative prerequisites for a democratic EU are emerging, paradoxically as effects of politicisation through contentious EU policy issues. If politicisation of EU-level issues is a necessary mechanism for promoting the Europeanisation of public spheres, the articulation of civil society voices is not yet sufficient to progressively engage Europeans with European decision-making. Whether by direct forms of engagement through referendums or European elections, or by indirect ones through national parliamentary processes, Europeanisation through politicisation requires three more conditions: first, at the EU level, ongoing processes of institutional and constitutional reform that are designed as catalysts for mass public politicisation of European integration; second, at the transnational level, mechanisms and arenas – including the European Citizens' Initiative and others – for framing issues of EU reform not exclusively within but across different national contexts; third, the predisposition of national and European political and media elites to reliably represent and respond to citizens' critical voices in a constructive manner. Provided these preconditions are met, politicisation of European integration should link in closely with effective and legitimate EU reform.

Acknowledgements

I want to thank the editors of this book for very useful comments and suggestions on a previous draft of this chapter.

Notes

1 For instance, despite considerable public debates and referendum turnout, the majority of the French and Dutch rejected the EU's Constitutional Treaty. The Lisbon Treaty is another case in point where EU leaders only succeeded with ratifying by forestalling referenda and thus the manifestations of popular opposition against it.

2 Building on Jürgen Habermas (1991, 2009a), the idea of European integration by deliberation has been developed by Bohman 2007a and Eriksen and Fossum 2000a; and, with a focus on different kinds of public spheres, by Eriksen 2007. For a sceptical account, see Peters 2005.

3 Bohman's conception of a 'transnational democracy' differs from the present third model in so far as he proposes a system of governance and not government; however, both conceptions converge in granting a pivotal role to civil society and public spheres for transnational processes of democratic legitimation.

4 This section further develops the 'process tracing approach' (see Gerhards and Neidhardt 1991; Liebert and Trenz 2009b).

5 The concept of 'civil society' as it is used here includes three distinct sectors, namely the 'civic sector' (also 'third sector', 'voluntary', 'community' or 'non-profit' sector) that is conceived as the sphere of social activity undertaken by organisations that are non-profit, non-governmental and represent general interests, the 'economic' or 'capital' sphere denoting the for-profit 'private sector', constituted by organised economic and professional interest groups, including employers' and business associations, and the political sphere, constituted by partisan organisations (see Galtung 1999; Liebert and Trenz 2010; Liebert and Trenz 2009a).

6 For a more detailed description of how these indicators have been set up, cf. Liebert and Trenz 2008; Liebert and Trenz 2009b. The empirical indicators proposed there for assessing mass media coverage of EU constitutional ratification debates have been extended here to compare different fields of European political communication, including parliamentary debates, European election campaigns and mass media coverage of EU issues.

7 I want to thank the members of the ConstEPS and RECON WP5 research teams at the Jean Monnet Centre for European Studies, University of Bremen, for collaboration on compiling and analysing the cross-national comparative data sets, namely Aleksandra Maatsch (Poland), Kathrin Packham (Germany, UK), Petra Rakušanová Guasti (Czech Republic) and Tatjana Evas (Estonia, Latvia); Ewelina Pawlak and Alexander Gattig for quantitative data analysis and research project management, including the summer school for international PhD students in 'Advanced methods of media analysis' (July/August 2007, University of Bremen). The empirical data sets on which the following summaries are based have been generated in collaborative coding sessions by teams of junior researchers with expertise from different member states, under the supervision of Aleksandra Maatsch and Kathrin Packham, and led by WP5 coordinator Ulrike Liebert (UniHB). Funding is acknowledged for ConstEPS to the Volkswagen Foundation (2005–2008) and for RECON WP5 to the European Commission, FP6 (2007–2010).

8 For the description of the qualitative samples compiled from three arenas of European political communication, see Appendix, especially Tables A7.1–A7.4. The structure of the coding scheme that was used for Atlas.ti-based ComPDA is provided by Table A7.5, and Table A7.6 shows the results of ComPDA for the parliamentary and media data sets.

9 This research cluster has been conducted by Aleksandra Maatsch (Jean Monnet Centre, University of Bremen), the comparative data set has been elaborated and analysed by Ewelina Pawlak. For a more elaborate presentation of the results, see Maatsch 2010.

10 A summary of the results from the quantitative analyses is provided in the Appendix, Tables A7.1, A7.2, A7.9 and 7.12.

11 However, the 2009 Lisbon Treaty has upgraded the rights for participation of national parliaments in an early phase of the EU's legislative process.

12 A similar argument has been made by Fossum and Trenz (2007: 211), however, referring to the French and Dutch ratification referenda in 2005 and not to national parliamentary ratification procedures as catalysts for politicisation and domestic sources of democratic legitimation of the EU.

13 The first print media survey covers six member states during 2004 and 2005 and has been compiled in the framework of ConstEPS, at the University of Bremen. The second one has complemented this database by an additional 'print media data set' covering 2005–2007, and elaborated in the framework of RECON WP5, co-coordinated by the University of Bremen and ARENA, Oslo; see Appendix data description and Table A7.1.

14 Regarding the extensiveness to which the media have covered EU treaty reforms and put them on the public agenda, a total of 8500 articles have been retrieved over the 25-month period from more than 30 news media outlets in the six countries under research (see Appendix, Table A7.4).

15 Substantively, media coverage of the EU's treaty reforms frequently refers to diverse topics of domestic public interest, among them Enlargement and Turkey, Common Foreign and Security Policy (CFSP), Union Budget, Social Policy, Energy and Transport, but also the Charter of Fundamental Rights (UK) and Majority Voting (Poland) (see Appendix, Table A7.7). But the news media coverage of the Constitutional Treaty and Lisbon Treaty also featured democratic frames, most of them reflecting institutional features and policies that indicate the supranational democratic model in the first place (Appendix, Table A7.12) and national democratic frames in the second.

16 Regarding media-based transnational communication dynamics, 15 out of 20 media outlets that have been more closely scrutinised by consteps and RECON participants Katherin Packham an Ewelina Pawlak have most vigorously developed cross-border dimensions of European political communication during the initial phase of constitutional treaty ratification and crisis (Appendix, Table A7.11).

17 A look at the substantive top three topics that the media associated with EU treaty reform (see Appendix, Table A7.7) shows that issues regarding the 'deepening' of European integration took precedence, but that 'widening' was high on the agenda as well. Namely in the Czech Republic and in France the potential accession of Turkey into the Union was on top of heated domestic debates, and also in Germany and Hungary enlargement-related issues received high attention. The Polish 'red line' on the terms of majority voting in the Council was not only important in the parliamentary debates but made it prominently into the news, too.

18 We have analysed the EU treaty reform coverage by 20 news media outlets from 6 member states qualitatively in depth, finding that only 8 of them devoted a limited space to public intellectuals, experts, civil society organisations or representatives from interest organisations.

19 For more information on both data sets, see Appendix; Table A7.8.

20 At the time of the European elections in June 2009, the ratification of the Lisbon Treaty was still pending because the second Irish Referendum was scheduled to be held in early October of the same year. This does not mean, though, that in the 2009 debates domestic topics did not play any role. For instance, in the Czech Republic, the fall of the Topolanek government and the scandal involving paparazzi pictures taken in Silvio Berlusconi's villa made the news. German public debates revolved around the 'Super Election Year' with national parliament elections coming up in September. In Hungary, Fidesz' call for new elections as well as the emergence of the far right were widely discussed. The British discourse focused on the expenses scandal involving a number of national MPs, and the success of the BNP, which was anticipated to take advantage of the voters' dissatisfaction over the performance of the main political parties.

21 In fact, in media communication on European election campaigns in the Czech Republic, France, Germany and Poland, European discourses or arguments outnumber national ones (see Appendix, Table A7.8).

22 Eurobarometer '2009 Post Election Survey'. Available at: http://www.europarl.europa. eu/pdf/eurobarometre/28_07/SA_EN.pdf
23 This finding from media analysis contradicts the 2009 Eurobarometer poll in a twofold way. First, the poll sees the 'vote of discontent' as a reason for voting, while in the media this is presented also as a reason for non-voting. Second, it concludes that 'The so-called "vote of discontent" is very weak' (p. 9), which is in net contrast to the media coverage.
24 The 2009 Eurobarometer post-election study confirms these findings: asking respondents to name the most important themes they wanted to express by voting, the responses pointed to matters of an 'economic nature' (41 per cent economic growth; 37 per cent unemployment; 22 per cent future of pensions; 22 per cent role of the EU on the international scene).
25 Cf. the discussion of the state of European public sphere research by Thomas Risse (2010) who engages the most comprehensive range of empirical findings from European public sphere research to date, however indicating two conspicuous lacunae: first, regarding the new East/East Central European member states, and, second, the developments following the EU's constitutional treaty failure.
26 For comparative analyses of the national media systems of Europe see, among others, Bajomi-Lázár and Hegedűs 2001; Hallin and Mancini 2004; Sparks with Reading 1997; Splichal 1994; Sükösd and Bajomi-Lázár 2003.
27 Conceiving European political communication in terms of social practices is defined here as a configuration of action and practical knowledge – that is actors' 'know how' – by which collective models of reality are generated and eventually changed through practical action; in this framework, discourses and texts acquire meaning only in the context of contingent historical social practices (see Raabe 2008: 370ff).
28 See also Nordenstreng 2000.

APPENDIX

Data description

The preceding chapter draws on seven comparative data sets from different arenas of European political communication that have been compiled from eight EU member states – Czech Republic, Estonia, France, Germany, Hungary, Latvia, Poland, United Kingdom in one case (2.b) including several cases more (Bulgaria, Denmark, Italy, Netherlands, Spain, Sweden and Turkey):

1. ConstEPS I. Media data set: TCE ratification 10/2004–10/2005 (7 member states; responsible researchers: T. Evas, A. Maatsch, P. R.Guasti, K.Packham, A. Wyrozumska); see Liebert *et al.* 2007 (PEPS).
2. RECON I. Media data set: TCE crisis and reflection 6/2005–7/2007 (12 member states plus Turkey; Bremen Summer School July/August 2007 co-coordinated by UniHB and ARENA; responsible researchers: A. Gattig, E. Pawlak); see Liebert and Trenz (2008b) RECON WP5 Media Report 2007.
3. RECON II. Media data set: 2009 European election campaigns 5–6/2009 (6 member states; responsible researchers: K. Packham; E. Pawlak).
4. RECON III. Parliamentary data set: Constitutional and Lisbon Treaty ratification debates 1/2004–1/2009 (6 member states; responsible researcher: A. Maatsch).
5. ConstEPS II. Civil Society data set on TCE 2007 (N = 148, from 6 member states; responsible researchers: T. Evas, A. Maatsch, P. R.Guasti, K.Packham, E. Pawlak).
6. RECON IV. European Elections data set 1999–2009 (6 member states; responsible researcher: E. Pawlak).
7. RECON V. TCE Referendum Data Set 2005 (4 member states, responsible researcher: A. Gattig).

TABLE A7.1 RECON I, II, III. Data description

	RECON I *TCE media data* *set 2005–07*	*RECON II* *European elections* *media data set 2009*	*RECON III* *Parliamentary* *data set 2009*
Timeframe of data set	TCE ratification debates June 2005–July 2007	European parliamentary election campaigns May–June 2009	Parliamentary EU Treaty ratification January 2004– January 2009
Scope of quantitative/ qualitative data set	Quantitative data set of 8,583 articles for 6 EU member states;[1] 240 articles selected for qualitative data set (40 articles percountry).	Quantitative data set of 2,841 articles for 6 EU member states;[2] 181 articles selected for qualitative data set (30 articles per country).	Qualitative data set of plenary debates in 6 EU member states:[3] in total 47 parliamentary debates.
Search strings for sampling	Articles dealing with the 'EU Constitutional Treaty'	'European election/ campaign'	'Constitutional or Lisbon Treaty ratification'

TCE, Treaty establishing a Constitution for Europe

Notes:
1 The Czech Republic, France, Germany, Hungary, Poland and the United Kingdom, selected from 14 countries.
2 The Czech Republic, France, Germany, Hungary, Poland and the United Kingdom, selected and consolidated from 14 countries.
3 The Czech Republic, France, Germany, Hungary, Poland and the United Kingdom.

TABLE A7.2 RECON III. Parliamentary data set

Country	*Plenary debates on Constitutional Treaty ratification*	*Plenary debates on Lisbon Treaty ratification*
Czech Republic	....	6 debates: March 2008, February 2009 by Chamber of Deputies; April 2008, May 2009 by Senat.
France	8 debates: 4 in the National Assembly, 4 in the Senate; January–February, April, May 2005.	3 debates: 2 in the National Assembly; 1 in the Senate; February 2008.
Germany	4 debates: 2 in the Bundestag, 2 in the Bandera: February, May 2005.	4 debates: 2 in the Bundestag, 2 in the Bundesrat; February –May 2008.
Hungary	4 debates: 2 in October 2004; 2 in December 2004.	1 debate: in December 2007.
Poland	3 debates: 2 in the Sejm – lower chamber, 1 in the Senat – higher chamber; February–April 2004/2005.	6 debates: 5 by Sejm, 1 in Senat; February – March 2008, July 2008, January 2009.
UK	2 debates: January – February 2005 in the House of Commons.	6 debates: 3 in the House of Commons, 3 in the House of Lords; December 2007, January– June 2008.

TABLE A7.3 ConstEPS II. Civil society data set

| | | Organisation category | | | | | Total |
		Civil society	Political party	Trade unions	Employers' organisations	Other	Civil society
Country	Czech Republic	10	6	4	4	0	24
interview	Estonia	6	6	3	3	1	19
	EU	1	4	6	2	0	13
	France	8	7	6	0	1	22
	Germany	9	9	3	4	0	25
	Poland	8	8	2	3	3	24
	UK	8	7	4	3	1	23
Total		50	47	28	19	6	150

TABLE A7.4 RECON I and II. Comparative media data sets

RECON Data sample		RECON Summer School Bremen 2007 Post-referenda debates		RECON Summer School Bremen 2009 EP election campaigns	
Country	Newspapers	Quantitative sample	Quantitative sample	Quantitative sample	Quantitative sample
		Total no. of articles	Total no. of articles	Total no. of articles	Total no. of articles
Czech	Hospodarske noviny	361	13	108	7
Republic	Pravo	295	17	194	9
	MF Dnes	260	8	324	12
	Respekt	106	2	. . .	. . .
	Reflex	21	0	13	2
	Blesk	6	0	26	1
	Totals	**1,049**	**40**	**665**	**31**
France	Le Monde	1,046	19	334	14
	Le Figaro	927	12	231	7
	Libération	716	9	124	6
	Le Parisien	. . .	. . .	137	3
	Totals	**2,689**	**40**	**826**	**30**
Germany	FAZ	927	15	. . .	. . .
	Süddeutsche Zeitung	646	10	336	12
	TAZ	371	5	78	6
	Welt	680	10	103	7
	Bild	. . .	. . .	31	3
	Spiegel	. . .	. . .	10	2
	Total	**2,624**	**40**	**558**	**30**
Hungary	Magyar Nemzet	303	19	153	8
	Népszabadság	275	21	126	10
	Blikk	5	0	21	3
	Heti Világ Gazdaság	. . .	. . .	83	5
	Heti Válasz	. . .	. . .	15	2
	Elet és Irodalom	. . .	. . .	16	2
	Total	**583**	**40**	**414**	**30**

Poland	Gazeta Wyborcza	428	19	28	11
	Rzeczpospolita	495	16	46	7
	Polityka	56	5	10	4
	Nasz Dziennik	...	...	16	5
	Super Express	...	...	11	3
	Total	**979**	**40**	**111**	**30**
UK	The Times	383	19	67	7
	The Guardian	276	21	135	12
	The Sun	...	...	30	4
	The Daily Mirror	...	...	21	4
	The Economist	...	...	14	3
	Total	**659**	**40**	**267**	**30**
Total		**8,583**	**240**	**2,841**	**181**

TABLE A7.5 Coding scheme for Atlas.ti-based ComPDA (print media, parliamentary)

1.	Basic document-level information	Source, title, author, origins of author, etc.
2.	Actors	Individual and institutional, actor's origin
3.	Topics	Divided into the following subcategories:

- Substantive topics (codes based on the topics in the Constitutional treaty)
- Constitution or treaty
- Procedures (constitutional process)

4. Argumentative strategies — Four major categories:
- definitive
- designative
- evaluative (positive, negative and neutral)
- advocative

5. Justifications — Five major categories:
- interest (European, state, sectoral, strategic)
- ideas (past, present and future visions of Europe)
- collective identities (subnational, national, European, group specific); democracy (i.e., transparency, accountability, participation, representation, deliberation, elite responsiveness)
- political ideologies

6. Interaction and relations among actors
- horizontal across national borders
- vertical, from EU level down to citizens on the domestic level
- type of relationship (alliance, co-ordination, co-operation, interdependence versus competition, collision, polarised conflict)

7. Context issues
- EU related
- national
- international

TABLE A7.6 ComPDA parliamentary and media data sets

Parliamentary data set

	CZ	FR	GE	HU	PL	UK
Plenary debates, no.	6	11	8	5	9	8
Primary documents, total no.	5	7	8	5	11	5
Quotations, total no.	222	598	730	190	743	##
Quotations, total no., models I, II, III	111	290	330	105	507	742
Quotations, total models★	123	312	371	110	614	801
★ with overlapping						

Media data set

	CZ	FR	GE	HU	PL	UK
Primary documents, total no.	31	30	30	30	30	32
Quotation, total no.	175	468	497	368	567	493
Quotations, total no., models I, II, III	62	120	140	87	222	106
Quotations, total models★	66	90	127	96	218	114
★ with overlapping						

Source: RECON II and III data sets

Comparative Tables and Figures

TABLE A7.7 Print media coverage of EU treaty reform

Topics		CZ	FR	GER	HU	PL	UK
Top three topics[1]		Reform Treaty	TCE (2004)	TCE (2004)	TCE (2004)	TCE (2004)	Reform Treaty
		9%	6%	9%	8%	9%	11%
		Turkey	Turkey	Enlargement	Enlargement	Majority voting	Constitution
		4%	6%	2%	4%	2%	4%
		CFSP	Union Budget	CFSP	Social Policy	Energy and Transport	Charter of Fundamental Rights of the Union
		1%	*2%*	*2%*	*2%*	*3%*	*1%*
Actors	National	67%	45%	26%	28%	70%	38%
	European	29%	55%	74%	72%	29%	61%
Positions	Positive	47%	44%	43%	43%	36%	42%
	Neutral	25%	14%	23%	30%	30%	12%
	Negative	27%	39%	29%	23%	21%	38%
Justifications	National	60%	24%	30%	26%	32%	34%
	European	22%	65%	52%	58%	56%	56%
	Universal	18%	11%	18%	16%	12%	10%

Source: RECON I data set.

Note

[1] 'Top three topics' are measured as percentage of total number of topics in country data set.

TABLE A7.8 Print media coverage of 2009 European Election campaigns

		CZ	FR	GER	HU	PL	UK
Topics	Top three topics¹	Lisbon Treaty	National parties: Conservatives Socialists	Social policy	National parties	EU institutions	National parties: Radical Right Conservatives Socialists
		10%	10%	6%	47%	8%	48%
		EP issues: expenses, MEP salaries, legislative powers	Institutional issues: Commission performance	Institutional issues: Commission	National executive	Lisbon Treaty	Lisbon Treaty
		9%	3%	6%	21%	8%	3%
		Economic and monetary policy, European Central Bank	Lisbon Treaty	Lisbon Treaty	Lisbon Treaty	Union and its neighbours	EU institutions, EP's legitimacy
		2%	2%	4%	0.5%	4%	3%
Actors	National	69%	78%	76%	84%	54%	72%
	European	31%	21%	24%	16%	28%	26%
Positions	Positive	33%	29%	41%	41%	49%	32%
	Neutral	15%	34%	23%	13%	30%	21%
	Negative	52%	37%	36%	46%	22%	47%
Justifications	National	31%	34%	36%	61%	44%	64%
	European	54%	46%	54%	21%	48%	36%
	Universal	15%	20%	10%	18%	8%	0%

Source: RECON media data set II.

1 Figures for 'Top three topics' are measured as a percentage of total number of topics in country-specific dataset.

TABLE A7.9 Parliamentary ratification discourses: topics, actors, positions, justifications

		CZ	FR	GER	HU	PL	UK
Topics	Top three topics[1]	Council decision-making: QMV	Referendum	Principle of subsidi-arity	Minority protection in Preamble of TCE	Ratification by President and Parliament	Popular referendum
		14%	6%	6%	10%	17%	17%
		Charter of Fundamental Rights	TCE and Lisbon Treaty	Charter of Fundamental Rights	Ratification referendum	Ratification referendum	Council decision-making QMV
		7%	5%	5%	9%	8%	7%
		National parliaments (Lisbon)	EU Presidency	Lisbon Treaty	Collective minority rights	Decision-making QMV	Lisbon Treaty
		6%	4%	4%	8%	4%	5%
Actors	Government	25%	32%	46%	34%	3%	12%
	Party groups	74%	65%	52%	61%	94%	84%
	Non-parties	1%	3%	2%	6%	3%	4%
Positions	Positive	49%	64%	70%	63%	59%	53%
	Neutral	19%	10%	21%	17%	20%	21%
	Negative	32%	25%	9%	19%	21%	27%
Justifications	National	21%	…	…	…	…	…
	European	28%	…	…	…	…	…
	Universal	13%	…	…	…	…	…

Source: RECON III data set.

[1] 'Top three topics' are measured as a percentage of the total number of topics in the country data set.

TABLE A7.10 Discursive quality of print media in European political communication

	Y: Transnational (non-national)	X: Socio-political diversity (non-state)	Y2: Justification (justified) +	X2: Argumentative mode (positive) +1
Czech Republic	0,55	0,38	0,59	0,44
Estonia	0,34	0,41	0,54	0,70
France	0,25	0,48	0,46	0,48
Germany	0,57	0,42	0, 42	0,46
Latvia	0,51	0,49	0,43	0,55
Poland	0,37	0,57	0,55	0,47
Sweden	0,32	0,56	0,35	0,53
UK	0,47	0,50	0,53	0,53

Note
[1] 'Argument mode' is measured by the relation between positive and negative positions towards the EU–TCE/Lisbon Treaty in argumentation strategies (positive = 1, negative = 0).

TABLE A7.11 Transnational democratic quality of EU coverage, by 20 news media outlets (2004–05)

	Indicator 1: transnational diversity	Indicator 2: sociopolitical diversity	Indicator 3: argumentative mode
MDF	1	0	1
Pravo	1	0	0
Respekt	1	0	1
Arvamus	0	1	1
Postimees	1	0	0
Le Monde	1	0	0
Le Figaro	0	1	0
SüddeutscheZeitung	1	1	1
FAZ	1	0	0
Diena	1	0	1
Neatkariga	1	1	1
TygodnikPowszechny	0	1	0
Rzeczpospolita	1	1	0
Wprost	0	0	0
GazetaWyborcza	1	0	0
Expressen	0	0	0
SvenskaDagbladet	1	1	1
DagensNyheter	1	0	1
Times	1	0	0
Guardian	1	1	0
Total	**15/20**	**8/20**	**8/20**

Note
For measuring transnational democratic quality of EU coverage, the results here from ComPDA for each news media outlet have been coded as 0 for below average and as 1 for above average performance.

TABLE A7.12 Three democratic frames in European political communication (RECON models)

National democracy frame (Model 1)							
Parliaments		*CZ*	*FR*	*GE*	*HU*	*PL*	*UK*
Values	A	19	21	5	4	79	130
Institutions	B	71	75	158	17	260	301
Policies	C	5	5	2	1	16	27
Print Media							
Values	A	4	6	7	6	40	11
Institutions	B	27	28	48	25	23	47
Policies	C	5	9	11	17	20	7
Supranational democracy frame (Model 2)							
Parliaments		*CZ*	*FR*	*GE*	*HU*	*PL*	*UK*
Values	A	6	38	16	19	46	18
Institutions	B	6	97	96	22	114	230
Policies	C	11	72	58	6	59	51
Print Media							
Values	A	5	6	13	6	51	17
Institutions	B	25	37	43	36	67	22
Policies	C	4	30	27	17	59	17
Cosmopolitan democracy frame (Model 3)							
Parliaments		*CZ*	*FR*	*GE*	*HU*	*PL*	*UK*
Values	A	5	4	35	6	37	40
Institutions	B	0	0	0	35	2	4
Policies	C	0	0	1	0	1	0
Print Media							
Values	A	0	1	4	4	7	2
Institutions	B	0	1	0	0	4	1
Policies	C	0	2	1	2	6	7

Source: RECON II, III data sets.

Notes
Figures refer to quantity of quotations coded as references to the values, institutions or policies – dimensions of the three RECON models.

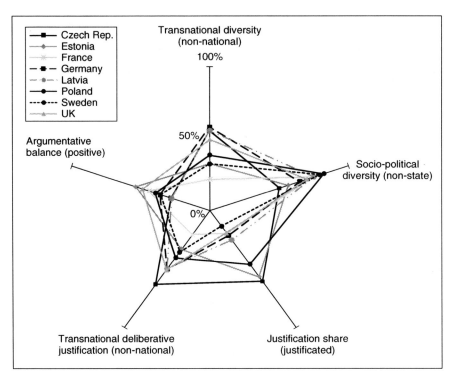

FIGURE A7.1 Discursive quality of media–based European public sphere (8 member states, 2004–05)

Source: ConstEPS I and RECON I media data sets.

8

DEMOCRATIC CHALLENGES TO THE EU'S FOREIGN AND SECURITY POLICY

Helene Sjursen

Introduction

The status of democracy in European foreign, security and defence policy is increasingly questioned among policy-makers and analysts alike. But if European foreign and security policy were to be democratic, what would it look like?

Following the analytical scheme established by Eriksen and Fossum in Chapter 2, three alternative ways of institutionalising democracy in European foreign and security policy are considered. These are linked to more general conceptions of the European Union (EU) *qua* polity, and respond to basic democratic requirements in different ways. Recognising that variation in the form and degree of integration may give rise to different democratic challenges, this analytical scheme allows for a more nuanced analysis of the status of democracy and possible, suitable remedies.

Focusing almost exclusively on the role of the European Parliament (EP), the literature on democracy and EU foreign policy has paid too little attention to the link between the nature of the polity and the putative democratic challenges. Thus there is a need to reconsider the diagnosis of a democratic deficit and the reasons presented for it, as well as the remedies suggested. It is only when we know what kind of polity we are actually faced with that we can say something about how (un)democratic it might be.

This is particularly so as the nature and form of integration in European foreign and security policy is contested. Formally, EU Common Foreign and Security Policy (CFSP) is subject to intergovernmental procedures of decision-making. However, it may well be that the range of policy-making and the many hands involved makes the intergovernmental model of delegatory control obsolete. If, as several studies of European foreign policy-making suggest, power and control have drifted away from national governments, where do they reside? And what are the implications for national constituencies and their ability to hold those in power to account? If the CFSP is no longer intergovernmental , what is it then, and (how) can it be democratic?

In order to answer these questions; the RECON models are developed and specified with regard to foreign and security policy. The empirical relevance of each model is discussed with reference to concrete examples.

The chapter starts out by briefly outlining the approach chosen and situating it in relation to the existing literature on the EU's foreign and security policy. Subsequently each conception is discussed in more detail. The first conception of audit democracy is in line with the conventional understanding of EU foreign and security policy as controlled by the member states. The second conception of a federal multinational democracy and the third one of a regional-cosmopolitan democracy challenge the idea of foreign policy as nationally controlled in different ways and to different degrees.

A democratic European foreign policy: conceptual and methodological challenges

Considerable attention has been given to the question of 'actorness' in European foreign policy (Allen and Smith 1990; Bull 1991; Duchêne 1972; Hill 1993; Keukeleire and MacNaughtan 2008; Sjøstedt 1977). The aim of their discussion is similar to that of this chapter in the sense that it is concerned with conceptualising the 'nature of the beast'. However, foreign policy analysts have focused on whether or not the EU could be defined at all as an international 'actor' given that it is not a state, and, further, on what might characterise the EU's 'actorness'. In so doing they have relied on knowledge regarding the substance of its external policies, rather than the institutional structures and procedures for foreign policy-making that arc in focus here. Moreover, little attention has been paid to the democratic credentials of the actor. It is efficiency and not democratic legitimacy that is the underlying concern of most studies of the EU's foreign and security policy. Thus, the approach taken in this chapter complements the existing literature through the emphasis on institutional structures and procedures of the polity, as well as the democratic qualities (or lack of such).

The starting point here is that foreign and security policy does not differ from domestic policy with regard to the need to comply with core democratic standards of autonomy and accountability. The autonomy requirement pertains to the ability of those affected by laws to also be their authors:

> Intrinsic to this criterion is the possibility of the authorised bodies of decision-making to react adequately on public support to determine the development of the political community in such a way that the citizens can be seen to act upon themselves.
>
> *(Eriksen 2009a: 36)*

When investigating to what extent this principle is properly respected, key questions are 'Who decides – and on what issues'? In order to find out if it is possible to trace decisions back to citizens' authorisation, a mapping of where and how decisions are made is required. As for accountability, the issue is whether those who decide can be held responsible for their decisions. The key, in other words, is the possibility (or not) of citizens to sanction those in power:

> Accountability designates a relationship wherein obligatory questions are posed and qualified answers required. It speaks to a justificatory process that rests on a reason-giving practice, wherein the decision-makers can be held responsible to the citizenry, and by which, in the last resort, it is possible to dismiss incompetent rulers.
>
> *(Eriksen 2009a: 36; see also Bovens et al. 2010)*

In this context we must ask not only *who* is held responsible, but also to whom and with regard to what issues? What rights and resources do citizens have in this regard?

Institutional 'solutions' to these requirements vary, and it is these solutions and their applicability to the field of foreign and security policy that are discussed in this chapter. Drawing on the above two requirements, and with the aim of ensuring a reasonably transparent analysis, the different models will be discussed with reference to the following four indicators: constituency, legitimacy, core function and executive power. While the latter two pertain mainly to the requirement of autonomy and the need to disentangle authorisation, the former two pertain mainly, although not exclusively, to the question of accountability. This is so because they aim to tell us something about the question of 'to whom' those in power are held responsible.

A particular challenge when discussing democracy in foreign and security policy arises with regard to the first indicator of 'constituency'. This is so because the 'affected parties' are not necessarily national citizens. In that sense the two first models suffer from the same one-sidedness or Janus-faced nature as besets state-based democracy in general: democracy is a vital matter internally to the state but can be virtually ignored in the realm of interstate relations (Archibugi 2008). The third model, the regional-cosmopolitan one, takes heed of the fact that the basis for the identification of 'affected parties' needs to be broadened. A key feature of this conception is the idea of a 'domestication of foreign and security policy'. This implies not only that foreign and security policy should be subject to law rather than the will of the most powerful, but also that the perspective of third parties must be taken into account. Nevertheless, as it does not entirely do away with borders and the idea of national/regional citizenship, it requires us to reconsider the basic understanding of what is foreign and what is domestic. This is not a simple task. Further, the question of specifying the required institutional structures to ensure that the voice of 'all those affected' at a global level is taken into account constitutes a major challenge and is not adequately solved.

In order to discuss the empirical relevance of the third model, the practical challenge is what to look for. It is necessary to establish what would be key institutions and organising principles for the foreign policy of a regional-cosmopolitan entity. The challenge is further compounded by the fact that the global cosmopolitan order is at best incomplete; thus the answer to the question of what a regional-cosmopolitan order operating in a non-cosmopolitan context would look like is more diffuse.

When discussing the models, I proceed in two steps. Each model is first operationalised. Subsequently, its empirical relevance and possible gaps between the ideal conception and the actual structure of the polity are discussed.

Audit democracy

In this first conception, the democratic legitimacy of any collective European foreign policy endeavour would rely on procedures and institutions established within the confines of each member (nation) state. The only actors in European foreign policy with power to decide would be the member states. They would dispose of the right to veto decisions at the European level. European foreign policy would in other words be decided upon according to intergovernmental procedures. It would be in line with the idea of sovereignty in the international system, where each member state would have equal rights, regardless of the size of its population or territory, economic or military capabilities, etc.

In order to ensure clear lines of authority, the member states would communicate through the traditional means of diplomacy, with national diplomatic missions representing each one. They would act on mandates defined by their home ministries and changes to the mandates would be subject to decisions in the capital. Information and knowledge would reside mainly within the national foreign ministries and only to a limited extent be subject to exchanges between member states. In such a system, democratic legitimacy would be indirect, derived from the domestic political systems.

The core function of foreign and security policy would be to assist the member states in their endeavour to protect and promote their particular interests and values. The expectation would be that in some cases there would be agreement that this could be done more effectively if the EU's member states acted collectively than if they acted alone. In so doing they might conceivably delegate certain tasks to the European level. A crucial criterion, however, would be that this should not affect the ability of member states to maintain control, or the possibility that the executive could be held accountable through national procedures and institutions. One could imagine the Union might be mandated to handle, for example, the task of defence procurement. Here member states might see an economic advantage in joining forces in the development of armaments. Further, joint training operations as well as education of military staff might very well be conducted in co-operation without jeopardising the sovereign control of each government over its troops. Finally, it should be possible to expect some *ad hoc* joint military activities, along the same principles as those followed in military alliances. That is, troops would be raised by the nation states, and it would be entirely up to them to decide for each specific task whether or not they would be willing to contribute to a common operation. The possibility to revoke powers that have been delegated would be crucial.

As noted, this is a conception of democracy that relies on the idea that 'it is only the nation state that can foster the type of trust and solidarity that is required to sustain a democratic polity' (Chapter 2, p. 22). It is a conception that is in line with the perspective outlined by Peter Hain, representative of the British government to the European Convention. In his view, 'If foreign policy is to enjoy legitimacy, there must be accountability through elected governments to national parliaments'.[1] It follows that the relevant constituency is explicitly confined to the borders of each individual member state. From the perspective of this model, there would not be any need for particular procedures or institutional constraints in order to ensure that the perspectives of any affected parties outside these borders were taken into account.

The empirical indicators of this model are summarised in Table 8.1.

Empirical relevance and democratic challenge

According to key European foreign policy-makers, such as France's prime minister François Fillon and Spanish foreign minister Miguel Moratinos,[2] power and authority lie exclusively with the member states in European foreign and security policy. The national veto is intact, and the final word does not reside with the supranational institutions such as the Commission, the Parliament and the Court. However, in order to respond to concerns and ambitions regarding the coherence, effectiveness and credibility of European foreign and security policy, member states have introduced a number of institutional innovations. As a result, one may question if policy-making within this field really follows an intergovernmental mode.

The institutional nexus of policy-making has become highly complex and a large variety of actors are involved. It is not only that the Commission's activities affect traditional foreign policy issues, and that it is often difficult to distinguish between its domain and that of the member states. Already in the late 1990s, reports of a move from intergovernmentalism towards a Brussels-based bureaucratic working method emerged. A process of Brusselsisation – that is, a shift in the locus of national decision-making to Brussels-based institutional structures of foreign policy – was identified and analysts talked of a policy process that was distinctive from the so-called Community method, but also from intergovernmentalism (Allen 1998;

TABLE 8.1 The empirical indicators of the audit democracy model

	Constituency	Executive power	Legitimacy	Core function
Audit democracy	National	National level	Via elected representatives in national parliaments	Assisting member states in protecting national interests and values

Howorth 2001; Tonra 2003). The institutional formations within the Council were reported to have developed an increasingly autonomous role in making and shaping European foreign policy. In 2007, Deirdre Curtin (2007) argued that, especially in the newer policy fields such as the CFSP, the Council had assumed executive functions in much the same way as the Commission does in other policy areas. And in spite of governmental inputs in these policy areas, what was becoming apparent in her view was the independent nature of the Council and its bodies. Prior to the signing of the Lisbon Treaty, the performers of this growing Council structure were Council General Secretariat bureaucrats as well as national bureaucrats participating in Council committees. Their important role in assisting the Presidency in agenda-setting and actual negotiations is, according to Curtin, often overlooked. Similar observations were made by Duke and Vanhoonacker who argued that 'the administrative level plays a crucial role in the CFSP policy cycle' (Duke and Vanhoonacker 2006: 179). And, further, 'the administrative role goes well beyond that of making sure that the machinery works smoothly, to include important if often unnoticed roles in agenda-shaping, decision-shaping and implementation' (ibid.). In combination with the increasingly political function of the High Representative and the Policy Unit, this entailed considerable modifications of intergovernmentalism in foreign policy.

The transformation of the organisation of the whole field of foreign and security policy that follows from the Lisbon Treaty and the establishment of the European External Action Service (EEAS) reinforces these tendencies. Among other things, the very logic of recruitment to the EEAS stands in contrast to intergovernmental principles because 60 per cent of staff in the EEAS will be permanent and all staff will be appointed 'on merit' rather than based on geographical or national origin. The difficulties in monitoring the borders between the intergovernmental and supranational strands of the EU's role in the world also remain, or are perhaps even reinforced with this new institutional set-up. Supranationalism and intergovernmentalism now live together under the same roof. It starts with the High Representative, whose authority is derived from the member states, and who is also part of the Commission. As for the EEAS, it exists to assist the High Representative, and thus must live down this distinction in its daily activities. The precise location of executive power has become diffuse. It is linked to national governments but not entirely controlled by them (Sjursen forthcoming).

With regard to the core functions of the CFSP, again, there does not seem to be a clear fit with the audit democracy model. An intergovernmental entity is there to serve the member states, to assist them in solving concrete problems, to ensure the protection of their interests and values and to enforce their preferences. However, in the case of the CFSP, there has been a conscious effort to go beyond this, to define *European* interests, as well as *European* values. The most coherent definition of these interests and values may be found in the European Security Strategy, adopted by the European Council in December 2003. The Security Strategy 'established principles and set clear objectives for advancing the EU's security interests based on our core values' (Council of the European Union 2008: 3. It set out three strategic objectives for European security: tackling key threats, building security in our neighbourhood and promoting an international order based on effective multilateralism (Council of the European Union, 2003. Further, one may read in the Lisbon Treaty that '*the Union* shall [. . .] assert *its identity* on the international scene' (Title I, art. 2). Thus, there is a clear expectation that the CFSP should do more than serve the interests and values of the member states. It should also serve those of the Union.

With regard to the core constituency as well as the legitimacy basis of executive power, they speak more easily to the audit democracy model. This is particularly so because the constituency is confined to the member states. The main challenge is the model's requirement of a European-wide assembly to assist the national parliaments in holding the European institutions accountable. This might be quite an alien structure to those of the national systems in which the executive has almost exclusive control of decisions in this field. This might also require communication between national parliamentary assemblies, which so far is virtually non-existent in this field. Existing parliamentary assemblies such as the North Atlantic Treaty Organisation (NATO) and the now defunct Western European Union (WEU) parliamentary assemblies do not in any way live up to democratic criteria (Wagner *et al.* 2010). At best, they may be considered 'talk shops'; at worst, they have been established with the aim of legitimising the decisions of the executives and not of scrutinising them.

Thus, to meet the requirements of the audit democracy model, reforms at the national levels are needed – as practice varies a great deal in terms of the extent to which national parliaments, for example, are involved in foreign and security policy. But even if such a reform were introduced, it might not be sufficient to ensure that those in power were held accountable, because a process of executive fragmentation has taken place. Most likely a strengthening of the influence of national parliaments would need to be supplemented with a scaling down of integration, in order for the requirements of this model to be fulfilled.

There is no precise answer to the question of how much this audit democracy model can sustain in terms of uploading of tasks and 'permanentisation' of institutions before its democratic credentials are jeopardised. However, it does seem that, even with regard to the CFSP, intergovernmental co-operation has been loaded with so many tasks that it has turned into something else.

Federal multinational democracy

In the second conception, that of a federal state-based multinational democracy, the democratic legitimacy of foreign policy is linked to institutions and procedures at the European level. As this is a *federal* state, decentralisation would most likely be much stronger than in many European states (Chapter 2). However, this would not have much effect on the foreign policy field. Rather, national foreign and security policies would be replaced by a European foreign, security and defence policy.[3] It would be headed by a European executive that would be accountable mainly to the federal level, and to a lesser extent to the national levels. The EU would also dispose of the traditional means of coercion that are normally available to states. That is, it would be able to raise military forces and they would be answerable to the Union. One would further expect that administrative structures similar to those of the nation state in foreign, security and defence policy would be replicated at the European level. Likewise, national diplomatic services would be replaced by a common European diplomatic service, which would use the Brussels-based, European institutions as the primary source of information and knowledge.

This model is to a large extent based on the replication of the state model at the European level. It follows that the main function of this single foreign and defence policy would be that of guaranteeing the inviolability of the EU's territory, and ensuring the promotion and protection of collective European interests and values. But although the EU would be a state, it would, as noted, be a *multinational* federal state, which would have to accommodate nation-building processes both at regional and 'national' levels. A question that arises in this regard is to what extent it would then have a sufficient identitarian basis to act collectively and be perceived as representative of a common interest at the global level. This could perhaps be constituted through a so-called constitutional patriotism where 'political agency [is] conceived as animated by a set of universalist norms, but enriched and strengthened by particular experiences and concerns' (Müller 2006: 2). It would mean that, contrary to what is usually assumed to be the case in European nation states, there would have to be a stronger reliance on democratic procedures and on an open public debate in order to ensure the legitimacy basis of the foreign and security policy. It would not, most likely, be sufficient to assume the kind of automatic 'rallying around the flag' that seems to be the expectation in states that rest on the idea of a 'thick' collective identity.

Assuming that criteria for accountability would be stricter than in some of the member states, the EP would not only have the right to be informed of decisions in foreign and security policy, it would be in a position to question the executive on any aspect of foreign security and defence policy as well as to veto decisions related to the use of force. As the EP would also hold the powers of the purse, its role in influencing the overall shape and direction of foreign and security policy would be considerable. The challenge noted with regard to the first model and the varying practice of member states with regard to democratic control of foreign and security policy might also arise in this model, to the extent that the transformed national parliaments would also expect to have a say in this policy field.

While the constituency is expanded in comparison with that of the first model, it is also here clearly delimited, because democracy is conceived of as linked to the confines of a state. To the extent that there is multinationality, this is *within* the European polity. Hence, it is not, from the perspective of this conception of European democracy, necessary to establish particular procedures to ensure that the viewpoints of affected parties outside the borders of the European federation are heard.

Key features and empirical indicators of a federal multinational democracy are summarised in Table 8.2.

TABLE 8.2 Key features and empirical indicators of a federal multinational democracy model

	Constituency	Executive power	Legitimacy	Core function
Federal multinational democracy	European	European level	Via elected representatives in a federal parliament	Protecting European (state) interests and values

Empirical relevance and democratic challenges

The idea of an EU establishing a single foreign, security and defence policy at the federal level that would replace national foreign and security policies breaks with established views of what is possible in foreign and security policy. Most observers would argue that the attachment to the principle of national sovereignty is so strong that such a move would not be made – at least not deliberately. As noted, however, there are several indications of a departure from the core principles of intergovernmentalism. The question is whether this thickening co-operation manifests itself in an unambiguous development towards EU statehood.

With the coming into force of the Lisbon Treaty, some state-like features are in evidence. First, the EEAS seems to be modelled on the very idea of the diplomatic services of states. This Service, which will comprise officials from relevant departments of the General Secretariat of the Council and of the Commission, and staff from national diplomatic services, may with time both look and act very much like a European diplomatic corps. Second, because the EU has now obtained legal personality, it has the capacity to enter into legal relations with other actors on the international stage. This is important in order to conduct an autonomous foreign and security policy, and further strengthens the argument of those who see the CFSP developing in a state-like direction. Incidentally, it has been argued that this development was already manifest prior to the Lisbon Treaty because the EU had, for example, entered into an agreement with the now defunct WEU as well as with NATO through the Berlin agreement (Tiilikainen 2001). However, with the Lisbon Treaty, the EU's status in international affairs should no longer be disputed.

Third, the case of the battle groups, where national troops are at the disposal of the Union for crisis management and peace enforcement tasks for six months at a time, also reveals some state-like features. Although this does not mean that the EU may raise military forces, it may decide to deploy such forces. Also, because the battle groups are integrated forces, and permanently at the disposal of the Union, they cannot be seen to be under the exclusive authority of the government that initially raised these forces. On the one hand, other governments may veto their use, against the will of their 'home government'. On the other hand, it may be difficult for the home government to go against deployment if a majority is in favour, because this would mean that the group as a whole could not be deployed (Peters et al. 2008).

In general, it may also be noted that the existence of clearly distinguishable national preferences within European foreign policy has been reduced. In fact, despite the well-known solo initiatives of some of the EU's member states in situations of crisis, it is increasingly difficult for member states to escape expectations of consistency between national foreign policy and the foreign policy positions of the EU. The establishment of a common framework for decision-making with regard to foreign policy issues, and the fact that the obligation to consult all other parties has become the standard in the CFSP – even though it is not consistently respected – suggest a move beyond a pure intergovernmental process. It is increasingly difficult for national foreign ministries to control all aspects of national foreign policy-making. The frequency of meetings among national representatives in the various institutional settings organised under the Council and located in Brussels, and the time spent on the preparation of these meetings as well as their duration may have contributed to this reduced sense of distinctive national foreign policies (Pijpers 1996; Tonra 2003).

Rather than point towards a single federal executive, however, this general observation points to the ambivalence of the EU's foreign and security policy. New institutions are crafted on the nation state model. Nevertheless, the attachment to national sovereignty remains. The system of decision-making and the complex web of executive institutions must be seen as the products of a strong attachment to this principle combined with the equally important, but contradictory, ambition of a coherent foreign policy. Although intergovernmentalism has been considerably modified, and some state-like features are in evidence, there is no unified executive at the EU level. The EU does not dispose of any legal means to force member states to comply if they do not wish to do so. One might also question the realism in the federal conception when foreign policy is characterised by such organisational heterogeneity. The institutional symmetry implied in the federal model may be impossible to uplift to the EU level, given the variation in power, policy instruments and global orientation among member states.

With regard to the core function of the CFSP, the Treaties say that the Union's foreign and security policy shall 'safeguard its values, fundamental interests, security, independence and integrity'. Clearly, the commitment to the integrity of the Union does not go as far as to promise to protect the inviolability of the borders of the Union, as a national security and defence policy would. However, to commit to the 'integrity' of the Union, a clause that was introduced in the Treaty of Amsterdam, as well as to its security, certainly goes a long way in this direction. Further underlining that the federal model has relevance, with regard to the core function of the CFSP, is the fact that there was already a debate during the discussions prior to the Amsterdam Treaty as to whether or not the inviolability of the EU's external borders should be added to the list of goals of the EU's foreign and security policy (Tiilikainen 2001).

With regard to the legitimacy basis of the CFSP, it is clearly not derived from a federal parliament. The EP does not authorise decisions in the field of foreign and security policy, and nor is it able to hold the executive accountable (Bono 2006; Crum 2009; Peters *et al.* 2008). Admittedly, certain developments in this direction have taken place. Over time, the EP has gained considerably more competencies in foreign policy than those foreseen in the Treaties. This is so, both in terms of the EP's supervisory and budgetary powers. The strengthening of the EP's power was introduced through an interinstitutional agreement from 1997, which extends the EP's information and consultation rights, confirms its budgetary powers and introduces concrete budgetary procedures in the field of foreign policy (Maurer *et al.* 2005: 187). This 1997 interinstitutional agreement was amended by a Joint Declaration of the Parliament, the Council and the Commission in 2002, which provided among other things for a regular political dialogue on the CFSP between the Council and the EP (Barbé 2004; Crum 2009; Maurer *et al.* 2005).

The general rule, however, is that the EP is only consulted on the main aspects and basic choices made in the field of foreign and security policy, and then kept informed of how those policies evolve. With the establishment of the EEAS, it has succeeded in strengthening its position a little further, as the High Representative is subject to Parliamentary questioning on the same basis as the Commissioners. Further, its role in deciding on the budget of the EEAS is important. And finally, its active involvement in the discussion on the entire set-up of the EEAS suggests that it may in future be a more influential actor. However, it is widely acknowledged that it neither authorises decisions, nor is able to hold those who make decisions accountable.

If the EU's foreign and security policy were to cohere with the core tenets of this model, it would not only be a matter of uploading certain powers to the EU level, or introducing qualified majority voting. It would require that the EU settled some very difficult issues pertaining to its territory, borders and citizenship. This, together with the need to bolster the role of the EP suggests that this conception of CFSP is too demanding. This is so even if the nation state remains the ideal type from which new institutions within this field take its inspiration.

But are fully fledged federal-like democratic institutions really required?

Regional-cosmopolitan democracy

In the third conception, a democratic European foreign policy would be akin to a regional-cosmopolitan democracy. In this 'pyramidal structure of autonomy and accountability' (Chapter 2, p. x), the democratic legitimacy of European foreign policy would be linked to processes and institutions at both regional and global levels. Because government is decoupled from the state, this conception entails a number of challenges to the established literature on foreign policy and international relations. As such, it speaks to much of the existing debate regarding the CFSP, which has been grappling with the question of whether it is possible to speak of a foreign policy without a state since the European Political Cooperation was launched by the European Council in the late 1960s (Allen and Smith 1990; Bull 1991; Duchêne 1972; Hill 1993; Keukeleire and MacNaughtan 2008; Sjøstedt 1977), as well as to the discussion of the 'model' nature of the CFSP (Aggestam 2004; Lucarelli and Manners 2006; Manners 2002; Smith 2000).

The regional-cosmopolitan model does not require a state at the EU level, and only limited means of coercion to ensure compliance. Nevertheless, it assumes a clear and identifiable executive at the EU level dealing with global issues. There would in other words, according to this model, be a kind of 'foreign' (and security) policy at work, although it would probably be less centralised than in the traditional state-conception. The executive would derive its legitimacy from democratic elections at the regional and national levels.[4] However, in addition, there would be a kind of 'top-down' process of democratic control, in the sense that the EU would also commit itself to be bound by higher order norms and procedures. Further, these would be a source of democratic legitimacy. Global cosmopolitan law would bind the EU, and the particular interests of the citizens of the EU would also have to be acceptable from the perspective of the citizens of the global community:

> The many 'accounts' that such a system necessarily fosters, presuppose a more central role for civil society and the public sphere in demanding and ensuring proper justificatory accounts; hence it locates democracy more explicitly in the civil society/public sphere than is the case in the previous two models.
>
> *(Chapter 2, p. x)*

As mentioned in the Introduction, this is the only conception that takes seriously the challenge that affected parties in foreign policy are *de facto* not only national citizens but also citizens of other regions or states. It entails some form of permeable constituency where the definition of affected parties might vary.

The main point is not only an assumed link between the roles of the polity in transforming political community within the region and outside it. One would not only expect that the internal standards of the polity – the principles of human rights, democracy and the rule of law – were also the ones that the entity would project externally. The model goes further than to raise this expectation of consistency between internal and external standards. The requirement that the entity should be bound by global cosmopolitan law already suggests the requirement of consistency and signifies a dismantling of the conception of sovereignty that is operative in studies of international relations. What comes in addition is that procedures would have to be in place also to ensure that, when decisions were made, the perspective of affected parties outside the borders of the regional entity were taken into account.

Thus, this conception is much more demanding than those of the EU as a civilian power, ethical power or normative power (Duchêne 1972; Manners 2002; Smith 2000), which are more linked to the availability of certain instruments than to the legal constraints that the EU subjects itself to. Further, as these conceptions rely on an indiscriminate view of norms, they are of little use if we are to investigate the democratic quality of a polity. As norms are simply associated with 'good things', a normative power may easily be the opposite of a regional-cosmopolitan entity as defined in this chapter, because it may simply seek to impose its own views of what is good without regard for the perspective of others (Sjursen 2006c).

Key indicators of this model are summarised in Table 8.3.

TABLE 8.3 Key indicators of the regional-cosmopolitan democracy model

	Constituency	*Executive power*	*Legitimacy*	*Core function*
Regional cosmopolitan democracy	Regional/ global	Shared between regional and global level	Via democratically elected representatives at regional and global levels	Upholding cosmopolitan law

Empirical fit

With regard to the executive, as already noted when discussing the first and second models, there is a shift towards a more diffuse transgovernmental level. This shift might speak quite well to the description of this third model, especially as the CFSP does seem capable of making decisions even though it does not dispose of any means of coercion. The EU cannot force member states to comply with collective decisions in foreign policy, nor does it have the option to sanction any state that chooses to go it alone rather than consult and act in co-ordination with its EU partners. It is the case that member states do not always act in concert or consult. However, the reaction when states go it alone, or choose not to follow agreed procedures, suggests that the expectation is that states will follow them – even though they cannot be forced to do so.

However, in this conception there is also a requirement of the executive being subject to global cosmopolitan law. Because the global cosmopolitan order is at best imperfect, the relevant empirical indicator must be whether the EU promotes such law as well as binding itself, and not only others, to it. There are in fact elements in the way in which the EU organises its relations with the rest of the world that echo such an idea of a 'top-down' process of democratic control of European foreign and security policy, or of what is defined as shared executive power in the analytical scheme developed in this chapter. The EU is often described as an entity that refrains from the use of force in global relations and that pursues an agenda of human rights, multilateral co-operation and a law-based international order. Reference in this regard is often made to the commitments made in the European Security Strategy (Council of the European Union 2003, 2008). The objectives identified here are to develop a stronger international society, well-functioning international institutions and a rule-based international order. Membership of key international institutions is to be encouraged and regional organisations are considered important in the effort to strengthen global governance. The cornerstone of a law-based international order is, according to the European Security Strategy, the UN. Its role must be strengthened; it must be equipped to fulfil its responsibilities and to act effectively.

Further, pointing towards the EU's policy of self-binding is the fact that a human rights clause has been standard content of all trade agreements established with third countries since 1992.

Lerch and Schwellnus (2006) also stress that the EU not only works to promote human rights, but that it aspires to change the valid rules of international law in order to accommodate a stronger human rights protection than what is found in international law today. As the EU is confronted with the challenge to present coherent arguments that go beyond the legal status quo, they have found that the EU 'leaves room for different human rights conceptions while pushing a debate and a gradual process towards a new international consensus on the interpretation of the right to life' (Lerch and Schwellnus 2006: 241). The EU differs from the USA, for example, in that it seems more willing to be bound by those very same rules that it seeks to promote to others.

Finally, the fact that the Charter is legally binding also for the CFSP goes in the same direction. It ensures that the EU is legally committed to consistency between it own policies and those promoted abroad. It remains, however, that the EU does not have formal mechanisms to sanction those that do not comply with the collectively agreed policy, or indeed any of the constraints introduced in the Treaties.

While the emphasis on strengthening the human rights dimension in international law is fairly clear in the way in which the EU organises its relations with the rest of the world, this does not appear to entail a clear idea of the need of citizens' participation either at the regional or the global level. An attempt to realise the objective of giving a voice in decision-making to third parties may be seen in the EU's so-called neighbourhood policy. The emphasis is on dialogue and reaching common understandings of what needs to be done as well as how it should be done. However, most observers argue convincingly that this ambition has yet to be satisfactorily realised. Thus, there is not much to show for the criterion of a legitimacy basis that should go via representatives at the global level (Tocci 2007).

There are processes of justification taking place and 'accounts' being given. However, these processes take place among the executives. Mechanisms such as the co-ordination reflex between member states, requiring that they take no final position on foreign policy matters before consulting with the other member states, may be seen as conducive to a form of interstate accountability. This requirement of consultation, in which national positions would have to be justified in a manner that makes it acceptable to all, does seem to cause member states to moderate their interest claims as well as bringing them to seek a certain consistency between their claims and the underlying constitutive principles of the EU (Mitzen 2006; Sjursen 2006c).

An example of the constraints on policy that results from such accounts may be the process of writing the EU's Security Strategy. Some of the more belligerent formulations regarding intervention disappeared from the first draft during the process of consultation with member states. Although this does not amount to democratic accountability, it subjects actors to intersubjective scrutiny and leads to the requirement that policy be consistent with the entrenched norms of the Union. This, then, may be said to provide a certain legitimacy basis to the foreign policy that is decided upon; however, the only way to fit this into the expectation of the regional-cosmopolitan model of a legitimacy basis that is derived via democratically elected representatives at the regional and global levels would be if the Council were transformed into a legislative body and its deliberation became open to public scrutiny.

In sum then, the CFSP speaks well to some aspects of the regional-cosmopolitan model. This is particularly so with regard to the absence of hierarchy combined with the ability to make decisions. This echoes with the expectations of the model regarding key characteristics of executive power. Further, the way in which the EU organises its relations with third countries does speak to the idea that both constituency should be regional and global and executive power should be shared, but most importantly to the core function of upholding (or further developing) cosmopolitan law. It remains, however, as is the case with the second and the third models, that the link to the citizens is fudged. Attempts are made to incorporate the fact that the constituency goes beyond the regional borders, yet it is not quite clear how decisions made may be traced back to an authorisation by their representatives (as well as by representatives at the regional level). It is also not clear how decision-makers may be held accountable to citizens and their representatives. 'Accounts' are given, as the model posits, but mainly among the executives and in closed quarters. The answer to the question of 'who decides' is difficult to get at. Hence, the CFSP is lacking with regard to the expectation of legitimacy as based on democratically elected representatives at regional and global levels.

Conclusion

The main focus in the chapter has been analytical and focused on the question of what the EU would need to look like in order to be democratic, rather than the empirical aim of systematically assessing the democratic status of the CFSP.

This analytical endeavour is important because it contributes to disentangling a number of empirical claims about the nature and form of integration in the CFSP as well as to reorienting scholarly debates in this field towards the question of democracy, in contrast to the predominant concern of efficiency. Although the nature and form of integration are contested, very little effort has been made to conceptualise alternatives to the intergovernmental model. This is a necessary exercise if the scholarly debate is to move beyond the diffuse claim that there is something 'more' to CFSP than intergovernmentalism. Such an exercise is also required in order to make possible a nuanced analysis of the status of democracy in this field. Only on the basis of a sufficiently explicit conception of the nature of the polity can a claim to democracy be established. In this respect, the third RECON model of a regional-cosmopolitan polity, that is, a polity that is not a state and that instead rests on an agenda of state transformation, proved useful. This conception captured some key features of the CFSP as a policy field where the executive emerges from the nation states but is no longer entirely within their reach. A semi-autonomous foreign policy community, with particular institutional structures and its own modus operandi, has developed in Brussels and escapes traditional conceptions of state and sovereignty.

Although the empirical aim of the chapter has been modest, it is quite clear that, if the CFSP is to be democratic, reforms are required. Merely strengthening the powers of the EP would not be enough to respond to these challenges. There is no clearly identifiable federal executive that the EP may authorise to act and be held accountable. In this field, it is not then only a matter of reconstituting democracy but of reconstitutionalising a field in which democracy has not been a main concern. Because of the 'permissive consensus', the executive has run further than the legislative. As long as the contents and orientation of European foreign and security policy remain within the bounds of a regional-cosmopolitan order, this might, in theory, hold. However, if the toolbox of military force is further expanded, the democratic anchoring of this policy will be important. The CFSP then most likely faces two options. In line with Model 1, it might scale down executive integration and strengthen parliamentary co-ordination, or, in line with Model 3, it might 'upload' and reorganise the representative dimension, and clarify lines of authority and power between the different levels and layers of decision-making.

Acknowledgements

With thanks to Erik Oddvar Eriksen and John Erik Fossum for helpful comments on an earlier draft.

Notes

1   External Action of the EU: General Debate', Comment Number 4–031m. Minutes of the Convention Meeting of 11 July 2002, at p. 16. Available at: http://www.diss. fu-berlin.de/diss/servlets/MCRFileNodeServlet/FUDISS_derivate_000000005252/ Hatakoy_Dissertation_4.pdf;jsessionid=A2C0C11FB5631D87C9D8EE7843565F84?h osts=
2   Debate on the European External Action Service, European Parliament, CRE 07/07/ 2010–12, Strasbourg, 7 July 2010. Available at: http://www.europarl.europa.eu/sides/ getDoc.do?pubRef=-//EP//TEXT+CRE+20100707+ITEM-012+DOC+XML+ V0//EN
3   All federal states, however decentralised, operate these core state functions at the central federal level.
4   The relevant configuration might be labelled a Multilevel Parliamentary Field. See Chapter 5 for more on this, including the questions it raises pertaining to constituency, authorisation and accountability.

9

SITUATING THE DEMOS OF A EUROPEAN DEMOCRACY

Magdalena Góra, Zdzisław Mach and Hans-Jörg Trenz

Introduction

Collective identities matter in the transformation of political order in contemporary Europe. There is a wide debate among European leaders and academics regarding how the European Union (EU) did become, or should become, influential and meaningful to the people of Europe (Checkel and Katzenstein 2009a; Fligstein 2008; Fossum 2003; Herrmann *et al.* 2004; Kantner 2007; Kraus 2008; Risse 2010; Trenz 2010). Given the importance of democracy to the EU's self-understanding, public attitudes and identifications with Europe as a political community will become increasingly important (Herrmann *et al.* 2004: 3). Changes in the identity formation in Europe are not solely pertinent to the process of European integration, which is undoubtedly the most unique and distinctive process on the continent. Traditional forms of identification in both Western and Eastern Europe are also challenged by globalisation and individualisation questioning traditional notions of confined nationness and popular sovereignty (Beck and Grande 2007). Ultimately, cross-border mobility, immigration and transnational citizenship rights have challenged the traditional notions of belonging and political community. In facing these challenges, some authors have concluded that by entering the era of post-modernity we also enter a new era of post-democracy, in which collective identifications of the people are becoming moving targets, increasingly restraining the possibilities of democratic will-formation (Crouch 2004). The question of how collective identities can sustain a democratic polity, therefore, needs to be addressed with new urgency.

Within social sciences and history, collective identities are commonly conceptualised within the paradigm of social constructivism (Eder *et al.* 2002; Eisenstadt and Giesen 1995). Against primordialism, it is assumed 'that interests and derived policies are shaped within particular framework of meaning and are not exogenously given.' (Larsen 2004: 64). Collective identity should therefore not be studied as something external to democracy. We will rather be concerned with how collective identities are given meaning and form through democracy and democratisation. The current processes of reconstituting democracy in Europe can in this sense be considered as the prime example for further developing this theoretical understanding of collective identities. They illustrate how democracy does not rely on pre-established identities of the people (in spite of the fact that many groups, especially in the new EU member states, insist on their ethnic, religious or cultural belonging), but should rather be conceived as a way of discursively constructing the collective identity of the people.

The major aim of this chapter is to introduce a discursive understanding of collective identity construction to systematise the relationship between European polity-building and democracy. Constructivist approaches to the analysis of collective identity transformation in Europe have become mainstream (Checkel and Katzenstein 2009a; Herrmann *et al.* 2004; Risse 2010). Following these authors, social constructivism often implies a view of politics and political institutions as the engines of collective identity constructions. The emphasis is thus on purposeful actors and their political choices in promoting particular identity projects (Checkel and Katzenstein 2009b). Our discursive approach to collective identity constructions adds to this an understanding of content and cultural form shaped by discourse, in our case the discursive forms and contents that are available for constructing the 'collective' of a European democracy. More specifically, the construction of collective identities in relation to democracy takes place through particular discursive practices that mark the boundaries of the underlying collective of political self-determination. This is done through codes of distinction that classify inclusive and exclusive relationships of belonging, and specify how the two can be meaningfully linked together (Giesen 1992). Collective identities are at the same time tied to justificatory practices, through which people *claim* belonging and recognition by others. Modern societies typically open up a public space for the contestation of identitarian projects and plural notions of the good life; a public communicative sphere that is confined by, but at the same time also constitutive of, the particular constitutional order in place. If we accept these basic insights about the correlation between the political order and the justificatory order of society, we can meaningfully ask how collective identity-building correlates with the efforts of polity-building as they were recently undertaken within the framework of the EU. The constitutionalisation of the EU as the attempt to provide an adequate framework for the justification of the EU polity implies a process of reconstructing collective identities (Morgan 2005). If the proposed polity models are primarily understood as blueprints for constructing the democratic polity in legal and institutional terms, they also need to correspond to specific modes of constructing the collective identification of the people that *constitute* the democratic polity.

In this chapter, we want to undertake the necessary steps for conceptualising EU democracy in relation to collective identities. The major question is how different options for the reconstitution of democracy in Europe can be related to the expression of collective identities. We proceed in two steps. In the first part, we will account for the micro-processes of identity transformation in Europe and the social activities that lead to the expression of collective belonging. In the second part, we examine the correspondence between democratic polity-building and collective identity-building. We will in particular focus on how collective identities can be sustained in the ongoing process of nation state transformation. What kind of political identification will emerge from this process, and how sustainable are these constructs for the stabilisation of political order and legitimacy?

Collective identities and democratic practice – a conceptual clarification

Before we can explore how collective identities can meaningfully be given expression within a macro-setting of political order, we need to understand the micro-dynamics of constructing social bonds through democratic practices. The concept of identity, as it is commonly used in social sciences, involves the idea of dynamism and contextuality. It is generally accepted that identity is a process of building social bonds through the exchange of meaning, the construction of images of the self, or the engagement in a dialogue with partners (Eder 2009). The creation of the self-image of a person or a group relies on the active *participation* of individuals in a common activity. It is equally relying on *representation* of the social bonds in terms of images and discourses, which express the internal coherence and the external boundedness of the group. At the same time, the identification of the self takes place in relation to a significant other. Significant others, in relation to whom we construct our identity, constitute a frame of reference in which identity can be given expression. Identity is a process, and not a fixed structure; it is a dynamic construction of images and discourses, interrelating with others. One can even say that there is no identity, but processes of identification, of mutual construction of symbolic images of self and other (Ardener 1989; Barth 1969; Elias and Scotson 1965; Mach 1993).

Identity seen as a dynamic process of negotiation of meaning is inseparably interconnected to the process of social activities, of involvement in meaningful relations with others. It does not, however, necessarily mean that the process of collective identity formation automatically assumes its full rationality and awareness of the participants. Very often, people use without reflection the traditional images to communicate or to express themselves. On the other hand, the more an identity formation process shifts the emphasis from the collective level to the individual, the more reflexive this process is supposed to be. The negotiation of meanings and processes of social activities are two sides of the same coin – in fact one socio-cultural process of negotiation of meaning in complex interactions in which, in particular, power relations play an important role (Cohen 1974). Identity is activity; it is action in relations with others, creating and transgressing all boundaries, active realisation of the feeling of belonging and symbolic identification. If the individual or a group remain passive, unable to develop action, then it is difficult or even

impossible to build or rebuild identity in a changing environment. This is especially important in a situation in which the frames of reference of identity, a social
environment within which identity is constructed, change. Migration would be an
obvious example, in which migrants must have a need and the opportunity to be
active, to develop meaningful activities in the new environment, in the new social
and symbolic frames of reference. Then their new identity may be created (see Mach
1998). One can ask if a similar process is developing in the EU after the last enlargement, in the changing social and symbolic frame of reference. New and old Europe
are undergoing a process of negotiation of new boundaries and with new partners of
interaction, of dialogue and negotiation with new 'significant others'.

There is also another question concerning the process of identity formation
in modern, anonymous media democracies. The normative expectation is that,
in a democracy, the collective identification of the citizens must be expressed
through public deliberations and equal consideration of the life projects and symbolic expressions of others. We want to propose that this requirement of active
involvement of the citizens needs to be qualified. Symbolic expression requires
linguistic competence, self-awareness and often courage to challenge commonly
accepted discourses. The active participation of citizens in the generation of collective identities is increasingly relying on the collective representations generated
through the mass media. Official identity discourses are heavily determined, and
often dominated by the mass media, which impose the language – the conceptual
framework in which identity may be expressed. Poland would be a good example of a situation in which the dominating identity discourse, as expressed by the
media, is nationalistic and Catholic, and requires a lot of courage and competence
to challenge it by expressing one's own different identity. It is therefore easier to
conform, and remain within the official frame of reference in the symbolic expression of identity, while at the same time being actively involved and participating in
actions and deliberations, in relations and dialogues that cross traditional boundaries and constitute the new belonging and effectively the new identity. One may
not even be completely aware of the symbolic meaning of one's involvement,
but when the question of identity is asked, and it may not be asked very often, it
becomes clear that traditional concepts and identity images do not correspond to
actual involvement.

One of the most important consequences of the change in political reality and
the processes of integration is the process of Europeanisation of collective identities
and the new and widely discussed concept of European identity. The empirical
research on micro-processes of identity formation in Western European countries
leads to the conclusion that in various countries under different circumstances the
process of Europeanisation constitutes an important element in changes of collective identity (cf. Risse 2001). This is occurring through the mechanism of 'resonance' between the national and the supranational level. According to Risse:

> [I]deas about European order and identity constructions about Europe and
> the nation-state emanating from the transnational level will interact with

given collective nation-state identities. Such political visions and identity constructions are the more likely to impact upon and to be incorporated in collective nation-state identities, the more they resonate with the ideas about the nation and political order embedded in this collective understanding.

(Risse 2001: 202)

In this kind of approach, 'Europe' is brought into national identities. This mechanism can have a significant impact on the reconstruction of the political identities under the changing context of political reality in the EU. As Risse rightly observed:

> [P]eople need to make sense and develop collective understandings of political processes in the EU. If more and more competences are transferred to the EU level and made subject to joint decision-making involving supranational institutions, we should expect that this emerging European polity impacts upon the way individuals and social groups view themselves and the nation-state.
>
> *(ibid.: 200)*

In this approach, the change of the political frames of reference will influence significantly the collective identification of the people of Europe, and with this also the kind of legitimacy on which democratic order and democratic political institutions can be built.

Situating collective identity-building in relation to democratic polity-building

After having clarified how collective identifications are generated at the micro-level of social interaction, we need to relate these basic processes of constructing social bonds back to the macro political setting of democratic order. Micro-processes of identity transformation and the question of the Europeanisation of collective identities help us to clarify the particular notion of the demos that is underlying democratic politics. The micro/macro link is taken for granted within the constitutional setting of the nation state that unifies the plural identitarian practices by forging the notion of a demos. Such a demos can then be claimed to constitute the democratic polity. The problem with the reconstitution of a European democratic order is how this micro/macro link of collective identification of the citizens as members of the demos can be meaningfully defended.

The uncertainty about the possibilities of a democratic settling of European integration is to a large extent related to the seemingly obvious absence of a European demos. In one way or the other, democratic legitimacy needs to be grounded in the collective will of the members of a constituted political community (Eriksen 2009a). As far as the EU is concerned, the plausibility and requisiteness of Europe as a demos is tested out in the long-term process of constitutionalisation. European integration has not only dismantled the old Europe of independent nation states, it has also formally embraced democratic principles and procedures, but it has not yet consolidated democratic practice engendering citizens' trust and solidarity. The search for the reconstitution of democracy in the EU correlates with the search for the expression of the collective identity of the underlying collective of a European democracy. For instance, the parliamentary principle located in the heart of constitutionalisation of the EU can become an important element to forge a European political identity. Parliamentary rule 'constitutes a vital common institutional denominator of European democracy' (Eriksen, 2009a: 228). It embodies rules for representation and as such corresponds to a notion of popular sovereignty that needs to find discursive form and expression. These processes of identification and representation of the 'collective' take place in parliamentary deliberations and contestations, which, last but not least, always address a broader audience as if it were a democratic constituent as well.

What can it mean to relate collective identity-building and democratic polity-building in the EU? Our discursive approach implies that we cannot aim at an operationalisation of collective identities as a form or a substance that relates to particular types of polity. There can be no 'ideal identity' in relation to an 'ideal polity'. There can be no indicators or criteria to tell us that there is a collective identity of a particular category (e.g., a strong or a weak identity, an ethnic or a civic identity). There can only be discursive practices that claim for one type of identity or the other. What we find empirically are not collective identities but discursive contestations about identity in the attempt to stabilise social relations within the polity (or beyond it). Collective identities in this sense cannot find a form or a resting point (like 'civic' or 'ethnic'); they can be said to always be salient and never latent. Identitarian practices are therefore seen as necessarily unconcluded, since the question of collective identities only opens up when there is an attempt to verify it.

If collective identities need to become salient in order for them to be seen, we cannot measure and categorise collective identities through opinion surveys. Our own concept corrects this common view on collective identities as the aggregation of individual attitudes in a couple of important respects. A first caveat refers to the measurement of belonging through the subjective positioning of individual actors in terms of proximity and distance to the political community. The 'subjective identity paradigm' is based on the assumption that, by providing citizens with good knowledge of the EU and good reasons to trust European institutions, individual identifications will follow automatically. It has been objected that there is a long way from individual identifications to collective identities (Eder 2009). A collective identity is different from what we measure with the degree of identification with a pre-established political category (such as the EU). For the operationalisation of the models in relation to collective identities, this means that we cannot allocate collective identities to polity models by simply asking people whether they feel national or European. We cannot, for instance, conclude that a European identity exists if the majority of Europeans feel attached to Europe and the EU or are proud to be European. We can also not measure support to the EU and to democracy as an indicator of the coming into being of a European demos that would substantiate a federal model of European democracy.

The demos that is underlying the delegated democracy model and the federal model, either in the form of the national community of citizens or in the form of a community of constitutional patriots, can only be given meaning in discursive contestations and not in substantial terms through socio-demographic indicators of groupness, culture or territoriality. The demos and its acclaimed identity only come into being as an act of representation; it is not a pre-existing sociological category. Collective identities do not exist as latent attitudes but only through the efforts to substantiate them. Opinion polls remain 'meaningless' as long as they themselves are not becoming the object of identity politics, for instance, by using the results of an opinion poll to claim for the existence of a European identity. This is the irony of the literature on a European collective identity, which in order to avoid producing 'meaningless results' is forced to enter itself into the arena of identitarian politics.

The discursive paradigm of collective identities does not take the indicators that are used to measure strong or weak identifications at face value, but as part of the storytelling of belonging to the political community (Eder 2009). Following this paradigm, the meaning of collective identities is not simply contested; the problem is rather that meaning is only constructed through such contestations. The political community as a reference object of collective identity contestations is a projection of discourse, not its underlying basis (Laclau 2005). The demos is the 'empty signi fier' of democratic discourse that functions as long as nobody notices that it cannot be given substance (Luhmann 2000: 333).

In this sense, identities cannot be rooted in the feelings of belonging to a particular group of citizens. The groupness to which collective identities relate, and the acclaimed strong or weak feelings of attachment it presupposes, do not exist prior to and independently of identity talk but because of its narrative constructs and performances. Thus, European identity can only relate to a new contested field of performing collective identities without being linked to any substantialist identities that would cause or underlie these conflicts.

The discursive practice of contesting the basic legitimacy of the EU is at the same time to be understood as an identitarian practice of differentiating possible states of worth within that polity. In the evolution of modern societies, there is a direct link between degrees of societal complexity and the proliferation of collective identities as narrative constructs, which demarcate the boundaries of social relations and establish rules of inclusion and exclusion (Eder 2009). A transnational, heterogeneous and internally differentiated setting such as the EU is therefore not in need of fewer, but of more collective identities. European integration creates an imbalance between new hegemonic expressions of unity and the continuous effort towards differentiation of its constituting parts. In debating the legitimacy of the EU, a new balance is sought between unification (integration) and differentiation, a process, which, for the time being, remains highly contested (the 'unfinished character' of the EU). The constitutionalisation of the EU therefore leads to a situation in which Europeans, who claim at the same time to be nationals or regionals or even internationals, revitalise old narratives and test out new expressions of the self of the political community. The search for democratic legitimacy of the EU provokes substantialist identity claims in terms of new practices of differentiation and new hegemonic expressions of unity.

Relating these conceptual thoughts back to the task of modelling collective identities in relation to different notions of the EU polity, we can now see that the question of how to introduce European identity and mobilise it in a multi-identitarian field has a clear political dimension. To the extent that European actors, institutions and even political scientists become engaged in a process of democratic polity-building and designing, they enter European identity politics by actively promoting trust and solidarity of European citizens. In this political struggle on the institutional-constitutional design of the EU, the question of how multiple identities can co-exist and co-evolve in Europe becomes vital for modelling different paths of reform and testing out their viability (Eriksen and Fossum 2007b).

The question of European democracy is then typically reconstructed as the confrontation between different identity projects, in which the designation of the constituting people through national democracy is put into question. In the political struggle on the democratic reconstitution of Europe, such competing solutions to the quest of allocating the popular sovereignty of the people crystallise in different master stories that are held together by a narrative that signifies a particular polity-constituency relationship. The proposed models provide three modes for constructing political narratives of collective identity projects with regard to the consolidation of democratic order in Europe. They correspond to such narratives or 'master frames' for locating public authority and popular sovereignty in Europe. As a political narrative, the models demarcate a *polity* in legal-institutional terms and they demarcate a *constituency* in identitarian terms. The status of collective identities is thus crucial for establishing the internal consistency of the model (or rather the consistency of the narrative that constructs the model), since collective identities refer to the differential principle that allows us to distinguish the democratic subject to which popular sovereignty is allocated.

Modelling a European democratic polity in relation to collective identity

For the analytical purpose of reconstructing collective identity formation in Europe, we propose that the models can be applied as narrative templates for signifying possible constituents of a European democracy. The model-building exercises should hence be considered as part of the storytelling of European democracy. The three different narratives for the institutional-constitutional design of the EU related to a particular vision of popular sovereignty can be distinguished as follows:

Audit democracy: zero-sum relationship between existing national identities

This story builds on the classical division of labour between fully sovereign nation states as the locus for allocating popular sovereignty, as well as negotiating the quest for collective identities, and an international or European arena of interest negotiation.[1] National governments appear in this story as delegated national interest representatives. The kind of trust and solidarity that is needed to make democracy work would be provided by relatively stable and historically rooted national identities. It is only on the basis of the particular notion of nationness that the citizens can participate in opinion-forming processes and put the decision-makers to account. Different national identities would stand in a zero-sum relationship and European integration is aimed at taming potential conflicts between them. A European identity would not only be unnecessary, it would also potentially harm the integrity of the national community. This is manifested in the increase of conflicts between the two levels that can only be overcome by a clear delimitation of competences and a self-restriction of the EU to market-building, negative integration and auditing the normative integrity of the member states.

Federal democracy: zero-sum relationship between European and national identities

This story applies elements of the history of nation-building to the EU. In a federal Union, the interrelation between collective identities is likewise perceived as a zero-sum game with the new elements of supranational identification slowly replacing the traditional elements of national and subnational identities. The European institutions appear in this story as common interest representatives. Democracy would be grounded in a thick European identity with the potential to overcome national identity, or at least allowing for restricted identity pluralism by territorially demarcating the sub-identities within the federal union. A strong political identity needs to prevail at the federal level, grounded in constitutional patriotism that gives expression to the will of unity of the new political entity. This has to be rooted in citizenship rights and practice and establishing bonds of mutual recognition between its plural cultural expressions (Magnette 2007). It should be noted that, in spite of these categorising efforts, there remains a basic ambivalence in the status of 'constitutional patriotism' in relation to collective identity formation. It is meant to be a 'thin identity' in the sense of being constituted by an attachment to abstract universal norms and principles, and thus giving expression to a cosmopolitan vocation. At the same time, it is meant to be a 'thick identity' in the sense of being anchored in a historically specific culture and in a particular institutional setting (Fossum 2007b; Kumm 2005). While the former refers to an undifferentiated and thus basically non-identitarian world, it is only through the latter operation of bringing in social differentiation that a principled need for demarcating an identitarian space emerges. Citizens' allegiance to the EU would thus be formed in purely political terms, '[hinging] on the validity of legal norms, the justification of policies and the wielding of power in the name of fairness' (see Chapter 2, p. 26). At the same time, this political loyalty to the EU needs to be strong enough to specify criteria of membership and set the terms of inclusion and exclusion. The federal political union would ultimately need to generate trust and solidarity among the European citizens as members of a sovereign political community to which persisting cultural particularities can be clearly subordinated.

Cosmopolitan Europe: positive-sum relationship between nested identities

This story combines elements of human rights universalism and global solidarity with a particular democratic arrangement. In a post-national, cosmopolitan Union, the interrelation between different identity discourses would lead to a positive-sum outcome. European identity would be nested happily in persisting patterns of national identification (Checkel and Katzenstein 2009a: 5). In order to be able to display this reconciliatory function, the European constitutional project needs to give expression to a cosmopolitan vocation that can be transposed to the universal and inclusive community of democracy (Eriksen 2006; see also Chapter 10). European institutions would appear in this story side by side with international organisations and global civil society, as elements of an inclusive and encompassing democratic process that represents humanity. The EU setting would thus be post-national, in the sense of renouncing a strong identity, and the persisting plural identities would be significantly constrained by the necessity to respect diversity and cosmopolitan values. In this sense, there would be an institutional guarantee that the particularity of collective identities would always be counterbalanced by reflexivity, which is displayed in the discursive references to the 'unity in diversity' of the shared political space of Europe. There would be only 'weak' and 'self-restrained' collective identities under the common principle of 'shared humanity'.

Democracy as a way of substantiating collective identities

Against the common view that holds the self-identified political community as prior to and independent of the design of the polity, we have proposed in the previous section that research on collective identity should clarify how democracy operates through the identification of popular subjectness. This should result in a distinction of specific political narratives or discourses on how the demos is signified and recognised through the unfolding of democratic practice within the European setting. Research into the dynamics of collective identity formation in Europe should therefore not be constructive, but reconstructive. It should not propose better or more coherent identity narratives to *construct* the distinct and internally coherent demos that is underlying European democracy. Research should rather *reconstruct* how people narrate their belonging, how and by whom such narratives are amplified and what effects they have on stabilising or de-stabilising the collective bonds and drawing the boundaries of the social bonds.

In light of this operationalising task, we believe that the polity models remain ambivalent with regard to the constitutive or constituting role of the demos and the constructive or reconstructive approach towards collective identities. As we will try to demonstrate in the following, this ambivalence originates in the double allocation of the people in the architecture of the democratic polity. The demos, or the collective will of the people, is the founding myth and the telos of democracy. This double allocation of the people has been referred to as the paradox of democracy (Mouffe 2000). It refers to the need to postulate the presence of the demos, before it can be claimed to come democratically into existence (Offe 2003b: 154).

Our central proposition is that, whenever the constituents of a democratic polity refer to collective identities, they confront this basic underlying paradox of democracy. The research task then consists of developing an operational understanding of democracy and of democratic practice as modes of de-paradoxisation of the undecided ability of collective identity. According to Niklas Luhmann (1997: 1061), complex societies *proceed* through displacements of their constitutive paradoxes in time. De-paradoxisation is achieved through proceduralisation, which does not resolve, but dissolves, the constitutive paradox of the social. The displacement of the paradox of the underlying unity takes place through practices of differentiation, which allow the demarcation of shifting boundaries and to establish flexible rules of inclusion and exclusion. This meets with our understanding of the polity models as narratives of postulating a polity-constituency relationship that is held valid for the particular social and political space that is demarcated by European integration. At the same time, the narratives are *operationalised* as scripts of social practices, which differentiate this polity-constituency relationship over space and time. The question then is not only how and by whom the narrative is generated, but also how it is taken up as a script that instructs democratic practice. Under these assumptions, operationalisation can only mean proceduralisation. Operationalisation should start with proceduralising the model assumptions to be able to test out how democratisation in Europe *proceeds* through images and discourses that claim for the existence of the collective will and popular sovereignty.[2]

The democratic undecidability of the *pouvoir constituant* thus results in a principal ambivalence of the polity models with regard to the status of collective identities. This is translated into two opposing views about the causal and directional processes of the constitutionalisation of the democratic polity. The first view holds the self-identified political community as – at least partially – independent of constitutional designing. European collective identity is thus seen as the basic infrastructure of a European democracy. The second view observes how EU democracy *operates* through the identification of popular subjectness (i.e., through discourses that signify the people as the constituent power of the EU). In this view, collective identity is seen as a product of entering into democratic practice.

By claiming a zero-sum relationship between collective identities, the audit democracy and the federal model are relying on a substantialist notion of collective identities. Democracy is claimed to be rooted in a popular subject, which again is given substance in a historically and culturally distinct identity. This view on collective identities as the cultural expression of unity and diversity of a political community replicates the self-description of democratically constituted nation states. In a democracy, any exercise of power needs to be justified as an articulation of popular will and subjectness. Whether emphasis is put on the idea of democracy as a process of collective will-formation or on the idea of democracy as a control of power, a strong voluntaristic assumption is made, which puts trust in the freedom and autonomy of the 'people' to be their own master in history.

The audit democracy model and the federal model can thus be said to continue a 'nationalistic' tradition of substantiating collective identities, by applying the basic rhetoric of popular sovereignty as a source of democratic legitimacy. They differ, however, in their assumptions of how the demos can come into existence. In the audit democracy model, we can assume that the mainstream of collective identity formation will still be within the national framework. The Europeanisation of the national identity in this model is limited and will not necessarily bring any changes in solid national foundations, while the resonance with the European substance will rather enforce national identification. The nature of the collective identities will be more stable than changing, and historically rooted in pre-political bonds.

Following the narrative of the audit democracy model, the democratic subject is searched for in the manifestations of culture, traditions and distinct ways of life, which demarcate the plurality of European nation states. It is assumed that such distinct national identities can be traced back in historical accounts, located in socio-structural terms or counted empirically (e.g., through public opinion surveys). With a view on Europe, such a model would also recognise the distinctiveness of Europe as a civilisation (Eisenstadt 1987; Giesen 2003; Kaelble 2001, 2009) or as a space of cultural diversity and multiple, historically rooted identities (Fossum 2001; Landfried 2002; Shelley and Winck 1995). The decisive point, however, is that this European commonness provides only weak indicators for an identity that would be able to sustain democracy. The audit democracy model therefore concludes that the EU suffers from a democratic deficit, which cannot easily be overcome by institutional reform and is partially grounded in a deficit of social and cultural integration (Cederman and Kraus 2005). The formal democratisation and constitutionalisation of the EU would remain incomplete for as long as the emerging polity cannot rely upon a robust, durable and self-identified political community (Bartolini 2005). Without such a constituted political community or demos, any democratic solution would be unfeasible.

In the 18th- and 19th-century process of nation-building, two historical modes of defining the exclusiveness of national identities have been developed in parallel and in partial demarcation to each other. National identity has been grounded in either a strong ethnic bond or a historically grown civic practice. Ethnic and civic identities constitute two competing, and often exclusive, trajectories of constructing national citizenship and belonging (Brubaker 1992). The ethnic type of belonging is oriented towards the past, emphasising tradition, common roots and cultural substrates (Eriksen 1993; Geertz 1973). As such, it was frequently implemented in Central and Eastern Europe, often explicitly as a counter-project to the French Revolution (Francis 1965). Nationalists of the ethnic type tend to be exclusive and anti-modern, sceptical about innovation and change that may bring new ideas and new identifications. Nationalists of the ethnic type do not trust 'national others' and foreign ideas in general. They are collectivistic, placing collective values, such as family or religion, above individual ones, such as freedom, human dignity and free choice. In facing European integration, ethnic nationalists frequently opt for closure and xenophobia, and express their unwillingness to be part of supranational structures.

The more open societies of Western Europe, which in the tradition of the French Revolution celebrate dialogue, plurality of ways of life and mutual respect have traditionally rejected such rigid constructions of a closed, ethnic, exclusive nation. Instead, a civic model of nation develops, which proposes to build collective identity on citizenship, civic values, liberalism and negotiation of meaning. Such a civic nation postulates an open, dynamic and future-oriented social bond. Membership is based on choice and negotiation, opening the possibility of inclusion and the establishment of different levels of social organisation (e.g., in a federation). In facing European integration, civic nationalists often emphasise the limited resources of trust and solidarity among the co-nationals, which cannot easily be transposed to the transnational level.

In facing new challenges of immigration, multiculturalism and shifting allegiances of citizens, we also observe how traditionally defined civic and ethnic components of collective identities can be quickly transformed and re-arranged. Although national identity remains the main frame of symbolic reference for many people (Smith 2001), European societies are on the move towards re-defining the bonds of the social. In particular, the ethnic concept of nation, traditionally developed in many European societies, is now more and more often seen as not only unfashionable and parochial, but also counter-productive in facing global and European challenges.

The federal model starts from the same premises of a plurality of cultural expressions that substantiate distinct national identities, but goes one step further by sustaining the transformative force of European integration in re-shaping collective identities. It further specifies the mechanisms through which such a political community of the Europeans can be given substance. This is basically achieved through the constitutional designing of the emerging European polity that is given a democratic form and thus would be able to re-direct citizens' allegiance and create the kind of trust and solidarity that is necessary to sustain a European democracy. The democratic reconstitution of Europe would in this sense be followed by the reconstitution of the social carriers of democracy. The research task would then go beyond the mapping of existing plural identities and embrace the conception of political strategies to overcome the deficit of social and cultural integration. Whereas the audit democracy model would stop with the diagnosis of collective identity cleavages that mark the European space, the federal model would need to address the question of the peaceful co-existence of different identity projects and how they could be put into a hierarchical order. For this purpose, notions of federalism are typically introduced and, for example, linked to some notion of constitutional patriotism to distinguish between 'strong' and 'weak' elements of collective identity.

On the basis of the federal model, it is also frequently sustained that political identities are mouldable through political intervention and can be actively promoted to supersede other residual forms of cultural identity, which are more resistant to change. In the literature on European collective identity formation, efforts have been made to demonstrate that co-existing plural identities are not only possible, but also normal (Herrmann *et al.* 2004). Academic work can thus indirectly back the identity-selling efforts of European institutions by demonstrating, for instance through opinion surveys, that individuals can, and in fact do, hold multiple identities (Risse 2004). It needs to be critically noted, however, that such surveys intrinsically replicate the substantialist notion of collective identity. By measuring collective identities at the aggregated level of individual attitudes, they are usually relying on predefined categories to which the respondents have to react, but in which the individual life histories of the people tend to disappear (Eder 2009).

Beyond identity?

Much of the debate about the possibilities of democracy beyond the nation state has focused on the question of whether collective identities are constitutive of or derivative from democracy – with the audit democracy model taking the former and the federal model the latter position. Many, and in particular liberal and deliberative theorists, have also argued, however, that democratic rules and procedures should be understood in purely universalistic terms and therefore detached from the particularity of collective identity. In the following, we will basically argue that there can be no 'beyond identity' in relation to democracy. There can be, however, a reflexive mode of dealing with collective identity contestations in democracy (Chapter 10).

The cosmopolitan model constitutes one possible political narrative to conceptualise democracy 'beyond identity' but also exemplifies the intrinsic contradiction such a project runs. In relation to collective identities, such a model does not negate the possibility of belonging and boundaries, but puts them under the constraint of universal discourse and procedures. This opens the possibility of a positive-sum relationship between nested identity games. Instead of searching for the possibilities of a peaceful co-existence and the harmonious relationship between plural identity projects under the European umbrella, the cosmopolitan model counts on the transformative power of identity talk and practice. The narrative of this model is therefore not simply based on the preservation of existing plural identities. It rather looks at identity transformation as a creative and open-ended process, in which the validity of the collective project needs to be constantly reconfirmed and the boundaries of the social remain contingent. This introduces a certain ambivalence into identity discourse, since the underlying constituents are no longer seen as fixed and homogeneous. It is sustained that criss-crossing public discourses linked to shifting allegiances can also generate democratic legitimacy (Chapter 2). Types of identity and degrees of attachment may vary and must be constantly renegotiated through the democratic process. Collective identity is then no longer seen as a stable resource on which democracy can draw, but a shifting target that is contingent on the democratic process.

Instead of relying on collective identity as a pre-political category or as a substantialist feature of individuals and groups (the participatory perspective of 'nationalists'), the cosmopolitan model self-reflexively recognises the contingent ways of narrating collective identities. It thus turns from a substantialist to an operational notion of collective identity formation as a consequential effect of entering into a shared discursive practice. This has consequences for how research on collective identity formation in relation to the reconstitution of EU democracy can proceed. One problem related to this notion is how research can still underlie collective identity as a category of analysis while at the same time recognising its character as a category of practice (Brubaker and Cooper 2000: 5). In searching for the essence of 'sameness' or 'groupness' of the Europeans, research can only find 'identity talk' and 'identity politics'. Second, research would need to look at social groups not as carriers of collective identities, but rather as containers of identity discourses and practices. We need to understand how different role ascriptions of European and national actors are embedded in a plural and multi-level representative field, which is given discursive form and which signifies the social groups or the 'people' as the carriers of identity.

Does the cosmopolitan model open the path for introducing a non-substantialist notion of collective identities? There are two readings of how to underlie a positive-sum relationship between nested collective identities as part of the narrative of a post-national democratic polity: the politics of recognition and the politics of deliberative supranationalism.

The first notion of how to narrate collective identities as elements of a post-national democratic union refers to the politics of recognition. Within this paradigm, the promoters of a European democracy would need to pay tribute to the existence of multiple identities. Democracy would be made possible through the recognition of diverse life forms and belongings (Honneth 1995). While it would no longer be necessary to ground democracy in a substantial and homogeneous demos (either the civic or the ethnic variant), the substantialist paradigm is nevertheless maintained with regard to the recognition of diversity. Democracy can in this sense always be seen as the positive-sum outcome of balanced conflicts and diversity. An encompassing legal and institutional framework provided by universal law, international organisations and global civil society would be sufficient to guarantee such positive-sum outcomes and could substitute the hierarchical institutions of the nation state or of a European constitutional order.

The solution proposed within the politics of recognition paradigm is thus that a positive-sum game between nested identities would facilitate democracy while preserving collective identity. Therefore the only criterion of European identity is acceptance of the basic principles that govern the process of negotiation and participation in the common social, political and economic space. Those values include in particular the rule of law, the principle of openness, tolerance and dialogue as the only methods of solving problems, and respect of human rights, especially freedom, equality, dignity and the principle of non-discrimination, as they are expressed in the Charter of Fundamental Rights.

The second notion of how to narrate collective identities as elements of a post-national democratic union refers to the politics of deliberative supranationalism (Eriksen and Fossum 2000b). The legitimacy of the proposed system stems from the process of deliberation based on reasoning. The basis for legitimacy in an internal sense is given by participation. Agreement is reached during the proceedings according to communicative rationality. Moreover, deliberative democracy:

> [D]isconnect[s] collective will-formation in modern politics from the notion of a pre-existing system of common values and affiliations. In this perspective, there is a separation of politics and culture, of citizenship and nationality, of ethnos and demos. Discourse theory departs from a substantive, or ethical conception of citizen autonomy, which emanates from the convergence of tradition and community-type bonds on the basis of which it is possible to reach an agreement and forge a common position.
>
> *(Eriksen and Neyer 2003: 8)*

The politics of deliberative supranationalism – in contrast to the politics of recognition – are characterised by the attempt to de-substantialise collective identities. Discourse is recognised as the driving force in the making of collective identities and rational discourse also constrains expressions of collective identities by introducing the universal moment of 'shared humanity'. The positive-sum outcome of 'shared humanity' is thus achieved through a reflexive operation by those who are involved in the 'making of' collective identities. Reflection is a way to overcome the conditionality of collective identities, because it confronts the participants of discourse with a notion of universal validity beyond the particularity of meaning. In this last sense, the 'cosmopolis' can be said to rely on discourse and 'shared humanity', and not on collective identity (Eriksen 2006). As we will argue in the following, this attempt to de-substantialise collective identities introduces a tension with the concept of democracy, because it de-substantialises at the same time the notion of popular sovereignty on which democracy is based. The question that needs to be raised in the last part of this chapter is how the 'shared humanity' of the cosmopolis can be turned into the collective will of the demos that underlies democracy. How can the 'cosmodemos' be constituted through the expression of a collective identity?

From 'shared humanity' to collective identity

By shifting from a substantialist to a discursive perspective on the 'making of collective identities', the cosmopolitan model attempts to reconstruct democracy as a justificatory order, in which individuals draw on particular principles and discourses to define their common world. From the research perspective, this 'linguistic turn' in the study of collective identities can be accommodated by analysing the narratives and discursive practices that claim for collective identities in relation to European integration in general, and European democratic polity-building in particular. In line with this, it is assumed that there can be no substance of collective identity that exists independently of its discursive representation. Notions of collective identity need to be discursively represented and have no existence 'beyond discourse'. The analytical programme that follows is linked to 'identity politics' as the dynamics of raising and contesting identity claims. The non-substantialist notion of collective identities would help to demarcate either a polity of recognition or a polity of deliberation, in which competing identity projects need to be accommodated by common rules and procedures.

The question that remains to be answered at the end of this chapter is whether such a non-substantialist notion of collective identity is also sustainable from the participatory perspective of democracy. To the extent that the cosmopolitan model embraces a project of democratic polity-building, it shifts back from a deconstructive to a constructive (and thus intrinsically political) notion of collective identities. It does not track further the operational understanding of democratic practice and identity talks, but returns to the substance of democracy and collective identity that is needed to defend the cosmopolitan project. The proposition to be made at the end of this chapter is that such a rhetoric shift is not inconsistent with democratic theory but intrinsic to any attempt of demarcating the collective will of the people. Democracy, in one way or the other, needs to signify popular sovereignty. It needs to identify the people, to give them a name and a substance. Collective identities fulfil precisely this purpose of giving hegemonic expression to popular sovereignty. They primarily help to stabilise and equip social relations and to *objectify* them in such a way 'as to give them body, performance and presence' (Boltanski and Thévenot 2006: 185). Under these premises, what are the conditions for turning the 'shared humanity' as the 'positive-sum outcome' of the cosmopolitan model into a collective identity that signifies popular subjectness and sovereignty?

In order to explore this intrinsic relationship between democracy and substantive identity claims, it is useful to recall once more the basic operational requirements in the making of collective identities. In the conceptual part of this chapter, we have claimed that collective identities do not exist as latent attitudes, but only through the efforts to substantiate them. From this perspective, a non-substantialist notion would be a contradiction in terms, precisely because the basic operation of signifying the popular subject of democracy remains incomplete.

One must therefore conclude that the cosmopolitan model provides an incomplete democracy narrative as long as it does not locate popular sovereignty in relation to substantive identity claims. In order to objectify the collective, a justificatory practice cannot rest uniquely on the requirement of 'shared humanity'. The identitarian moment is introduced only at the point of combining the cosmopolitan principle with the principle of differentiating possible states or worths for the members of the collective. Collective identities specify commonness through distinction. They are thus made up of two opposing forces: the first aspiration consists in what the cosmopolitan model has identified as the requirement of 'shared humanity' – that is, in the escape from singularity, individualism and distinction. As an identitarian narrative, democracy postulates a relation of equivalence among human beings in as far as they all belong to a collective that includes and transcends them. Democracy consequently works to attain what is naturally common, what belongs to all, to break down isolation and to unite. This cosmopolitan aspiration for 'shared humanity' is counterbalanced by the requirement of differentiation and isolation of the popular will and subjectness. As an identitarian narrative, constitutional democracy justifies a relation of difference among human beings, which is found in the dignification of the personal, the individual right and the authorisation of the singular will. This includes formulas to express the worth of the particular group and to embody the collective, to draw the boundaries of belonging and to set the rules of inclusion and exclusion.

By applying this operational perspective, the positive-sum outcome of a reconciled collective identity of the cosmopolitan model is revealed as a new hegemonic expression of popular sovereignty. This model remains an incomplete identity narrative as long as it does not designate a polity-constituency relationship that unites the universal moment of 'shared humanity' with the particular moment of differentiating popular subjectness. Such a specification of the conditions of how democracy works could classically rely on the citizenship narrative of the audit democracy model and the federal one. Yet, our change of research perspective allows us to turn from the substance of the 'demos' to the process of its substantialisation. Democracy is precisely about this process of signifying popular will and sovereignty (Laclau 2005) and it remains dubious whether this can be done without raising a substantialist claim for collective identity. If the cosmopolitan model in turn rests merely on the cosmopolitan denotation of shared humanity, the popular sovereignty remains unsignified. The cosmopolitan Europe would fall back to naturalism by delineating a primordial state, that would be a-social and a-political in the sense of barely relying on natural signifiers of shared humanity.

The corresponding research programme consists in analysing discourses, which substantiate collective identities by signifying the people as the constituent power of the EU. This is a reconstructive task, which analyses how the discourse of EU democracy constructs its own object or how the 'represented' of a European democracy is constituted through the acts of representation. Comparative research on EU constitutional debate provides a prime example for these dynamics of underlying notions of 'collective will', 'the people', 'popular sovereignty' or claiming belonging and identity (Liebert and Trenz 2008a, 2008b; Trenz 2008; Trenz et al. 2009 ; Vetters et al. 2009). As a further research strategy for linking 'EU-polity narratives' to collective identities, it is proposed to reconstruct more systematically and also critically *how* and *at which points* 'European cosmopolitanism', as manifested in the unspecified claims for overcoming the particularity of collective identities by reference to universalism, is turned into new identitarian practices. In particular, this implies normative consistency tests of the underlying model assumptions on how particularism and universalism are related. In its existing form, the polity models have a tendency to treat particularism and universalism as special cases, the former opening up to collective identities and contextualised versions of democracy (the first and second models), and the latter demarcating a basically identitarian free world of a cosmopolitan version of democracy (the cosmopolitan model). From a discourse theoretical notion of collective identities, the models would rather need to specify the mechanisms of substantiating collective identities at the interface between claims for universalism and particularism. References to 'shared human- ity' and to 'differentiating parts' need therefore to be singled out in each model in order to be able to arrive at a consistent account of collective identity. The model- building exercise of relating the polity and the constituency of a European democ- racy should in this sense be considered as part of the narrative construction of Europe. European identity discourse would not be exceptional but rather follow the general rules of debating democratic legitimacy, which combines the cosmo- politan rhetoric with a differentiating identitarian practice. This could contribute to our understanding of how and why the attempts to initiate a positive-sum game of collective identities continuously (and inevitably) fall back into a zero-sum logic of demarcating collective identities (the paradox of cosmopolitanism).

Conclusion

In this chapter, we have argued that collective identities are tied to particular dis- cursive forms and practices that mark the boundaries of the social and, in relation to democracy, the collective of self-determination. However, in its double refer- ence to popular sovereignty and universal rights, democracy remains ambivalent with regard to the demarcation of collective identities. This intrinsic ambivalence of democracy in relating to collective identities is also informing the current recon- stitution of democracy in Europe. Ongoing processes of identity transformation are driven by the uncertainty of allocating popular sovereignty in a world of dis- persed authority and constitutional reshuffling of the basic polity-constituency relationship.

The RECON models reflect this ambivalence of collective identities in Europe. It has become clear that any attempt to consolidate democracy and politi- cal rights in a transnational setting such as the EU remains bound to the narrative of popular will and sovereignty and, as such, needs to rely on the demarcation of collective identity in relation to a particular type of polity. At the same time, this ambivalence of identity discourse in relation to democracy explains the con- tested nature of the ongoing struggles over the European integration project and its underlying legitimacy. The question of which form a European collective iden- tity should take to comply with the standards of democracy cannot therefore be resolved by theoretical modelling. It is rather the practice of reconstituting democ- racy in Europe that remains tied to a practice of re-defining the boundaries of the social.

Notes

1 See Risse (2004: 248) and Checkel and Katzenstein (2009b) for an understanding of zero-sum and positive-sum identity games.
2 For such a procedural translation of the polity model assumptions, see the contribution by Ulrike Liebert to this volume (Chapter 7).

10

COSMOPOLITANISATION IN EUROPE AND BEYOND

John Erik Fossum

Introduction

This chapter is explicitly focused on the third democratic polity model, namely the notion of the European Union (EU) as a democratic post-national Union. This model sees the EU as a regional subset of an emerging global cosmopolitan order. The EU has from the outset been considered a regional arrangement, set up to deal with the specific challenges facing Europe after two devastating wars in less than one generation. Cosmopolitanism did not figure as an explicit political doctrine, or as an intrinsic part of the EU's self-conception.[1] But the effort to institutionalise interstate cooperation under a new supranational order no longer based on narrowly defined nationalism has, if not an explicit cosmopolitan vocation, at least cosmopolitan features. A rapidly growing body of literature then also discusses the EU in cosmopolitan terms (Beck and Grande 2007; Delanty and Rumford 2005; Eriksen 2006, 2009a; Eriksen and Fossum 2007a). There are also those such as Ulrich Beck who see the EU as 'institutionalised cosmopolitanism' (2006: 114) and as a cosmopolitan vanguard.

Does the EU qualify as a cosmopolitan vanguard? To establish that it is necessary not only to consider how cosmopolitan the EU is, but also to make clear whether the EU is more suitable for cosmopolitanism, or better able to promote it, than other types of political or social entities such as global institutions, an increasingly globalised civil society, and states. The nation state with its exclusivist propensity – based on the need for preserving national distinctness – appears the least likely candidate for cosmopolitan vanguard. But does that apply foremost to the *nation* state, or to the *state form*, as well? State-based democratic constitutionalism is, after all, founded on a set of universal principles (Habermas 1996), and many analysts see states as compatible with cosmopolitanism (Archibugi 2008; Beck 2006; Holton 2009; Kendall *et al.* 2009; Turner 2008). Might then states serve as cosmopolitan vanguards? If so, what features of states would make them cosmopolitan forerunners? We should expect such states to propound basic human rights, and to understand the individual not only as an autonomous being but also as the ultimate unit of concern, and that this status would be recognised as universally applicable. The requisite type of community would be inclusive (post-national). Since states with explicit post-national vocations are hard to come by, we might instead consider as possible candidates those democratic constitutional states that are explicitly committed to inclusive community (frequently labelled as multinational, cf. Gagnon and Tully 2001).[2]

This chapter devises an analytical framework that will enable us to discern whether, and the extent to which, different forms of political entity – state (Canada) and non-state (EU) alike – can be cosmopolitan forerunners. Canada is a particularly interesting state to consider from a cosmopolitan perspective because it has distinct cosmopolitan traits. Might such traits qualify it as a vanguard? This is of interest because a positive conclusion might challenge the widely held notion that regional supranational (non-state) entities are more conducive to and supportive of cosmopolitanism than states. However, the main obstacle to cosmopolitanism may reside not in the state as such, but in nationalism and how it programs sovereign statehood. One path to cosmopolitan democracy would then be through the (hierarchical) state form, but reconfigured along post-national or even multinational lines. Peaceful and democratic contestation over community may thus be conducive to cosmopolitanism.

The chapter first proceeds to define cosmopolitanism. Based on this, it establishes a set of criteria for assessing degree or magnitude of cosmopolitanisation (i.e., the process of entrenching cosmopolitanism). The criteria must work for different political entities, thus enabling us to capture how this process unfolds along state and non-state lines alike. The two cases (EU and Canada) are obviously shaped by global (cosmopolitan) institutional developments, which are, however, unlikely to exert such a strong pressure as to harmonise cosmopolitanisation processes across these differently structured political entities (which may not even be about the same underlying understanding of cosmopolitanism). I therefore devise the two cases as different cosmopolitan paths, and specify criteria along each, with the EU understood as a non-state-based cosmopolitanising entity, and Canada as a state-based cosmopolitanising entity. In the concluding section, I briefly contrast the two, in order to say something about their cosmopolitan-democratic character and quality.

What is cosmopolitanism?

Cosmopolitanism's structuring normative intuition is moral universalism (Habermas 1997: 135, 2006). The modern version of cosmopolitanism can be traced back to Immanuel Kant, notably his *Zum Ewigen Frieden* which was first published in 1795. Kant's vision is that of the emergence of a global legal order, which unites all peoples and abolishes war. Jürgen Habermas's position builds on Kant but addresses the weaknesses in the Kantian position and updates it so as to make it relevant to the contemporary world (Habermas 1997, 2006, 2010). Habermas, the specifics of whose position have changed over time, nevertheless underlines how cosmopolitan restructuring pertains to: (a) the external sovereignty of states; (b) states' internal sovereignty; and (c) the very meaning of peace. On the first point, each world citizen has rights that have to be institutionalised so as to be able to bind individual governments. The overarching community thus needs sanctioning powers. Within such a construction: 'The external relationship of contractually regulated international relations among states, where each forms the environment for the others, then becomes the internally structured relationship among the members of a common organisation based on a charter or a constitution.' (Habermas 1997: 127). The second point, that of internal sovereignty, pertains to a world community that is made up of citizens rather than a world made up of sovereign states:

> The point of cosmopolitan law is . . . that it goes over the heads of the collective subjects of international law to give legal status to the individual subjects and justifies their unmediated membership in the association of free and equal world citizens.
>
> *(ibid.: 128)*

The third and final requirement speaks to the reciprocal democratisation of individual states and the community of states. The ensuing conception of war and peace then also changes: the cosmopolitan notion does not simply refer to crimes committed *during* war; war itself becomes a crime: the crime *of* war can be prosecuted.

We see from this reading of cosmopolitanism that it presupposes a major process of transformation, wherein all states succumb to a global order, either by ceasing to be states, or by transforming so much as to cohere with the core tenets of cosmopolitanism. It is this latter point of magnitude of state transformation that is of particular interest when considering whether states can be cosmopolitan vanguards. Is it about the magnitude of contemporary transformation brought about by globalisation? Then the issue differentiating vanguards from run-of-the-mill or laggards is the degree of 'global cosmopolitan uplink' or exposure to globalisation.

Cosmopolitanism has deep historical roots, is not confined to the West, has waxed and waned over time (Delanty 2009; Holton 2009). This also suggests that there may be particular historical circumstances that can be quite decisive in terms of opening or closing cosmopolitan windows or opportunities. The same argument will likely apply with added force in specific states or entities. One possible factor differentiating vanguards from others can therefore be certain 'historical dispositions', that is, some states may have historical traits and arrangements that particularly dispose them towards cosmopolitanism. One such can be historical failure to establish an unambiguous, substantively robust shared sense of national community. This sits well with Kant's starting assumption pertaining to cosmopolitan right, namely that 'we are always likely to find ourselves alongside others who disagree with us about justice . . .' (Waldron 2010: 172). Peaceful and democratic handling of such conflicts requires more universal solutions and an inclusive sense of community. This point does apply to Canada, which 'has passed from a pre-national to a post-national phase without ever having become a nation' (Frye cited in Lipset 1990: 6).

The definition of cosmopolitanism presented earlier presupposes transformation. The problem, as we saw with regard to the EU, is that even entities that scholars hold up as cosmopolitan vanguards may not have explicit cosmopolitan self-conceptions or credos. They will likely not be powered by explicit cosmopolitan doctrines. We therefore have to discern their cosmopolitan orientation from *actual practice* and the *process of cosmopolitanisation*.[3] The added problem that Robert Holton's (2009) comprehensive multi-disciplinary survey brings up is that there are many different strands of cosmopolitanism. Thus, precisely where we stand today in relation to a cosmopolitan world requires far more systematic attention. Further, research on the type of practical arrangements that might sit with cosmopolitan principles, coupled with assessments of the extent to which practical arrangements *actually* work according to cosmopolitan principles, is still in its infancy. Some analysts attribute that to what they see as social science's inherent nation state bias, or 'methodological nationalism'.[4] This implies that there are arrangements and practices that might at closer scrutiny qualify as cosmopolitan, but have not been understood as such, because they have not been explicitly couched in cosmopolitan terms, whether by decision-makers or by analysts.

There is therefore a need for proper translation. We need to consider which concepts, polity designations, procedural arrangements, identities and conceptions of self and other are directly translatable into cosmopolitanism. Such an act of translation is necessary also because of nationalism's prestige in today's world. Nationalists define political communities in national terms whether the label fits or not, because there is such a great legitimacy gain in successfully doing so. Proper translation is therefore also a way of avoiding nationalism's 'reification fallacy', the propensity to accept as an already established fact that which one wants to have come into existence.[5]

The criteria for cosmopolitanisation must be tailored to that which translation helps to uncover, namely the *processes of entrenching* cosmopolitanism across different entities. It is obvious that such processes must be steeped in the notion of moral universalism. Core elements of moral universalism, notably pertaining to human rights, must be legally entrenched in positive – cosmopolitan – law. Moral universalism is not necessarily footloose; all cosmopolitan arrangements are steeped in distinct institutional-cultural contexts. The cosmopolitan thrust hinges on compliance with the requirements of inclusion (or openness) and reflexivity. With inclusion I refer both to the physical inclusion of others (non-nationals, members of other cultures, etc.), as well as to the taking into account of the interests and concerns of non-nationals. Further, the institutional and cultural setting must leave space for, or be compatible with, reflexivity, which, as Habermas underlines, is closely connected with moral universalism.

In order to clarify the institutional implications of this, it is useful to keep in mind that the nation state makes up a particular – and distinctive – configuration where limited scope for exit and entry (of persons, groups, and territorial systems of rule) is important for the system's ability to ensure the type of loyalty that is considered necessary for the sustenance of the national community over time.[6] Cosmopolitanism is based on a different configuration of exit, entry, loyalty and voice.[7] It operates with far lower barriers to exit and entry (for individuals, groups/collectives and territorial systems of rule) than does the nation state. The far lower barriers to exit and entry will shape the system's ability to instil loyalty and the relationship between loyalty and critical voice. Such a configuration places a greater onus on *reflexivity*: the extent to which the polity is open to challenge, reinterpretation and amendment. It entails a process that is open to deliberative challenge, a process of critical self-examination on who we are, who we should be, and who we are thought to be. Rights that ensure individual autonomy – private and public – are critical institutional preconditions for reflexivity.

A cosmopolitan vanguard is thus a political entity that is imbued with moral universalism, and is open to the world and inclusive of others and otherness – it is reflexive in the sense that it does not integrate them into a fixed (national) mould, but adapts itself and its self-conception as part of the process of inclusion.

A changing global context

Many analysts see the prospects for cosmopolitanism today foremost from globalisation (Beck 2006). The assumption is that globalisation does away with or reconfigures state sovereignty, and helps to erect a global structure of norms and institutions of cosmopolitan character. How much merit this assessment has is disputed.

There is no doubt that states are becoming more closely linked together across a broad range of domains: political, social, cultural, economic and legal. Tight links are amplified by the revolution in microelectronics and information technology. New international and transnational actors have emerged. States are also faced with a whole range of boundary-spanning problems pertaining to environmental degradation, international crime, terrorism, tax evasion and so forth. In response to the recent financial crisis and the ensuing economic downturn, states across the globe have been compelled to take drastic measures to face a crisis that is clearly global in character and whose global character has exacerbated its severity and effects.

Many analysts conclude that these developments are *unprecedented* in spatio-temporal and organisational terms. The argument is that global flows are far more extensive, intensive, and have a far higher velocity and impact than was the case in earlier processes of globalisation. Contemporary globalisation is also more strongly institutionalised than before, through international organisations, treaties, regimes and conventions, and networks and patterns of interaction and contact. The upshot is that the present situation is seen as unique, notably in its *confluence* of factors and processes (Held *et al.* 2000).

The argument is, further, that developments within the realm of international law challenge and/or transform state sovereignty. Individuals and groups are recognised as legal subjects of international law. The realm of international law is shifting from being focused primarily on political and geopolitical matters to an increased focus on regulation of economic, social, communication and environmental matters. This also relates to changes in the sources of international law – which far more than before include international treaties or conventions, international custom and practice, and 'the underlying principles of law recognised by "civilized nations"' (Held *et al.* 2000: 63). This has also led to an increased focus on the relation between the individual and his or her own government:

> International law recognises powers and constraints, and rights and duties, which have qualified the principle of state sovereignty in a number of important respects; sovereignty *per se* is no longer a straightforward guarantee of international legitimacy. Entrenched in certain legal instruments is the view that a legitimate state must be a democratic state that upholds certain common values.
>
> *(Held et al. 2000: 65)*

But globalisation unfolds unevenly, in the different functional realms and in the different parts of the world, and its democratic impetus is highly uneven across states, and in relation to the global level.[8] There is no reason to assume that globalisation will necessarily lead to cosmopolitan democracy.

At the global level, we see the emergence not of a coherent order but rather what Waldron (2010) has called an interlocking and growing thicket of global norms. There are international institutions, but they do not really constitute a world government. The international norms lack a binding commitment and a proper ability to enforce these. The United Nations (UN), established in the wake of the two devastating world wars, represented an effort to overcome the destructive forces built into the Westphalian system of nation states. The very forging of the UN bears testimony to a 'cosmopolitan opening', but one that also faces many constraints on cosmopolitanism in today's world. The UN is not capable of systematically enforcing human rights and securing peace, and is still privy to the decisions of the great powers which often run roughshod over international law. This even applies to Western governments, which 'protest against the lack of democracy inside the organisation . . . and do all they can to prevent any radical reform in that direction.' (Archibugi 2008: 11) The present global system is caught between sovereignty and hospitality (Benhabib 2006).

The significant institutional structure that regulates the economic realm (notably through such institutions as the World Trade Organisation (WTO), International Monetary Fund (IMF) and World Bank) has taken on a strong neoliberal orientation that empties out the space for politics (Habermas 2006, 2010), in a context of extreme and dramatic social and economic disparities. Some underline that this system is giving rise to the emergence of a new transnational ruling class (Brunkhorst 2009).

Nevertheless, we see the development of a global quasi-constitutional structure. It does lack proper democratic authorisation, and the links back to the democratic institutions in those entities that are democratic are also very weak. Much of the requisite democratic infrastructure is missing, certainly at the institutional level, but to a considerable extent also at the societal level. There is no real common political culture or shared democratic identity. There are international organisations steeped in an embryonic global civil society, but these are relatively underdeveloped global publics with weak ties to the global institutional structure. In this context, the main democratic thrust must come from below (Brown 2010: 262).

Strengthening the global institutions raises important challenges: How to fashion a global state or state-type structure without it becoming oppressive? The main problem is of course lack of democracy, but many also hold up the problem of scale: even when a global system of government is entrenched in democratically accountable institutions, this might produce a pattern of centralisation that is insensitive to difference and diversity. The fear of oppression has made many analysts, including Habermas and even Held, to argue that cosmopolitanism does not entail abolishing states but rather reconfiguring state sovereignty to suit a system based on cosmopolitan law. The legal developments that have already taken place lend some credence to such approaches. But there are clear limits to the effective reach of these legal provisions because they all depend on states (including oppressive authoritarian ones such as Russia and China) for their proper systematic effectuation.

Another problem stems from the fact that the pattern of globalisation that drives much of this process is highly asymmetric (Bohman 2007a: 13); hence it offers limited assurance of sustaining a *global* or universal pattern of transformation.

The problems that beset global solutions have prompted many analysts to cast their glance below the global level and focus on those parts of the world that hold the greatest potential to cosmopolitanise. This takes us to the regional level, what Habermas (2009b) labels as the second, the transnational level. The focus in this chapter is on the EU, which is the only trans/supranational regional entity with explicit cosmopolitan-democratic traits.

Regional cosmopolitanisation

The EU does not have an explicitly articulated cosmopolitan vocation. But the fact that the basic principles that the EU appeals to are universal, and because the EU is an attempt to foster an inclusive community, it makes sense to consider it as a possible vanguard for an emerging democratic – cosmopolitan – world order. This argument in effect relies on a process of translation to render clear to what extent the EU – in structural and operational terms – complies with key cosmopolitan tenets. In Chapter 2, Eriksen and I have presented a set of criteria that helps to render clear what institutional form such a regional-cosmopolitan entity could take to comply with cosmopolitan norms. These criteria need to be attuned to capture the process of cosmopolitanisation. In the following assessment, I only focus on the internal aspects of the EU; lack of space prevents a proper assessment of the EU's 'global uplink' and the extent to which the EU propounds cosmopolitanism in its foreign and external relations.[9]

The post-World War II situation (as, for instance, revealed through the establishment of the UN) represented a 'cosmopolitan opening', which provided the fledgling EU with a certain regional-cosmopolitan disposition. The EU, as Habermas (1998b) has noted, is a case of learning from disaster. The atrocities committed during the Second World War, with the Holocaust as the most egregious European manifestation, figured centrally in the minds of state officials and members of civil society who looked for institutional solutions to ensure that this would never again occur in Europe. Self-sufficient national communities were seen as a core element of the problem, and a system of European-level human rights protection, coupled with binding interstate cooperation that would tie former combatants together, were seen as vital parts of the solution. The cosmopolitan imprint becomes apparent once we consider how the cosmopolitan ethos manifested itself in certain social practices, which were institutionalised in the EU.[10] To get integration off the ground required reconciliation through forgiveness,[11] and the logic of *preventive foresight*: the European Coal and Steel Community (the forerunner of the European Communities) was explicitly set up with the aim of preventing further wars between Germany and France through tying their economies and societies together in the strategic areas of steel and coal production and use. Provision of aid and the fostering of solidarity figured as central elements in the broader entrenchment of cosmopolitan peace and democracy on the European continent and beyond.

Thus, the EU was born in a period with a certain cosmopolitan opening, but this was also a period marked by deep distrust. The structures that were set up to ensure cooperation were specifically designed to prevent further violent catastrophe on European soil. The EU was equipped with a 'cosmopolitan integrationist licence', albeit a highly *conditional* one, which presupposed effective measures to contend with the deep animosities that the two world wars in less than one generation had brought about.

This highly conditional cosmopolitan licence is clearly reflected in the rights-basis and the institutional-constitutional development of the EU (see also Chapter 4), a development that in turn came to equip the EU with its distinct characteristics. On rights, the most explicit symbolic manifestation is the European Charter, which equips European citizens with civil, political and social rights. The extent of rights that the EU provides to individuals is unprecedented at the supranational level. At the same time, the effective enforcement of these, and their ability to program the EU in a clear cosmopolitan direction, depends on the EU's institutional-constitutional development.

The EU of today has clear traits of supranational government (in line with the criteria for a regional-democratic Union, as outlined in Chapter 2), but it nevertheless also falls well short of this model because of how the supranational dimension combines with important intergovernmental features (which most likely will persist under the Lisbon Treaty).

To get at this, it is useful to think of the EU as departing from the standard, uniform conception of internal sovereignty that marks states, even federal ones.

The EU is perhaps best understood as a two-tracked or even two-headed construction.[12] This can be traced back to its inception (1957) where one track consisted in the relatively rapid process of legal and economic integration that resulted in the supranational European Community (EC), and where the other had its roots in the protracted effort to establish a common European military and security arrangement after the French Parliament in 1954 rejected the European Defence Community (EDC). This was first given institutional expression in the (separate from the EC) intergovernmental system of European Political Cooperation from 1970, which was subsequently incorporated as a separate pillar (II) in the EU (established with the Maastricht Treaty 1991),[13] under the heading of Common Foreign and Security Policy (CFSP). From this was gradually singled out a European Security and Defence Policy (ESDP).[14]

The EU of today remains organised along two sets of institutional structures, associated with two conceptions of integration. We can summarise these, on the one hand, in the supranational Community, and, on the other, in the so-called intergovernmental but more fittingly labelled *transgovernmental* (Wallace 2005) component, mainly pertaining to the CFSP/ESDP, although core elements of this Council-led institutional procedure is also applied to what remains of Pillar III (Justice and Home Affairs). What is notable regarding this second 'head' is that it has changed from a mere intergovernmental to a more institutionalised transgovernmental system (Smith 2004), with decision-making increasingly being lifted to the European level.[15] This transgovernmental component is still based on national democratic authorisation (the European Parliament (EP) has some limited powers of scrutiny).

This shows that the EU's institutional make-up falls well short of a fully fledged system of supranational government, according to the criteria laid out in Chapter 2. The institutional entrenchment of this second 'head' exerts a certain countervailing centrifugal pull on the EU structure and induces it towards 'soft-law' governance solutions. It gives the heads of state and government a unique position (notably in the EC) to navigate (manipulate) their domestic and international tasks and obligations in manners far from always respectful of the EU treaties and human rights.[16] This structure has important constitutional implications in that it also helps to sustain ambiguity as to the EU's constitutional status and character. The structure enables member states to place significant constraints on the EU's cosmopolitan orientation and thrust. To what extent are such constraints overcome through the EU's distinct configuration of exit-entry-voice-loyalty?

A distinct configuration of entry-exit-voice-loyalty

The EU makes up a distinct configuration of exit, entry, voice and loyalty in the sense that it has different barriers to entry and exit, and lacks strong measures for instilling loyalty. That sets it far apart from the configuration of exit-entry-voice-loyalty that we associate with the sovereign nation state (with high barriers to exit-entry and strong mechanisms for instilling loyalty), and directs it towards cosmopolitanism.

With regard to territorial entry, the EU does not operate with specific ethnic or other communal – linked to a specific identity – requirements; it is open to all European states that qualify as democratic. It is confined to Europe, but that need not rule out the prospect of the EU operating as a *regional*-cosmopolitan entity. The terms of entry are important. State-based entry is of course voluntary, and the EU's criteria for entry are not culturally coded. EU enlargement is based on democratic conditionality. It ensures that only constitutional democracies become members. The logic behind this arrangement is broadly speaking consistent with regional-cosmopolitan democracy. Because the institutions at the EU level are operating the democratic entrance criteria, the process feeds back on the EU, whose own democratic credibility is assessed in relation to its monitoring of the applicant's democratic credentials. Thus, the process can reinforce both the vertical and the horizontal entrenchment of democracy (see Chapter 4). But the process is demo-cratically sustainable only so long as the institutions at the EU level can effectively ensure democracy at the EU level, and so long as the member states (new and old) provide mutually reinforcing support for democracy. Acceding states must adapt their systems to the EU; thus the cosmopolitan quality of the process ultimately hinges on the cosmopolitan quality of the EU.

How this process is practised places important limitations on the cosmopolitan thrust of these measures. Many recently added member states have receded back to non-democratic practices because of a structural problem: the monitoring arrange-ments are too weak once they have become members. Such reversals place added stress on EU-level democratic institutions, which in turn can give rise to negative spirals when reinforced by the undemocratic practices of certain old member states (for instance, Berlusconi's Italy). Many member states have actively sought to con-fine enlargement. This has become part of a broader struggle for 'Europe's soul', with strong Christian-religious overtones and which seeks to confine the EU's territorial reach to Western Christianity. This includes efforts to bar Turkish EU membership in line with a rising xenophobic populism that targets Muslims and non-Europeans in general. This spills over into efforts to limit the EU's openness to asylum-seekers and immigrants in general (thus in effect raising the threshold against individual entry). Several member states are also in violation of UN provi-sions in terms of how they treat asylum-seekers and immigrants (Greece, Italy and Denmark, for instance). These comments show that, whereas the EU has proce-dures for dealing with territorial entry with clear cosmopolitan traits, entry does depend on political consensus. At present, the political support for a cosmopolitan orientation to entry appears to have weakened.

Ensuring exit from a *nationally* constructed past is part of the cosmopolitan attempt to forge a distinct *post-national* mode of belonging (Fossum 2008; Hab-ermas 1998a, 2001b). This could mean either to forget the past, or to invoke Europe's common past and history as a resource. Both options have been tried, but neither has really succeeded. The member states have not abandoned their national pasts and have largely retained their national socialising mechanisms. Efforts to draw on Europe's common past and history to foster agreement on a constitutional arrangement have largely backfired and generated negative voice. On territorial exit, the EU permits it, and the Treaty of Lisbon has formalised it. The threshold of territorial exit is low. It is also lower than that of Canada, the only major state-based democracy with democratic procedures for secession.

On the question of loyalty, the EU's socialising ability is very low and significantly lower than that of any nation state. It lacks many of the socialising levers (school system, conscription, etc.) and the financial resources that modern nation states possess.

On the question of voice, the EU has steadily expanded procedures for including critical voice, through entrenching democratic arrangements, increasing transparency, sounding out and consultation, etc. but these still suffer from important defects, as is reflected in the debate on the EU's democratic deficit.

This brief assessment shows that the EU has a distinct configuration of exit-entry-voice-loyalty that shares more in common with the cosmopolitan than with the nation state configuration. But this is a very fragile structure, which has become readily apparent at this time of financial crisis.

One structural feature that the crisis exposes is how much weaker than the national the EU's means for instilling loyalty are. This manifests itself, for instance, in the member states' unwillingness to equip the EU with the fiscal means to offset crises and imbalances. One bias that is often noted is what many see as an institutionally entrenched imbalance between a narrowly based monetary union and the lack of a compensatory fiscal union (De Grauwe 2011). A similar argument underlines that the EU is structurally imbalanced: a rapidly proceeding neo-liberal economic integration outpaces weak and insufficient social compensatory measures with significant legitimacy costs (Scharpf 2010).

To sum up, at the beginning of this section it was noted that the EU has a clear rights-based cosmopolitan thrust, the salience of which must be considered in relation to the EU's institutional-constitutional make-up. The EU is democratically deficient, offers inadequate institutional-constitutional rights-based supports, and is too weak as a system of government. Its complex ('two-headed') institutional structure constrains citizens' public (self-governing) and private (rights protection) autonomies. And whereas the EU has proven remarkably inclusive through enlargements, this process is facing political opposition. The question that the financial crisis has raised is whether the altered configuration of exit-entry-voice-loyalty that the EU has thus far configured might be based on an excessively narrow resource base and an institutional structure with a built-in bias against many of those elements that we from the nation state context understand as sustaining of the loyalty required to hold a community together. The interesting question for the future sustainability of the EU and for cosmopolitanism more broadly is whether the EU's configuration of inordinately low barriers against entry and exit, combined with very weak mechanisms for instilling loyalty but considerable scope for voice, can be sustained.

This is an experiment that no states have willingly embarked on. But many have had to deal with similar challenges. We will consider the most advanced such democratic instance, namely Canada.

Canada – cosmopolitan vanguard or 'stumbling into cosmopolitanism'?

Stephane Dion, a political scientist and former Minister of Intergovernmental Relations and leader of the federal Liberal party, noted a few years ago that 'Canada is a country that works better in practice than in theory.'[17] This is certainly the case when considered in relation to nationalism; the question is whether the same conclusion pertains to cosmopolitanism. Canada does not propound cosmopolitanism as an explicit doctrine. Therefore, any attempt to uncover its cosmopolitan traits must rely on translation. In doing so, we need to consider history as well as the present.

Canada's historical disposition inclines it to cosmopolitanism. Broadly speaking, this has two important sources. One stems from the historical onus on accommodation of difference and diversity (cf. LaSelva 1996; Mendes 2008), notably but far from exclusively, in response to Quebec's demands for constitutional recognition of its cultural and linguistic distinctness and possible separation. The question of the role of Quebec within the Canadian federation has sparked other issues (such as the federal make-up and the plight of aboriginals), that have given the political system an almost constant focus on *constitutive constitutional politics*: 'existential questions that go to the very identity, even existence, of the political community as a multinational political entity' (Choudhry 2008: 168). Struggles for sub-state minority nationalism, for indigenous rights/self-government and for immigrant ethnic recognition, have long been at the core of Canada's complex constitutional and political agenda. Insofar as contestation over community inclines towards cosmopolitanism, Canada is a prime cosmopolitan candidate.

The other cosmopolitan source stems from the strong links with the UK and the British empire (with Canada's constitution being formally patriated as late as 1982). Canada's gradual transition from colony to nation was greatly complicated by the fact that Canada was the offspring of *two* colonial settlers in North America, Britain and France. This produced two important historical traits with significant cosmopolitan conditioning effects on Canada. As part of a British Empire, many British-Canadians felt a strong tension between imperial and national belonging, which heightened the sense of communal ambiguity: 'The unending debate over the appropriateness of any particular boundary between imperial and domestic always had one set of protagonists arguing, in effect, for a transnational definition of community that encompassed United Kingdom kin' (Cairns 1995: 104). Further, Quebec's insistence on distinct community status effectively thwarted any effort to establish a Canadian nation based on ethnic linguistic and religious homogeneity.

Neither source has given rise to any conscious or programmatic effort to promote cosmopolitanism. But the Canadian experience with accommodating diversity has generated a sense in Canada (however contested this may be) that its uniqueness and its struggles have brought forth something valuable, and that this is distinctly different from traditional nationalism: 'The Canadian approach to diversity strengthens Canada's reputation as a just and fair society. Canada is renowned for its rich cultural mosaic and the Canadian model has become an example for the rest of the world' (Department of Canadian Heritage 1999). The general principles that are used to depict Canada are cultural and linguistic tolerance, inclusive community, federalism, interregional sharing, democracy, rule of law, and equality of opportunity, as well as respect for and accommodation of difference.

Historically speaking, three terms have played a central role in depicting Canada's approach to the accommodation of difference and diversity, namely federalism, bilingualism and multiculturalism. In Canada there has been broader recognition that federalism, when understood as a principle and as a mode of attachment, is distinct from nationalism, and also that a federation need not be a state.[18] Further: 'the federal principle represents an alternative to (and a radical attack upon) the modern idea of sovereignty.' (LaSelva 1996: 165) Analysts have sought to extend the term to encompass the distinct challenges facing Canada.[19]

One important reading of the Canadian experiment that goes back to one of the founders, George-Étienne Cartier, understands it as that of creating a political nationality through federalism. To Cartier, the existence of a French-Canadian (mainly Catholic) and an English-Canadian (majority Protestant) community meant that the essential challenge was to create a sense of common allegiance, while also respecting the uniqueness of each group. This was a very different challenge from that facing the American founders. 'Canadian nationalism presupposes Canadian federalism, which in turn rests on a complex form of fraternity that can promote a just society characterised by a humanistic liberalism and democratic dialogue.' (LaSelva 1996: xiii) To address this, Canada had to develop its own special version of federalism. According to La Selva, George-Étienne Cartier's notion of federalism was as a way of life:

> For Cartier, the justification of federalism was . . . that it accommodated distinct identities within the political framework of a great nation. The very divisions of federalism, when correctly drawn and coupled with a suitable scheme of minority rights, were for him what sustained the Canadian nation.
>
> *(LaSelva 1996: 189)*

Such accommodation of difference presupposed tolerance, co-operation, mutual accommodation and minority justice. The requisite sense of attachment is not nationalism but *fraternity*. Nationalists appeal to the value of fraternity but confine it to one group, or culture or language community, whereas federalists *expand* it: 'The idea of fraternity looks two ways. It looks to those who share a way of life; it also looks to those who have adopted alternative ways of life.' (LaSelva 1996: 27). Fundamental to this idea of fraternity are a reflexivity and other-regard that break down the distinction between us and them intrinsic to nationalism. There is a clear affinity between this notion of fraternity and Kant's notion of cosmopolitan right.

The failure to agree on a common cultural nationality has helped to keep alive a practice of accommodation of difference that has spawned numerous other efforts to develop conceptions of community that are more inclusive than nationalism.

Canada has officially embraced multiculturalism and multilingualism;[20] it has developed specific provisions for aboriginal self-government; and it has been committed to a cosmopolitan-oriented notion of human security (which has been greatly weakened or perhaps even undercut in recent years, notably under the Harper government). From a cosmopolitan perspective, these doctrines and policy stances may be seen as efforts to give meaning to and to offer more principled justifications for an ongoing practice.

The way they have been adopted, that is, largely from an ongoing practice, does not mean that they are devoid of inspirational content or principled orientations. Consider multiculturalism: understood *as a doctrine*, it is premised on the notion of integrating immigrants from diverse cultural backgrounds into society – without eliminating their characteristics. Multiculturalism as a doctrine is about the just integration of immigrants. It seeks to avoid the twin evils of assimilation and ethnic separation or ghettoisation. It is also an ideology that speaks to interethnic tolerance and the benefits that accrue to society from its diversity (Norman 2001). This doctrine is premised on the notion that integration or incorporation of people from different backgrounds is a two-way process, which places requirements on those who integrate, but also on those who are already there. The essence is to heighten social inclusiveness as well as self-reflection on the part of both the arriving minority(ies) and the receiving majority, to ensure a process of mutual accommodation and change.

Will Kymlicka (2007: 61) understands Canada's approach, that of liberal multiculturalism, to represent 'a rejection of earlier models of the unitary, homogeneous nation-state.' But he does not see it as a departure from nationalism, as such. Rather, 'the resulting approach is best described as one in which robust forms of nation-building are combined and constrained by robust forms of minority rights' (Kymlicka 2007: 83). It is easy to see why Kymlicka could reach this conclusion. The Canadian state at its several levels does not lack national socialising mechanisms, and it seeks to integrate immigrants through low citizenship thresholds. But there are many socialising agents that are directed at the maintenance of several distinct national (and provincial) communities, including First Nations communities. The critical issue is what keeps this system together. Or what is there to reconcile these often conflicting processes? What is it that keeps relations between them peaceful and basically respectful of liberal-democratic principles? It is not possible to appeal to an overarching national identity because every such appeal will be interpreted as a partial and a biased appeal to strengthen that particular community. My contention is that what keeps these processes together has been the historical experience with accommodating diversity through a distinct sense of fraternal federalism. What I would further claim is that this is best understood as a cosmopolitan-type approach for how to deal with deeply entrenched and highly politically charged differences and conceptions of distinctness.

Over time it became clear that this version of fraternal federalism did not match up to modern democratic requirements because it was not sufficiently attentive to individual rights. Prior to the 1960s, this approach was practised within a constitutional setting without an explicit bill of rights or charter. Further, the main parties to the process of accommodation were governments operating through a comprehensive yet largely informal system of intergovernmental relations with obvious democratic defects.

The most important change was the patriation of the Constitution in 1982, which included the Charter of Rights and Freedoms. The Charter spoke to every citizen as a rights holder and a stake-holder in the constitution and the process of constitutional change. The Charter institutionalised and constitutionalised reflexivity through rights. There was also a clear political purpose associated with introducing the Charter, namely to deflect political attention away from Quebec nationalism and federal-provincial concerns. To this end, the Charter included provisions that gave special constitutional attention to minority language rights, aboriginal rights, gender rights and rights for ethnic minorities. These provisions have later been called group-based rights and have been touted as vehicles to weaken territorially based nationalism, and notably the hold of governments – in particular provincial ones – on the population.

The introduction of the Charter contributed to the mobilisation of a great number of self-conceived constitutional stake-holders, in particular women's groups, gays and lesbians, Aboriginals, immigrants and people with disabilities. Some of the groups given special attention in the Charter issued demands for direct participation in the process of intergovernmental negotiations, and Aboriginals or First Nations groups later obtained this. The Charter has been handled by the courts in a manner that exhibits considerable sensitivity to Canada's diversity; thus this institutional mechanism represents a clear case of injecting a cultural dimension to the rights-based universalism we normally associate with charters and bills of rights. But the Charter also reconfigured legislative-judicial relations. The system of competitive parliamentary government referred to earlier was made to co-exist with – to compete with and to be harmonised with – court-based litigation. But the 1982 Constitution Act, which the country abides by, has not been signed by the province of Quebec and did not settle the constitutional conflicts that sparked a decade-long process of 'mega constitutional politics'.[21]

Nevertheless, three decades later, it is evident that Canada has experienced a major constitutional break, and indeed unleashed a 'Charter Revolution' (Cairns 2003; Morton and Knopff 2000) or 'constitutional catharsis' (Fossum 2007b). The notion of constitutional catharsis reflects three important changes: the first is a reconfigured conception of justice: weak and disenfranchised groups received some form of constitutional recognition. Canada's constitutional transformation helped to shift the standards of justice. In the pre-Charter period these were shaped by the perceived need to accommodate Quebec nationalism. Now this has to compete with the need to rectify historical injustice wrought on Aboriginals, as well as the accommodation of demands from other groups in Canadian society (i.e., women's groups, gays and lesbians and disabled people). The second feature of constitutional catharsis pertains to heightened constitutional reflexivity: the Canadian political system appears to have developed a more principled approach to the settlement of issues that have not gone away (more on this later on exit). The third aspect refers to more inclusive democratic norms permeating the political system. For instance, Quebec separatists have increasingly justified separation in more inclusive terms, to the extent of understanding Quebec as a multicultural society and hence echoing the multicultural character of Canada. Some separatists now argue that a future independent Quebec will have to be a multicultural state.

These brief comments reveal that the country has a historical disposition for difference-accommodation, which in recent years, through constitutional and other institutional changes, has obtained a stronger anchoring in individual rights and thus become more explicitly cosmopolitan.

A different configuration of exit, entry, voice, loyalty?

The question is whether this historically disputed country has a configuration of exit-entry-voice-loyalty that is systematically different from that of a nation state in a cosmopolitan sense. When discussing this in relation to a sovereign state, the question is whether Canada has lower barriers to entry and exit, and also whether it has a different inclination and ability with regard to instilling national allegiance and loyalty. Every state has numerous means for instilling loyalty. In the cosmopolitan polity, citizens' allegiance to the polity is shaped by universal principles that are institutionally embedded. These principles ensure that the threshold for subjecting citizens' allegiance to deliberative challenge remains low. The upshot is that citizens' sense of attachment exhibits considerable ambivalence. Allegiance is thus necessarily conditional. In contrast, every nation state seeks to reduce ambiguity and increase citizens' sense of loyalty and allegiance. Such efforts include provisions for regulating entry and exit for persons, and for communities and territorial sub-units. High (nation state) thresholds increase loyalty whereas low (cosmopolitan) ones make allegiance more conditional and much harder to take for granted. What kinds of thresholds does Canada have?

For Canada, territorial entry is not an issue, because there is no more territory that is available for inclusion. In terms of individual entry, Canada is exceptionally inclusive. It welcomes large-scale immigration, from across the world.[22] Canada is one democracy, if not the democracy, in the world with the largest proportion of foreign-born persons in its population.[23] This greatly increased diversity has not undermined the solidarity required to sustain a welfare state.[24]

Canada is exceptional when it comes to territorial exit because it includes explicit provisions for the democratic exit of a province. To install democratic provisions for territorial exit (which may result in the break-up of the state) has profound implications for community and identity; the option of territorial exit greatly reduces the state's ability to instil loyalty and allegiance, notably in those areas with a penchant to leave.

Can such procedures be conducive to cosmopolitanism? For one, the procedures must be consistent with basic human rights; and the operation must be set out so as to be properly reciprocal. Unilateral provisions, or provisions that do not include proper consultation and reciprocity, are incompatible with cosmopolitanism. I will now briefly spell out how these provisions have been set out in Canada in order to establish their compatibility with cosmopolitanism.

In Canada, the issue of territorial exit has its roots in the spectre of Quebec separation, which has been high on the political agenda since the 1970s. Two secession referenda have been held in the province of Quebec. The latest referendum in 1995 saw 49.4 per cent voting Yes, with a mere 50.58 per cent voting No (the No side won by only 54,288 votes). In the aftermath of the referendum, the question of Quebec separation was taken to the Supreme Court, which handed down its advisory opinion in 1998.[25] It stated that Quebec has no legal right – under Canadian or international law – to unilaterally secede from Canada. But it went on to note that:

> Our democratic institutions accommodate a continuous process of discussion and evolution, which is reflected in the constitutional right of each participant in the federation to initiate constitutional change. This implies a reciprocal duty on the other participants to engage in discussions to address any legitimate initiative to change the constitutional order. A clear majority vote in Quebec on a clear question in favour of secession would confer democratic legitimacy on the secession initiative which all of the other participants in Confederation would have to recognise.
>
> *(Supreme Court of Canada 1998)*

The federal government in 1999, through the so-called Clarity Act (an Act to give effect to the requirement for clarity as set out in the opinion of the Supreme Court of Canada in the Quebec Secession Reference) established a set of more specific procedural guidelines for how secession might proceed. Canada is thus the only major country in the world to have spelt out a set of *democratic* procedures for separation or break-up.[26] These apply not only to Quebec, but to any province. The provisions coupled with the obligation to negotiate (subject to certain conditions) ensure at least some elements of reciprocity. Actual negotiations with a province would not be bilateral – between the federal government and the relevant province – but would be conducted among all the governments of the provinces and the federal government.[27]

It follows that, when the threshold for territorial exit of a part of the country is greatly lowered and made subject to democratic procedures, the overarching community's ability to appeal to nationalism as a unifying bond is *procedurally* curtailed, thus opening up for a different configuration of voice and loyalty. Rather than being able to exercise relatively freely a whole range of instruments to instil loyalty, the larger community must offer justifications – in a continuous manner – for *why* the country should stay together. Such a justification requirement forms an intrinsic part of the procedures guiding secession. There is nothing automatic about secession. The procedures in the Clarity Act set the terms for how secession has to be justified, including what counts as compelling evidence of a democratically viable will to secede. They serve as benchmarks also for the larger community; they spell out the terms under which the larger community is compelled to enter into secession negotiations. The reciprocity built into this arrangement thus alters the terms of co-existence: from the sovereign constellation, where the question of community is bracketed off, to a situation in which the terms of community and the conditions under which different collectives live together are intrinsic parts of the legal-political deliberations of the communities (federal and provincial).

This represents an important modification in the doctrine of state sovereign territorial rule, and traces back to Canada's centuries-long historical experience of seeking to work out a mode of co-existence that accommodates multiple nation-building projects. Perhaps more explicitly than in the EU, several of these modifications in the doctrines of state sovereign territorial rule and nationalism can be traced back to doctrines of territorial governing and social co-existence.

Provisions for territorial exit can therefore spur reflexivity, because the very availability of a set of procedures for exit makes it more important for those seeking to hold the entity together to justify the merits of staying together, in order to ensure that exit remains a distant prospect. Further, in line with what has been said before about cosmopolitanism being based on the need to be open to the world, it should be clear that provisions for territorial exit should only really be considered under the cosmopolitan heading insofar as the world community is asked to serve as an impartial referee. This point figured in the Canadian Supreme Court secession reference:

> The ultimate success of [an unconstitutional declaration of secession leading to a *de facto* secession] . . . would be dependent on recognition by the international community, which is likely to consider the legality and legitimacy of secession, having regard to, amongst other facts, the conduct of Quebec and Canada, in determining whether to grant or withhold recognition.
>
> *(Supreme Court of Canada 1998)*

This statement can be construed as a warning not to proceed unless the condition of reciprocity is complied with. But its emphasising legitimacy can also be seen as a powerful reminder of the need to act in a manner consistent with global standards of legitimacy.

A final dimension with significant impact on the distinct character of Canada's exit-entry-voice-loyalty configuration is its very close relationship with the USA. This is formalised in the North American Free Trade Agreement and represents an important sovereignty constraint,[28] but also reinforces Canadian identity (as being different from the USA).

Conclusion

This chapter focused on the third, regional-democratic model of the EU, as initially presented in Chapter 2. The model is one representation of the EU as a regional-cosmopolitan vanguard. The question that this chapter has addressed was whether the status of cosmopolitan vanguard could be directly associated with this model or whether states could also be cosmopolitan vanguards. To that end, I discussed Canada as a possible state-based cosmopolitan vanguard.

It was shown that the EU is a distinct political entity with a regional reach. It was forged in a setting with a certain cosmopolitan opening; it was imbued with universal principles, albeit without an explicit articulated cosmopolitan doctrine and with variable cosmopolitan political support over time. The EU is clearly embedded in a distinct configuration of exit-entry-voice-loyalty with cosmopolitan traits. It alters the European political landscape and can rein in untrammelled nationalisms, although many would argue that the EU's ability to do so is too weak. Recent events also suggest that some of this cosmopolitan thrust has abated. Much of this will hinge on whether or the extent to which the EU manages to work through the current crisis. A critical question is whether the EU will be able to sustain its distinct configuration of exit-entry-voice-loyalty or reform it in a manner that strengthens the cosmopolitan-democratic dimension.

The global setting can only be relied on to offer partial but hardly unambiguous support for regional cosmopolitanisation processes. But the EU might not be the only cosmopolitan vanguard. This chapter has shown that Canada's historical failure to develop a common national sense of community and identity has compelled it to develop more inclusive conceptions of communal belonging, which in turn have predisposed it in a cosmopolitan direction. There is no explicit doctrine; it is more a case of stumbling into cosmopolitanism. The example of Canada shows that the state form can be as conducive to cosmopolitanism as can a supranational entity, but with the important proviso that this state's form has been substantially modified through a reflexive handling of communal contestation. At the base of Canada's distinct exit-entry-voice-loyalty configuration, we found a distinct combination of a historically entrenched tradition of accommodation of difference as part of an ongoing contestation over community; exceptionally high rates of inclusion of outsiders *combined with* lower thresholds against territorial exit. Because Canadians have been committed to dealing with the challenges in a peaceful and democratic manner, they have learnt to deal with communal conflict and contestation in an inclusive manner. These learning processes hold distinct cosmopolitan prospects.

Notes

1 Cosmopolitanism 'is not part of the self-identity of the EU . . .' (Rumford 2005: 5).
2 Many analysts understand inclusive community under the heading of liberal nationalism (cf. Kymlicka 2007; MacCormick 1999; Tamir 1993). I prefer to discuss it instead under the heading of cosmopolitanism, because I do not find liberal nationalism to be sufficiently inclusive (cf. Fossum 2011a).
3 Ulrich Beck devises an analytical framework with a set of criteria for discerning how cosmopolitanised a given society is. His distinction between normative cosmopolitanism and concrete patterns of cosmopolitanisation is devised so as to permit normative evaluation of the cosmopolitan practices that are uncovered, although it should be added that the normative position is greatly underspecified (Smith 2008: 259).

4 Ulrich Beck asserts that:

> the social-scientific stance is rooted in the concept of nation state. A nation state outlook on society and politics, law and justice and history governs the sociological imagination. To some extent, much of social science is a prisoner of the nation state.
>
> *(Beck 2003: 454)*

5 Jacob Levy has cogently argued that:

> "Nation" does not denote a kind of community describable apart from nationalist projects and the claim of national self-determination. Once we have a sociologically persuasive account of where a "nation" is, we find that one way or another the political mobilisation that nationalist theory is supposed to justify is already part of how we have picked the community out. In other words the political program of nationalism is built into the category of nation to begin with; the normative argument is always circular.
>
> *(Levy 2004: 160)*

6 Nationalism, when embedded in a nation state, limits exit from the past and erects high barriers against territorial exit as well as placing clear restrictions on or conditions for entry. Taken together, these constraints permit the nation state to instil a strong sense of attachment among the members of the community, an attachment that is considered essential to the community's sustenance over time.

7 I have adapted (Fossum 2008) and extended (with entry) Hirschman's (1970) three categories of exit, voice and loyalty in order to capture core dimensions of polity transformation (Fossum 2010). Other efforts to use Hirschman's categories are found in Bartolini, (2005) and Rokkan (1975).

8 Archibugi (2008: 33) reports a decline in the number of democracies since 2003.

9 Article 5 of the Lisbon Treaty states that:

> In its relations with the wider world, the Union shall uphold and promote its values and interests and contribute to the protection of its citizens. It shall contribute to peace, security, the sustainable development of the Earth, solidarity and mutual respect among peoples, free and fair trade, eradication of poverty and the protection of human rights, in particular the rights of the child, as well as to the strict observance and the development of international law, including respect for the principles of the United Nations Charter.

See Chapter 8 for more details on the EU's foreign and security policy.

10 I draw here on the social practices that Kurasawa (2007) identifies as intrinsic to the 'work of global justice'. Kurasawa explicitly links these to civil society actors only, whereas I argue that we may think of specific cosmopolitan openings where they can be entrenched in institutional arrangements and new forms. See also Fossum (2011b).

11 The process was conducted through state and civil society channels. See, for instance, Edward Luttwak (1994).

12 Lionel Jospin portrays the EU as a federation of nation states: 'Europe is an original political structure, a unique precipitate, an indissoluble mixture of two different elements: the federalist idea and the reality of European Nation States.' (Lionel Jospin, 'On the Future of an Enlarged Europe', address given to the Ministry of Foreign Affairs, Paris, 28 May 2001). My argument is that the integration process has unfolded in such a manner that Jospin's indissoluble mixture has manifested itself in a system with two heads.

13 The Maastricht Treaty contained three pillars. The first pillar (see earlier chapter) was

initially the institutional configuration that made up the EC (the mode of integration is generally referred to as the Community method). Today it has absorbed much of the third pillar (Justice and Home Affairs) and parts of the second (CFSP). Much of the second pillar and what is now left of the third pillar is associated with the Council (the mode of integration is generally understood as the Intergovernmental method).

14 Christiansen and Vanhoonacker (2008) list 1999 as the year when the decisive change took place.

15 It is more than a simple aggregation of disparate national voices; it works to facilitate common national positions; it has a legal basis in the Treaties; and there is a gradual strengthening of Brussels-based institutional capacity, so-called 'Brusselising' (Allen 1998; Christiansen and Vanhoonacker 2008; Duke and Vanhoonacker 2006a; Smith 2004).

16 This applies both to the handling of the financial crisis and to the conduct of foreign and security policy.

17 http://www.economist.com/node/8173164

18 Federalism is distinct from nationalism and a federation need not be a state. Daniel Elazar (1987: 230) has observed that 'the federal idea and its applications offer a comprehensive alternative to the idea of a reified sovereign state and its applications'.

19 They use such terms as 'multinational federation' (Gagnon and Tully 2001; Resnick 1994), 'asymmetrical federalism' (Webber 1994) and pluralist federalism, executive federalism and federalism as cultural compact.

20 The Canadian multiculturalism policy was introduced in 1971 and in 1988 it became officially enshrined in the Multiculturalism Act. The policy had four objectives:

> to support the cultural development of ethnocultural groups; to help members of ethnocultural groups overcome barriers to full participation in Canadian society; to promote creative encounters and interchange among all ethnocultural groups; and to assist new Canadians in acquiring at least one of Canada's official languages.
>
> *(Kymlicka 1998: 15)*

21 This is a process that:

> goes beyond disputing the merits of specific constitutional proposals and addresses the very nature of the political community on which the constitution is based [. . .] When a country's constitutional politics reaches this level, the constitutional question tends to dwarf all other public concerns.
>
> *(Russell, 1993: 75)*

22 Statistics Canada reports that out of the 1.8 million immigrants who arrived to Canada between 1991 and 2001, 58 per cent were from Asia; 20 per cent were from Europe; 11 per cent were from the Caribbean, Central and South America; 8 per cent were from Africa; and 3 per cent were from the USA (Census 2001, 'Canada's Ethnocultural Portrait: The Changing Mosaic', Statistics Canada, available at: http://www12.statcan.ca/english/census01/products/analytic/companion/etoimm/canada.cfm)

23 Canada is also the country that scores highest on Banting and Kymlicka's Multiculturalism Policy Index (Banting and Kymlicka 2006; Kymlicka 2007).

24 Canada does not face the progressive's dilemma, which refers to the tension between diversity and solidarity: 'Public attitudes in Canada reveal remarkably little tension between ethnic diversity and support for social programs, and the trajectory of attitudinal change does not raise red flags.' (Banting 2010: 798–99).

25 Supreme Court of Canada (1998) *Reference Re Secession of Quebec*, 2 S.C.R. 217, 20 August, available at: http://www.sfu.ca/~aheard/827/SCC-Que-Secession.html

26 Note that the Draft Treaty establishing a Constitution for Europe contains a provision

(Article I-60) that permits voluntary withdrawal from the Union. Available at: http://www.cap.lmu.de/transatlantic/download/howorth.pdf

27 S.C. 2000, c. 26:3.1. Available at: http://laws.justice.gc.ca/eng/acts/C-31.8/FullText.html

28 Some analysts underline not only its asymmetrical nature (in favour of the USA and of capital) but that it has taken on the shape of a kind of 'economic superconstitution' (Clarkson and Wood 2010).

11

CONCLUSION

Erik Oddvar Eriksen and John Erik Fossum

This book has dealt with the question of European democracy in a context where the familiar vectors that democracy has been traditionally anchored in are undergoing change and transformation. It is therefore hardly an exaggeration to state that democracy is one of the, if not the, most central issues at stake in the Europe of today. Further, it is hardly a surprise that there is a very broad debate on democracy, but there appears as of now to be an almost inverse relationship between the magnitude of attention that is paid to this issue on the one hand and the degree of normative and empirical agreement on the other. The debate is really three-dimensional: it is about what should be the appropriate *form* of democracy (from narrowly Schumpeterian to broadly participatory), what should be the most appropriate (senior) *level* of locating democracy (national, supranational or global), and what form of political-constitutional configuration democracy should be situated within (the question of the 'nature of the beast').

Properly addressing these issues entailed that the book had to provide conceptual clarification of the meaning and status of democracy in Europe today. That was necessary also to establish the right standard of evaluation in order to make sure that we actually recognise democracy when we encounter it in today's Europe.

The requisite conceptual exercise produced three democratic polity models, which we outlined in Chapter 2. In devising, applying and testing out this framework, the book represents a systematic attempt at making sense of the status of democracy in today's Europe, with specific emphasis on the main agent of change, the multilevel configuration that makes up the European Union (EU). A key message is that such an effort at clarification requires quite a comprehensive theoretical-methodological effort.

The book has shown that, in order to understand the character and status of democracy in Europe, we need to pay explicit attention to democratic theory. An important question that the transnationalists and cosmopolitans have raised is to what extent we need to devise a new theory of democracy in order to capture what is going on in Europe. To that end, we devised the third, regional-democratic, polity model – a conception of democracy that no longer relies on the sovereign state form. What this book has done is to develop this and examine it systematically in relation to (two) state-based versions of democracy. That way we have sought to capture novel trends and developments, while also examining how far we can rely on democratic theory devised for modern states – in order to capture the core features of the EU.

The ensuing framework is comprehensive. Thus, *if* the EU is systematically diverging from all three models, there are good grounds for questioning the continued presence of democracy in Europe. In that sense, the framework is useful to detect both democratisation and de-democratisation processes.

In Chapter 3, Christopher Lord developed a democratic audit framework that he tailored along the lines of these three models. This framework represents a vital step forward in terms of devising an encompassing democratic audit that permits systematic comparison of state-based and non-state-based modes of democracy. How specific and accurate this framework could be to a large extent hinged on the degree of specification available in the RECON framework. That was necessarily quite low, and reflects the difficulties we face when seeking to specify the third democratic polity model – which had no real-life example or counterpart to draw on. As an intellectual construct, it required specification and 'filling in'. This task was rendered more important by the sheer complexity of the EU on the one hand, and the problems associated with developing a viable model of non-state-based or supranational democracy on the other. These factors suggested to us that we had to spell out the analytical framework in more detail, and in relation to a range of quite specialised debates (within highly diverse policy fields such as gender justice or foreign security policy, as well as in relation to specific institutions such as the Commission or the European Parliament [EP]), in order to make sense of and try to clarify the status of democracy in Europe.

In other words, the complex EU compelled us to devise the framework in such a manner as to capture democratic traits across different institutional realms and policy fields. We saw, for instance, that with regard to the constitutional dimension it was necessary to devise a new constitutional theory that could capture the distinct manner in which the EU's constitutional construct had been devised – which we in turn showed had implications for how we would understand and analyse the question of constitutional democracy in Europe.

Beyond intergovernmentalism

The first model was based on an expanded intergovernmental position so as to enable it to supplement national democracy with a limited set of limited-function EU-level democratic structures. All the chapters in the book have unequivocally shown that the EU is beyond intergovernmentalism in polity and constitutional terms. It has integrated to such an extent and across such a broad range of policy fields as to have moved beyond this model. At stake in the European integration process is supranational not audit democracy, and the integration process has deeply affected nation state democracy. The attempt to devise a distinct European democratic constitutionalism is currently facing serious challenges but represents a fundamental and constitutionally salient case of legal Europeanisation. The upshot is that the democratic legitimacy of the EU's member states cannot be established independently of the EU, because they have become so deeply entangled that their patterns of legitimate authority have been transformed. What that also means is that the relevant standard of democracy that is required to assess this complex multilevel configuration cannot be based on this model (which relies on a combination of *audit democracy* at the Union level and representative democracy at the member state level). The Union's democratic ambitions are greater than what this model presupposes; the Union's implications for the workings of the established member state democratic arrangements are also so profound as to render this model basically irrelevant as the appropriate standard. Readers who are well familiar with the EU might think that in reaching this conclusion we have bracketed out the area of foreign and security policy, but that is not the case. As Helene Sjursen has shown in Chapter 8, even in this policy area the integration process has proceeded beyond what we should expect from an intergovernmental entity, but, as she also notes, integration has not been accompanied by democratisation.

The second democratic polity model that we devised understood democracy in the EU to be best served through establishing the EU as a *multinational* federal state. The book has shown that the EU does not qualify as a state – it lacks key state vestiges at the EU level and also transforms the member states. There is little to suggest that the EU is on a clear track towards statehood. But there are at least three points to show that this model still exerts a certain directional pull on the EU. The first is that the EU appeals to those very principles, the core constitutional-democratic ones that animate the modern democratic *Rechtsstaat*. These also, it was shown in Chapter 4, have served as the regulatory ideal for the EU's distinct approach to constitution-making. Second, the EU is structured as a system of government at the supranational level. This governing arrangement comes with elements of hierarchy – that fall well short of the system of hierarchical rule we associate with the sovereign state, but that nevertheless set the EU's supranational system apart from the less hierarchical and network-based structure of transnational governance. The EU gains a significant element of *stateness* through the manner in which the member states submit to EU decisions and effectuate these. However, the member states have not provided the institutions at the EU level with the instruments of territorial control and penetration that we associate with the sovereign state – and have retained significant checks on the ability of the central EU institutions to pursue policies independently of the member states. Third, we have seen that the system at the EU level copies and emulates institutional arrangements and policy measures from the member states.[1] However, these have not been put together in the same manner as we find in a state.

These observations suggest that we cannot rule out this model as entirely irrelevant for the EU, but must underline that the structure we have thus far seen emerging at the EU level has on balance taken a distinct non-state-based shape, certainly when considered in relation to a traditional conception of sovereignty. Further, as noted in Chapter 10, it was shown that the EU rests on a configuration of exit-entry-voice-loyalty that is systematically different from the one we find in the sovereign nation state. The book thus confirms that the EU, at least from what we see at present, represents an attempt to entrench a form of supranational democracy that does not rely on the nation state format.

How close, then, is the EU to the third democratic polity model? This model was an intellectual construct without any real-life analogy to draw on – except whatever we could model from the incomplete experience that makes up the EU. It posited that European democracy could be reconfigured through the EU serving as a regional *post-national* Union with an explicit cosmopolitan imprint.

The model of a regional-cosmopolitan Europe sheds light on the character of the broader international context and the move beyond Westphalia. But the cosmopolitan condition, which requires the constitutionalisation of international law, cannot draw its legitimacy from the international law regime itself or from the putative validity of humanitarian norms. It fails to meet the democratic requirements of autonomy and accountability. The problem of the expanded role of non-consented decision-making at the international level, which has increased the scope for jurist-made law, is a democratic one. The idea that there already exists a constitution at the international level, for example in the form of the United Nations Charter, is dangerous. It gives the false impression that the power of the state has already become a servant of legitimate international law. At the European level, it is, moreover, not a question of solving the problem of order in a state of nature, because European integration takes place among already constitutionalised and politically integrated states where the coercive functions are taken care of. The EU can stabilise behavioural expectations and achieve collective 'bindingness' for its laws with reference to the legal form in which they are dressed. This model's conception of the Union as a government based on differentiating state functions, downplaying the coercive elements and upgrading the normative-institutional elements, presents us with an organisational template that possesses a limited set of measures for ensuring implementation and compliance. Such an organisation can accommodate a higher measure of territorial-functional differentiation than can a state-type entity, because it does not presuppose the kind of 'homogeneity' or thick collective identity that is widely held to be needed for comprehensive resource allocation and goal attainment. It is based on a division of labour between the levels, a 'sharing' or pooling of sovereignty that relieves the central level of certain demanding decisions.

The various chapters have documented – to different degrees – that the EU holds traits that make it useful to consider in relation to this third model. What has been established at the EU level is a system of supranational government based on authorised jurisdictions. It implies that a proper evaluation of EU democracy should be based on the standards embedded in this democratic polity model. The problem with this being an intellectual construct was lack of information on how it would play out in the various institutional realms and policy fields, information that was vital to make this a reliable gauge. This is one of the book's contribu-tions: the various chapters of the book have sought to spell out this model in more operational detail; thus they have provided us with a more rich and nuanced set of criteria for evaluating the quality of supranational democracy.

One important observation is that the third model must be understood in light of the distinct approach to constitution-making that the EU has adopted (which we have labelled 'constitutional synthesis', see Chapter 4). This approach shows how the EU's constitutional arrangement has come about. It brings out what should be seen as a distinguishing feature of the system of supranational democracy (that is established at the EU level), namely that it initially came equipped with a *conditional* constitutional-democratic licence from the member states that was based on the need for compliance with democratic norms. It authorised supranational integra-tion. But it is important to underline that the democratic requirement applies to the entire multilevel structure. This structure is also exceptionally frail, it should be added, and highly vulnerable to upsets. In this setting, de-democratisation processes in one state or at one level can quite easily have systemic implications.

A second observation is that the book may enable us to discern more explicit democratic conditions for EU enlargement, which are: (a) the applicant must dem-onstrate full compliance with democratic criteria; (b) the institutions at the EU level must be able to effectively ensure democracy at the EU level; and (c) the member states (new and old) must be able to provide mutually reinforcing support for democracy. These conditions provide a more robust set of criteria to ensure that EU expansion through addition of new members will be a democratically viable process. Any process that falls short of these three criteria is likely to become democratically unstable or even unsustainable over time.

A third observation pertains to the structure of representation in the EU. We have seen in Chapter 5 that the regional-democratic model is compatible with the notion of a Multilevel Parliamentary Field (based on all parliaments' ability to entrench will-formation in legislation and hold the executives to account). The field is entrenched through formal structures of interaction, consultation and co-operation among parliaments and parties across states and levels of governing, and is marked by a distinct functional delimitation. The model understands parliaments as strong publics, and as effective legislators, at all three main levels. This parlia-mentary system is set up with a division of tasks between levels, where each level has some functions over which it is supreme. This model is capable of accom-modating far more diversity among parliaments than would, for instance, a federal model. For example, the model can accommodate differences in parliamentary structures because of the isomorphic and learning effects that the linking of parlia-ments together can produce. This structure raises important questions pertaining to constituency and accountability that require more attention. We need to establish what kind of representation-deliberation interface would be able to support such a structure. This point shows that there is still need for more theoretical work before we have a fully fledged conception of how this model can be properly configured in representative terms.

A fourth observation relates to the difficult question of identity and how this figures in a regional-democratic model with a clear *cosmopolitan* imprint. The standard notion of cosmopolitanism is premised on human rights and a shared humanity as the identitarian notion, which locates it in a deeply ambivalent relationship to any particular collective identity. What might keep such an entity together? Through its 'linguistic turn' to the study of collective identities, Chapter 9 suggests a way of injecting a necessary component of collective identity into the regional-democratic model. The chapter adopts a discursive approach to collective identity construction through positing that content and cultural form are shaped by discourse; thus what requires attention are those discursive forms and contents that are available for constructing the 'collective' of a European democracy. In this perspective, democratic discourse signifies popular will and sovereignty; thus the ability to forge EU democracy hinges among other factors on whether EU democracy is seen to be, as well as actually depicted as, operating through the identification of popular subjectness. The ability to sustain such discourses in turn hinges on the presence of institutions with ability to foster and sustain such discourses.

A fifth observation pertains to the model's contribution to issues of justice and democracy, as examined in this context in Chapter 6 through the model's contribution to 'gender democracy' – the notion that democracy is imprinted by gendered assumptions that influence processes and practices that go unquestioned in the course of decision-making. It is noted that this model highlights public debate; multiple access points for an autonomous, transnational civil society, of which women's organisations are an integral part; consensus and attention to deliberative quality; and a more fluid and less hierarchical system of identifications than we find in the state framework. At the same time, as the chapter makes clear, how well this model is set up to deal with the social dimension, including social security and social guarantees that underpin equality, is less well established and requires further attention.

A sixth and final observation pertains to foreign policy. Even though there is no hierarchy, it is possible to make collectively binding decisions in this policy field. Mechanisms such as 'the coordination reflex' between member states require that they take no final position on foreign policy matters before consulting with the other member states. This fits with the expectations of the model regarding key characteristics of executive power. Chapter 8 provides guidelines for how the EU should organise its relations with third countries to ensure that constituency should be regional and global, that executive power should be shared, but, most importantly, in relation to the core function of upholding cosmopolitan law. This chapter also sheds light on the realism of the cosmopolitan assumptions in this model through focusing on the character of the broader international context and whether it is moving beyond Westphalia.

European democracy at a crossroads

The book's main purpose was conceptual. It also contains empirical assessments but confined to a highly selective approach because a proper empirical assessment of three such macroscopic models would be a truly gargantuan task, an overwhelming challenge. But the various chapters have shown that the EU does not only suffer from a democratic deficit when assessed against the third model; post-Lisbon it appears to be moving away from this model. There are grounds to challenge the widely held assertion of a positive or mutually supportive relationship between integration and democracy: this relationship is far more complex and composite. In the EU it is exposed through what we may call the 'constitutional problem'. When the self-ordained constitutional chaperons in the European Council determine that the EU's legal construct cannot be officially designated a constitution, they also implicitly raise the question as to whether the democratisation that the EU has already wrought can be sustained without a proper constitutional justification. At present we see an EU that is democratically deficient and too weak to systematically uphold democratic standards, but which also simultaneously constrains the workings of national democracy. This generates pleas for unravelling or downscaling the EU, over and above what might be the fallout of the present crisis. Such pleas also face the questions of where to stop and how to stop. The process of unravelling can itself impose costs, and contains serious risks for relapse into less benign forms of rule.

The EU's dynamic character and sheer intrusiveness raise a number of questions of salience to theorists and practitioners alike. There is a clear continued need for basic research to connect this development with the accumulated knowledge that sits across academic fields with often significant translation costs to this complex setting. The nature of the challenge makes it no less important to handle. At the same time, researchers often find themselves in the situation of active process-chasing rather than the more comfortable process-tracing. The EU is a moving target. It is also a system that challenges the conventional wisdom of politics and established conceptions of political order, and not least of the processes that make it tick.

Note

1   See Chapters 4, 5 and 8, and also Fossum and Menéndez (2011), for a comprehensive overview.

REFERENCES

Abels, G. and Mushaben, J. M. (eds) (2011) *Gendering the European Union: New Approaches to Old Democratic Deficits*, Basingstoke: Palgrave Macmillan.

Abromeit, H. (1998) *Democracy in Europe: Legitimising Politics in Non-State Polity*, New York: Berghahn Books.

Ackerman, B. (1991) *We the People, vol. 1, Foundation*, Cambridge, MA: Harvard University Press.

—— (1998) *We the People, vol. 2, Transformations*, Cambridge, MA: Harvard University Press.

Aggestam, L. (2004) 'A European Foreign Policy? Role Conceptions and the Politics of Identity in Britain, France and Germany'. Doctoral dissertation. Department of Political Science, Stockholm University.

Allen, D. (1998) 'Who Speaks for Europe? The Search for an Effective and Coherent External Policy', in J. Peterson and H. Sjursen (eds) *A Common Foreign Policy for Europe?*, London: Routledge.

Allen, D. and Smith, M. (1990) 'Western Europe's Presence in the Contemporary International Arena', *Review of International Studies*, 16(1): 19–37.

Alter, K. J. (2002) *Establishing the Supremacy of European Law*, Oxford: Oxford University Press.

Archibugi, D. (1998) 'Principles of Cosmopolitan Democracy', in D. Archibugi, D. Held and M. Köhler (eds) *Re-imagining Political Community: Studies in Cosmopolitan Democracy*, Cambridge: Polity Press.

—— (2008) *The Global Commonwealth of Citizens: Towards Cosmopolitan Democracy*, Princeton, NJ: Princeton University Press.

Ardener E. (1989) *The Voice of Prophecy*, Oxford: Blackwell.

Arendt, H. (1958) *The Human Condition*, Chicago, IL: University of Chicago Press.

—— (1969) *On Violence*, New York, NY: Harcourt, Brace and World.

—— (1970) *On Revolution*, Hammondsworth: Penguin.

Bagehot, W. (1865) [2001] *The English Constitution*, Oxford: Oxford University Press.

Bajomi-Lázár, P. and Hegedűs, I. (eds) (2001) *Media and Politics: Conference Papers on the Interplay of Media and Politics*, Budapest: Uj Mandatum Publishing House.

Banting, K. G. (2010) 'Is There a Progressive's Dilemma in Canada? Immigration, Multiculturalism and the Welfare State', *Canadian Journal of Political Science*, 43(4): 797–820.

Banting, K. G. and Kymlicka, W. (eds) (2006) *Multiculturalism and the Welfare State: Recognition and Redistribution in Contemporary Democracies*, Oxford: Oxford University Press.

Barbé, E. (2004) 'The Evolution of CFSP Institutions: Where Does Democratic Accountability Stand?', *The International Spectator*, 39(2): 47–60.

Barth, F. (ed.) (1969) *Ethnic Groups and Boundaries: The Social Organization of Culture Difference*, Boston, MA: Little, Brown and Co.

Bartolini, S. (2004) 'Old and New Peripheries in the Processes of European Territorial Integration', in C. Ansell and G. Di Palma (eds) *Restructuring Territoriality*, Cambridge: Cambridge University Press.

—— (2005) *Re-Structuring Europe: Centre formation, System Building and Political Structuring between the Nation State and the European Union*, Oxford: Oxford University Press.

—— (2006) 'Should the Union be "Politicised?" Prospects and Risks', *Notre Europe Policy Papers*, 2006(19): 32–56.

Bauman, Z. (1999) *In Search of Politics*, Cambridge: Polity Press.

Beck, U. (2003) 'Toward a New Critical Theory with a Cosmopolitan Intent', *Constellations*, 10(4): 45–68.

—— (2004) 'Cosmopolitical Realism: On the Distinction between Cosmopolitanism in Philosophy and the Social Sciences', *Global Networks*, 4(2): 131–56.

—— (2006) *Cosmopolitan Vision*, Cambridge: Polity Press.

Beck, U. and Grande, E. (2005) *Das kosmopolitische Europa*, Frankfurt: Suhrkamp.

—— (2007) *Cosmopolitan Europe*, Cambridge: Polity Press.

Beetham, D. (1991) *The Legitimation of Power*, Basingstoke: Palgrave Macmillan Education.

—— (ed.) (1995) *Defining and Measuring Democracy*, London: Sage.

—— (1999) 'The Idea of Democratic Audit in Comparative Perspective', *Parliamentary Affairs*, 52(4): 567–81.

Beetham, D. and Lord, C. (1998) *Legitimacy in the European Union*, London: Longman.

Beetham, D., Carvalho, E., Landman, T. and Weir, S. (2008) *Assessing the Quality of Democracy: A Practical Guide (IDEA)*, International Institute for Democracy and Electoral Assistance. Available at: http://www.idea.int/publications/aqd/upload/AssessingOverview-Web.pdf

Bellamy, R. and Castiglione, D. (1998) 'Between Cosmopolis and Community: Three Models of Rights and Democracy within the European Union', in D. Archibugi, D. Held and M. Köhler (eds) *Re-imagining Political Community: Studies in Cosmopolitan Democracy*, Cambridge: Polity Press.

Benhabib, S. (1994) 'Deliberative Rationality and Models of Democratic Legitimacy', *Constellations*, 1(1): 26–52.

—— (2006) *Another Cosmopolitanism: Hospitality, Sovereignty and Democratic Iterations*, Oxford: Oxford University Press.

Beveridge, F. (2010) 'Going Soft? Analysing the Contribution of "Soft" and "Hard" Measures in EU Law and Policy', paper presented at the European Conference on Politics and Gender, Budapest, 13–15 January 2011.

Bisio, L. and Cataldi, A. (2008) *The Treaty of Lisbon from a Gender Perspective: Changes and Challenges*, Brussels: Women in Development Europe (WIDE).

Bohman, J. (2005) 'Reflexive Constitution-making and Transnational Governance', in E. O. Eriksen (ed.) *Making the European Polity: Reflexive Integration in the EU*, New York, NY: Routledge.

—— (2007a) *Democracy across Borders: From Dêmos to Dêmoi*, Cambridge, MA: MIT Press.

—— (2007b) 'Democratizing the Transnational Polity: The European Union and the Presuppositions of Democracy', in E. O. Eriksen (ed.) *How to Reconstitute Democracy in Europe? Proceedings from the RECON Opening Conference* 26 January, RECON Report No. 3, Oslo: ARENA.

Boltanski, L. and Thévenot, L. (2006) *On Justification: Economies of Worth*, Princeton, NJ: Princeton University Press.

Bono, G. (2006) 'Challenges of Democratic Oversight of EU Security Policies', *European Security*, 15(4): 431–49.

Bourdieu, P. (1980) *Questions de Sociologie*, Paris: Minuit.

Bovens, M. (2007) 'New Forms of Accountability and EU Governance', *Comparative European Politics*, 5(1): 104–20.

Bovens, M., Curtin, D. and Hart, P. (eds) (2010) *The Real World of EU Accountability: What Deficit?*, Oxford: Oxford University Press.

Brown, G. W. (2010) 'Moving from Cosmopolitan Legal Theory to Legal Practice: Models of Cosmopolitan Law', in G. W. Brown and D. Held (eds) *The Cosmopolitanism Reader*, Cambridge: Polity Press.

Brubaker, R. (1992) *Citizenship and Nationhood in France and Germany*, Cambridge, MA: Harvard University Press.

Brubaker, R. and Cooper, F. (2000) 'Beyond "Identity"', *Theory and Society*, 29(1): 1–47.

Brunkhorst, H. (2004) 'A Polity without a State? European Constitutionalism between Evolution and Revolution', in E. O. Eriksen, J. E. Fossum and A. J. Menéndez (eds) *Developing a Constitution for Europe*, London: Routledge.

Brunkhorst, H. (2005) *Solidarity: From Civic Friendship to a Global Legal Community*, Cambridge, MA: MIT Press.

Brunkhorst, H. (2009) 'States with Constitutions, Constitutions without States, and Democracy: Skeptical Reflections on Scheuerman's Skeptical Reflection', *Ethics & Global Politics*, 2(1): 65–81.

Buchanan, A. (2002) 'Political Legitimacy and Democracy', *Ethics*, 112: 689–719.

Bull, H. (1991) *The Anarchical Society: A Study of Order in World Politics*, London: Palgrave Macmillan.

Burke, E. (1774) [1975] 'Speech to the Electors of Bristol', in B. Hill (ed.) *Edmund Burke on Government, Politics and Society*, London: Fontana.

Cairns, A. C. (1995) *Reconfigurations: Canadian Citizenship and Constitutional Change*, Toronto: McClelland and Stewart Inc.

—— (2003) 'The Canadian Experience of a Charter of Rights', in E. O. Eriksen, J. E. Fossum and A. J. Menéndez (eds) *The Chartering of Europe: The Charter of Fundamental Rights and its Constitutional Implications*, Baden-Baden: Nomos.

Castiglione, D. (2004) 'Reflections on Europe's Constitutional Future', *Constellations*, 11(3): 393–411.

Cederman, L.-E. and Kraus, P. A. (2005) 'Transnational Communication and the European Demos', in R. Latham and S. Sassen (eds) *Digital Formations: Information Technology and New Architectures in the Global Realm*, Princeton, NJ: Princeton University Press.

Chalmers, D., Hadjiemmanuil, C., Monti, G. and Tomkins, A. (2006) *European Union Law*, Cambridge: Cambridge University Press.

Checkel J. T. and Katzenstein, P. J. (2009a) *European Identity*, Cambridge: Cambridge University Press.

—— (2009b) 'The Politicization of European Identity', in J. T. Checkel and P. J. Katzenstein (eds) *European Identity*, Cambridge: Cambridge University Press.

Choudhry, S. (2008) *Constitutional Design for Divided Societies: Integration or Accommodation?*, Oxford: Oxford University Press.

Christiansen, T. and Vanhoonacker, S. (2008) 'At a Critical Juncture? Change and Continuity in the Institutional Development of the Council Secretariat', *West European Politics*, 31(4): 751–70.

Clarkson, S. and Wood, S. (2010) *A Perilous Imbalance: The Globalization of Canadian Law and Governance*, Vancouver: UBC Press.

Clavero, S. and Galligan, Y. (2010) 'Gender Equality in the European Union: Lessons for Democracy?', RECON Online Working Paper 2010/23, Oslo: ARENA. Available at: http://www.reconproject.eu/main.php/RECON_wp_1023.pdf?fileitem=5456426

Closa, C. (2004) 'Ratifying the EU Constitution: Referendums and their Implications', US-Europe Analysis Series, The Brookings Institution. Available at: http://www.brookings.edu/fp/cuse/analysis/closa20041101.pdf

Cohen, A. (1974) *Two-Dimensional Man: An Essay on the Anthropology of Power and Symbolism in Complex Society*, London: Routledge.

Cohen, B. C. (1963) *The Press and Foreign Policy*, Princeton, NJ: Princeton University Press.

Cohen, J. (1997) 'Procedure and Substance in Deliberative Democracy', in J. Bohman and W. Rehg (eds) *Deliberative Democracy*, Cambridge, MA: MIT Press.

Cohen, J. and Sabel, C. F. (1997) 'Directly-Deliberative Polyarchy', *European Law Journal*, 3(4): 313–42.

—— (2003) 'Sovereignty and Solidarity: EU and US', in J. Zeitlin and D. M. Trubek (eds) *Governing Work and Welfare in the New Economy: European and American Experiments*, Oxford: Oxford University Press.

—— (2005) 'Global Democracy?' *NYU Journal of International Law and Politics*, 37(4): 763–97.

—— (2006) 'Extra Rempublicam Nulla Justitia?', *Philosophy and Public Affairs*, 34(2): 147–75.

Council of the European Union (2003) 'A Secure Europe in a Better World: European Security Strategy', Brussels, 12 December. Available at: http://www.consilium.europa.eu/uedocs/cmsUpload/78367.pdf

—— (2008) 'Reporting on the Implementation of the European Security Strategy: Providing Security in a Changing World', S407/08, Brussels, 11 December. Available at: http://www.consilium.europa.eu/uedocs/cms_data/docs/pressdata/en/reports/104630.pdf

Craske, N. and Molyneux, M. (eds) (2002) *Gender and the Politics of Rights and Democracy in Latin America*, Basingstoke: Palgrave Macmillan.

Crouch, C. (2004) *Post-Democracy*, Cambridge: Polity Press.

Crum, B. (2009) 'Accountability and Personalisation of the European Council Presidency', *European Integration*, 31(6): 685–701.

Crum, B. and Fossum, J. E. (2009) 'The Multilevel Parliamentary Field: A Framework for Theorizing Representative Democracy in the EU', *European Political Science Review*, 1(2): 249–71.

Curtin, D. (1993) 'The Constitutional Structure of the Union: A Europe of Bits and Pieces', *Common Market Law Review*, 30: 17–69.

—— (2007) 'Transparency, Audiences and the Evolving Role of the EU Council of Ministers', in J. E. Fossum and P. Schlesinger (eds) *The European Union and the Public Sphere: A Communicative Space in the Making?*, London: Routledge.

—— (2009) *Executive Power of the European Union: Law, Practices and the Living Constitution*, Oxford: Oxford University Press.

Dahl, R. A. (1971) *Polyarchy, Participation and Opposition*, New Haven, CT: Yale University Press.

—— (1999) 'Can International Organizations be Democratic? A Skeptic's View', in

I. Sharpio and C. Hacker-Cordón (eds) *Democracy's Edges*, Cambridge: Cambridge University Press.

De Grauwe, P. (2011) 'The Governance of a Fragile Eurozone', Centre for European Policy Studies (CEPS) Working Document 2011/346.

Delanty, G. (2009) *The Cosmopolitan Imagination*, Cambridge: Cambridge University Press.

Delanty, G. and Rumford, C. (2005) *Rethinking Europe: Social Theory and the Implications of Europeanization*, London: Routledge.

Della Porta, D. and Tarrow, S. (eds) (2005) *Transnational Protest and Global Activism: People, Passion and Power*, Lanham, MD: Rowman and Littlefield.

Department of Canadian Heritage (1999) 'Foreword by the Prime Minister' in the *10th Annual Report on the Operation of the Canadian Multiculturalism Act*, Ottawa: Minister of Public Works and Government Services Canada.

Dewey, J. (1927) [1999] *The Public and its Problems*, London: George Allen and Unwin.

Dicey, A. V. (1866) *Introduction to the Study of the Law of the Constitution*, London: Palgrave MacMillan.

Dryzek, J. S. (2006) *Deliberative Global Politics*, Cambridge: Polity Press.

Duchêne, F. (1972) 'Europe's Role in World Peace', in R. Mayne (ed.) *Europe Tomorrow: Sixteen Europeans Look Ahead*, London: Fontana.

Duke, S. and Vanhoonacker, S. (2006) 'Administrative Governance in the CFSP: Development and Practice', *European Foreign Affairs Review*, 11(2): 163–82.

Dunn, J. (2005) *Setting the People Free: The Story of Democracy*, London: Atlantic Books.

Easton, D. (1971) *The Political System*, New York, NY: Alfred Knopf.

Eberlein, B. and Grande, E. (2005) 'Beyond Delegation: Transnational Regulatory Regimes and the EU Regulatory State', *Journal of European Public Policy*, 12(1): 89–112.

Economist Intelligence Unit (2007) *Index of Democracy 2007*. Available at: http://www.economist.com/media/pdf/democracy_index_2007_v3.pdf

Eder, K. (2007) 'The Public Sphere and European Democracy: Mechanisms of Democratisation in the Transnational Situation', in J. E. Fossum and P. R. Schlesinger (eds) *The European Union and the Public Sphere: A Communicative Space in the Making?*, London: Routledge.

—— (2009) 'A Theory of Collective Identity: Making Sense of the Debate on a "European Identity"', *European Journal of Social Theory*, 12(4): 427–47.

Eder, K., Giesen, B., Schmidtke, O. and Tambini, D. (2002) *Collective Identities in Action: A Sociological Approach to Ethnicity*, Aldershot: Ashgate.

Egan, M. P. (2001) *Constructing a European Market: Standards, Regulation and Governance*, Oxford: Oxford University Press.

Eisenstadt, S. N. (1987) *The European Civilisations in Comparative Perspective*, Oslo: Norwegian University Press.

Eisenstadt, S. N. and Giesen, B. (1995) 'The Construction of Collective Identity', *European Journal of Sociology*, 36: 72–102.

Elazar, D. J. (1987) *Exploring Federalism*, Tuscaloosa, AL: University of Alabama Press.

Elias, N. and Scotson, J. L. (1965) *The Established and the Outsiders*, London: Frank Cass.

Eriksen, E. O. (ed.) (2005) *Making the European Polity: Reflexive Integration in Europe*, London: Routledge.

—— (2006) 'The EU: A Cosmopolitan Polity?', *Journal of European Public Policy*, 13(2): 252–69.

—— (2007) 'Conceptualising European Public Spheres: General, Segmented and Strong Publics', in J. E. Fossum and P. R. Schlesinger (eds) *The European Union and the Public Sphere: A Communicative Space in the Making*, London: Routledge.

—— (2009a) *The Unfinished Democratization of Europe*, Oxford: Oxford University Press.

—— (2009b) 'The EU: A Cosmopolitan Vanguard?', *Global Jurist*, 9(1), article 6.

Eriksen, E. O. and Fossum, J. E. (2000a) *Democracy in the European Union: Integration through Deliberation?*, London: Routledge.

—— (2000b) 'Postnational Integration', in E. O. Eriksen and J. E. Fossum (eds) *Democracy in the European Union: Integration through Deliberation?*, London: Routledge.

—— (2002) 'Democracy through Strong Publics in the European Union?', *Journal of Common Market Studies*, 40(3): 401–24.

—— (2004) 'Europe in Search of Legitimacy: Strategies of Legitimation Assessed', *International Political Science Review*, 25(4): 435–59.

—— (2007a) 'Europe in Transformation. How to Reconstitute Democracy?', RECON Online Working Paper 2007/01, Oslo: ARENA. Available at: http://reconproject.eu/projectweb/portalproject/AbstractRECONwp0701.html

—— (2007b) 'Reconstituting Democracy in Europe', in E. O. Eriksen (ed.) *How to Reconstitute Democracy in Europe? Proceedings from the RECON Opening Conference 26 January*, RECON Report No. 3, Oslo: ARENA.

—— (2009) 'Europe's Challenge: Reconstituting Europe or Reconfiguring Democracy', in E. O. Eriksen and J. E. Fossum (eds) *RECON: Theory in Practice*, RECON Report No. 8, Oslo: ARENA.

—— (2010) 'Introduction' in E. O. Eriksen and J. E. Fossum (eds) *What Democracy for Europe? Proceedings from the RECON Midterm Conference*, RECON Report No. 11, Oslo: ARENA.

Eriksen, E. O. and Fossum, J. E. (forthcoming) 'Representation through Deliberation: The European Case', *Constellations*.

Eriksen, E. O. and Neyer, J. (2003) 'Introduction: The Forging of Deliberative Supranationalism in the EU', in E. O. Eriksen, C. Joerges and J. Neyer (eds) *European Governance, Deliberation and the Quest for Democratisation*, ARENA Report No 2003/02, Oslo: ARENA.

Eriksen, E. O., Fossum, J. E. and Sjursen, H. (2005) 'Widening or Reconstituting the EU?', in E. O. Eriksen (ed.) *Making the European Polity: Reflexive Integration in Europe*, London: Routledge.

Eriksen, T. H. (1993) *Ethnicity and Nationalism*, London: Pluto Press.

Estlund, D. (1993) 'Making Truth Safe for Democracy', in D. Copp, J. Hampton and J. R. Roemer (eds) *The Idea of Democracy*, Cambridge: Cambridge University Press.

EUobserver (2011)'The Junta of Experts Tells Us: "Vote how you Like, but Policies Cannot Change"', 17 June. Available at: http://euobserver.com/7/32501

Eurobarometer (2005) 'The Future Constitutional Treaty: First Results'. Available at: http://ec.europa.eu/public_opinion/archives/ebs/ebs214_en_first.pdf

Eurobarometer 62 (2005) 'Public Opinion in the European Union'. Available at: http://ec.europa.eu/public_opinion/archives/eb/eb62/eb_62_en.pdf

Eurobarometer (2009) '2009 Post Election Survey'. Available at: http://www.europarl.europa.eu/pdf/eurobarometre/28_07/SA_EN.pdf

European Commission (2010) 'Strategy for Equality between Women and Men 2010–2015', COM (2010)491 FINAL. Available at: http://eur-lex.europa.eu/LexUriServ/LexUriServ.do?uri=COM:2010:0491:FIN:EN:PDFhtt

European Council (2007) 'Presidency Conclusions of the European Council of 21–22 June 2007'. Available at: http://www.consilium.europa.eu/uedocs/cms_data/docs/pressdata/en/ec/94932.pdfht

Evas, T. (2007) 'Elitist with a Russian Twist: Mass Media Discourses on European Constitutional Ratification in Estonia and Latvia', *Perspectives on European Politics and Society*, 8(3): 374–413.

Falkner, G., Treib, O. and Holzleither, E. (2008) *Compliance in the Enlarged European Union: Living Rights or Dead Letters*, Aldershot: Ashgate.

Fischer-Lescano, A. and Teubner, G. (2006) 'Regime-collisions: The Vain Search for Legal Unity in the Fragmentation of Global Law', *Michigan Journal of International Law*, 25(4): 999–1046.

Fligstein, N. (2008) *Euro-clash: The EU, European Identity, and the Future of Europe*, Oxford: Oxford University Press.

Flora, P., Kuhnle, S. and Urwin, D. (1999) *State Formation, Nation-Building, and Mass Politics in Europe: The Theory of Stein Rokkan: Based on his Collected Works*, Oxford: Oxford University Press.

Føllesdal, A. and Hix, S. (2006) 'Why There is a Democratic Deficit in the EU: A Response to Majone and Moravcsik', *Journal of Common Market Studies*, 44(3): 533–62.

Forst, R. (2007) 'Cosmopolitan Republicanism or Republican Cosmopolitanism? Comment on James Bohman', in E. O. Eriksen (ed.) *How to Reconstitute Democracy in Europe? Proceedings from the RECON Opening Conference*, 26 January, RECON Report No. 3, Oslo: ARENA.

Fortunato, J. A. (2005) *Making Media Content: The Influence of Constituency Groups on Mass Media*, Mahwah, NJ: Lawrence Erlbaum Associates.

Fossum, J. E. (2001) 'Identity-politics in the European Union', *Journal of European Integration*, 23(4): 373–406.

—— (2003) 'The European Union in Search of an Identity', *European Journal of Political Theory*, 2(3): 319–40.

—— (2004) 'Still a Union of Deep Diversity? The Convention and the Constitution for Europe', in E. O. Eriksen, J. E. Fossum and A. J. Menéndez (eds) *Developing a Constitution for Europe*, London: Routledge.

—— (2005a) 'Conceptualising the EU's Social Constituency', *European Journal of Social Theory*, 8(2): 123–47.

—— (2005b) 'Contemporary European Constitution-making – Reflexive or constrained?', in E. O. Eriksen (ed.) *Making the European Polity: Reflexive Integration in Europe*, London: Routledge.

—— (2007a) 'On Democratizing European Constitution Making: Possible Lessons from Canada's Experience', *Supreme Court Law Review*, 37: 343–81.

—— (2007b) 'Constitutional Patriotism: Canada and the European Union', RECON Online Working Paper 2007/04, Oslo: ARENA. Available at: http://www.reconproject.eu/projectweb/portalproject/AbstractRECONwp0704.html

—— (2008) 'Constitutional Patriotism: Canada and the European Union', in P. Mouritsen and K. E. Jørgensen (eds) *Constituting Communities: Political Solutions to Cultural Difference*, London: Palgrave.

—— (2010) 'The Future of the European Order', in P. Birkinshaw and M. Varney (eds) *The European Union Legal Order after Lisbon*, The Netherlands: Kluwer Law.

—— (2011a) 'Review Essay: A Cosmopolitan Constellation?', *European Journal of Social Theory*, 14(2): 235–48.

—— (2011b) 'Nationalism, Patriotism and Diversity: Conceptualising the National Dimension in Neil MacCormick's Post-sovereign Constellation,' in A. J. Menéndez and J. E. Fossum (eds) *Law and Democracy in Neil D. MacCormick's Legal and Political Theory: The Post-Sovereign Constellation*, Dordrecht: Springer Law.

Fossum, J. E. and Menéndez, A. J. (2005) 'The Constitution's Gift? A Deliberative Democratic Analysis of Constitution Making in the European Union', *European Law Journal*, 11(4): 380–410.

—— (2011) *The Constitution's Gift: A Constitutional Theory for a Democratic European Union*, Lanham, MD: Rowman and Littlefield.

Fossum, J. E. and Schlesinger, P. R. (2007) 'The European Union and the Public Sphere: a Communicative Space in the Making?', in J. E. Fossum and P. Schlesinger (eds) *The European Union and the Public Sphere. A Communicative Space in the Making?*, London: Routledge.

Fossum, J. E. and Trenz, H.-J. (2007) 'The Public Sphere in European Constitution-making', in J. E. Fossum and P. R. Schlesinger (eds) *The European Union and the Public Sphere. A Communicative Space in the Making?*, London: Routledge.

Francis, E. (1965) *Ethnos und Demos*, Berlin: Duncker and Humbolt.

Frankenberg, G. (1996) *Die Verfassung der Republik: Autorität und Solidarität in der Zivilgesellschaft*, Baden-Baden: Nomos.

—— (2000) 'The Return of the Contract: Problems and Pitfalls of European Constitutionalism', *European Law Journal*, 6(3): 257–76.

Fraser, N. (1992) 'Rethinking the Public Sphere: A Contribution to the Critique of Actually Existing Democracy', in C. Calhoun (ed.) *Habermas and the Public Sphere*, Cambridge, MA: MIT Press.

—— (1997) *Justice Interruptus: Critical Reflections on the Postsocialist Condition*, London: Routledge.

—— (2005a) 'Reframing Justice in a Globalising World', *New Left Review*, 36: 69–88.

—— (2005b) '*Transnationalizing* the Public Sphere', in M. Pensky (ed.) *Globalizing Critical Theory*, Lanham MD: Rowman and Littlefield.

—— (2007) 'Feminist Politics in the Age of Recognition: A Two-dimensional Approach to Gender Justice', *Studies in Social Justice*, 1(1): 23–35.

Fraser, N. and Honneth, A. (2003) *Redistribution or Recognition? A Political-Philosophical Exchange*, London: Verso.

Gagnon, A.-G. and Tully, J. (eds) (2001) *Multinational Democracies*, Cambridge: Cambridge University Press.

Gaisbauer, H. (2010) *Nizza oder der Tod!: Zur negativen Dialektik von Erweiterung und Vertiefung der Europäischen Union von Nizza bis Lissabon*, Baden-Baden: Nomos.

Galligan, Y. and Clavero, S. (2009) 'Applying the RECON Models to Gender Democracy in Europe', in E. O. Eriksen and J. E. Fossum (eds) *RECON: Theory in Practice*, RECON Report No. 8, Oslo: ARENA.

Galtung, J. (1999) 'State, Capital and the Civil Society: the Problem of Communication', in R. C. Vincent, K. Nordenstreng and M. Traber (eds) *Towards Equity in Global Communication: MacBride Update*, Cresskill, NJ: Hampton Press.

Geertz, C. (1973) *The Interpretation of Cultures*, London: Basic Books.

Gerhards, J. (2002) 'Das Öffentlichkeitsdefizit der EU im Horizont normativer Öffentlichkeitstheorien', in H. Kaelble, M. Kirsch, and A. Schmidt-Gernig (eds) *Transnationale Öffentlichkeiten und Identitäten im 20. Jahrhundert*, Frankfurt: Campus.

Gerhards, J. and Neidhardt, F. (1991) 'Strukturen und Funktionen moderner Öffentlichkeit. Fragestellungen und Ansätze', in S. Müller-Dohm and K. Neumann-Braun (eds) *Öffentlichkeit, Kultur, Massenkommunikation. Beiträge zur Medien- und Kommunikationssoziologie*, Oldenburg: Universitätsverlag.

Gerstenberg, O. (2002) 'The New Europe: Part of the Problem – or Part of the Solution to the Problem?', *Oxford Journal of Legal Studies*, 22(3): 563–71.

Giesen, B. (1992) *Die Intellektuellen und die Nation*, Frankfurt: Suhrkamp.

—— (2003) 'The Collective Identity of Europe: Constitutional Practice or Community of Memory', in A. Triandafyllidou and W. Spohn (eds) *Europeanisation, National Identities and*

Migration: Changes in Boundary Constructions between Western and Eastern Europe, London: Routledge.

Goodin, R. E. (2005) *Reflective Democracy*, Oxford: Oxford University Press.

Graf Kielmansegg, P. (1996) 'Integration und Demokratie', in M. Jachtenfuchs and B. Kohler-Koch (eds) *Europäische Integration*, Opladen: Leske and Budrich.

Greenwood, J. (2007) 'Organized Civil Society and Democratic Legitimacy in the European Union', *British Journal of Political Science*, 37: 333–57.

Greven, M. (2000) 'Can the European Union Finally Become a Democracy?', in M. Greven and L. Pauly (eds) *Democracy Beyond the State?* Toronto: University of Toronto Press.

Grimm, D. (1995) 'Does Europe Need a Constitution?', *European Law Journal*, 1(3): 282–302.

—— (2004) 'Treaty or Constitution? The Legal Basis of the European Union after Maastricht', in E. O. Eriksen, J. E. Fossum and A. J. Menéndez (eds) *Developing a Constitution for Europe*, London: Routledge.

—— (2005) 'Integration by Constitution', *I-CON*, 3(2–3): 193–208.

Haas, E. B. (1968) *The Uniting of Europe: Political, Social, and Economic Forces 1950–57*, Stanford, CA: Stanford University Press.

Habermas, J. (1976) 'Legitimationsprobleme im modernen Staat', in J. Habermas, *Zur Rekonstruktion des Historischen Materialismus*, Frankfurt: Suhrkamp.

—— (1981) *The Theory of Communicative Action*, vol. 1, Boston: Beacon Press.

—— (1991) *The Structural Transformation of the Public Sphere*, Cambridge: Polity Press.

—— (1994) 'Struggles for Recognition in the Democratic Constitutional State', in A. Gutmann and C. Taylor (eds) *Multiculturalism*, Princeton, NJ: Princeton University Press.

—— (1996) *Between Facts and Norms. Contributions to a Discourse Theory of Law and Democracy*, Cambridge, MA: MIT Press.

—— (1997) 'Kant's Idea of Perpetual Peace, with the Benefit of Two Hundred Years' Hindsight', in J. Bohman and M. Lutz-Bachmann (eds) *Perpetual Peace. Essays on Kant's Cosmopolitan Ideal*, Cambridge, MA: The MIT press.

—— (1998a) *The Inclusion of the Other: Studies in Political Theory*, Cambridge, MA: MIT Press.

—— (1998b) 'Learning by Disaster: A Diagnostic Look Back on the Short 20th Century', *Constellations*, 5(3): 307–20.

—— (1998c) 'Three Normative Models of Democracy', in J. Habermas (ed.) *The Inclusion of the Other*, Cambridge, MA: MIT Press.

—— (2001a) *The Postnational Constellation: Political Essays*, Cambridge: Polity Press.

—— (2001b) 'The Postnational Constellation and the Future of Democracy', in J. Habermas *The Postnational Constellation: Political Essays* [ed. and trans. M. Pensky], Cambridge: Polity Press.

—— (2004) 'Why Europe Needs a Constitution', in E. O. Eriksen, J. E. Fossum and A. J. Menéndez (eds) *Developing a Constitution for Europe*, London: Routledge.

—— (2006) *The Divided West*, Cambridge: Polity Press.

—— (2009a) 'Political Communication in Media Society: Does Democracy Still have an Epistemic Dimension? The Impact of Normative Theory on Empirical Research', in J. Habermas (ed.) *Europe: The Faltering Project*, Cambridge: Polity Press.

—— (2009b) 'The Constitutionalization of International Law and the Legitimation Problems of a Constitution for World Society', in J. Habermas (ed.) *Europe: The Faltering Project*, Cambridge: Polity Press.

—— (2010) 'A Political Constitution for the Pluralist World Society', in G. W. Brown and D. Held (eds) *The Cosmopolitanism Reader*, Cambridge: Polity Press.

Habermas, J., Lennox, S. and Lennox, F. (1974) 'The Public Sphere: An Encyclopedia Article (1964)', *New German Critique*, 3: 49–55.

Hallin, D. C. and Mancini, P. (2004) *Comparing Media Systems: Three Models of Media and Politics*, Cambridge: Cambridge University Press.

Hegel, G. W. F. (1821) [1967] *Philosophy of Right*, Oxford: Oxford University Press.

Held, D. (1995) *Democracy and the Global Order: From the Modern State to Cosmopolitan Governance*, Cambridge: Polity Press.

—— (1996) *Models of Democracy*, Cambridge: Polity Press.

Held, D., McGrew, A. Goldblatt, D. and Perraton, J. (2000) *Global Transformations*, Cambridge: Polity Press.

Herrmann, R. K., Risse-Kappen, T., Brewer, M. B. (eds) (2004) *Transnational Identities: Becoming European in the EU*, Lanham, MD: Rowman and Littlefield.

Hill, C. (1993) 'Shaping a Federal Foreign Policy for Europe', in B. Hocking (ed.) *Managing Foreign Relations in Federal States*, London: Leicester University Press.

Hirschman, A. O. (1970) *Exit, Voice, and Loyalty: Responses to Decline in Firms, Organizations, and States*, Cambridge, MA: Harvard University Press.

Hix, S. (2008) *What Went Wrong with the EU and how to Fix it?*, Cambridge: Polity Press.

Hix, S., Noury A. G. and Roland, G. (2005) 'Power to the Parties: Cohesion and Competition in the European Parliament, 1979–2001', *British Journal of Political Science*, 35(2): 209–34.

—— (2007) *Democratic Politics in the European Parliament*, Cambridge: Cambridge University Press.

Holmes, M. (ed.) (1996) *The Eurosceptic Reader*, Basingstoke: Palgrave Macmillan.

Holst, C. (2008) 'Gender Justice in the European Union: The Normative Subtext of Methodological Choices', RECON Online Working Paper 2008/18, Oslo: ARENA. Available at: http://www.reconproject.eu/projectweb/portalproject/AbstractRECONwp0818.html

Holton, R. J. (2009) *Cosmopolitanisms: New Thinking and New Directions*, Basingstoke: Palgrave Macmillan.

Honneth, A. (1995) *The Struggle for Recognition: The Moral Grammar of Social Conflicts*, Cambridge: Polity Press.

Hooghe, L. (2007) 'What Drives Euroskepticism?' *European Union Politics*, 8(1): 5–12.

Hooghe, L. and Marks, G. (2003) 'Unraveling the Central State, but How? Types of Multilevel Governance', *American Political Science Review*, 97(2): 233–43.

—— (2007) 'Sources of Euroscepticism', *Acta Politica*, 42: 119–27.

—— (2008) 'A Postfunctionalist Theory of European Integration: From Permissive Consensus to Constraining Dissensus', *British Journal of Political Sciences*, 39(1): 1–23.

Hoskyns, C. (1996) *Integrating Gender: Women, Law and Politics in the European Union*, London: Verso.

Hoskyns, C. and Newman, M. (2000) *Democratizing the European Union: Issues for the Twenty-first Century*, Manchester: Manchester University Press.

Howorth, J. (2001) 'European Defence and the Changing Politics of the European Union: Hanging Together or Hanging Separately?' *Journal of Common Market Studies*, 39(4): 765–89.

Imig, D. and Tarrow, S. (eds) (2001) *Contentious Europeans: Protest and Politics in an Emerging Polity*, Lanham, MD: Rowman and Littlefield.

Jachtenfuchs, M. and Kohler-Koch, B. (eds) (1996) *Europäische Integration*, 1st edition, Opladen: Leske and Budrich.

—— (eds) (2003) *Europäische Integration*, 2nd edition, Opladen: Leske and Budrich.

Jeffery, C. and Savigear, P. (eds) (1991) *German Federalism Today*, New York, NY: St. Martin's Press.

Joerges, C. and Neyer, J. (1997) 'From Intergovernmental Bargaining to Deliberative Political Processes: The Constitutionalisation of Comitology', *European Law Journal*, 3(3): 273–99.

Joerges, C. and Vos, E. (eds) (1999) *EU Committees: Social Regulation, Law and Politics*, Oxford: Hart.

Joerges, C., Sand, I.-J. and Teubner, G. (eds) (2004) *Transnational Governance and Constitutionalism*, Oxford: Hart.

Kaelble, H. (2001) *Europäer über Europa. Die Entstehung des modernen europäischen Selbstverständnisses im 19. und 20. Jahrhundert*, Frankfurt: Campus.

—— (2009) 'Identification with Europe and Politicisation of the EU since the 1980s', in J. Checkel and P. J. Katzenstein (eds) *European Identity*, Cambridge: Cambridge University Press.

Kantner, C. (2007) 'Collective Identity as Shared Ethical Self-understanding: The Case of the Emerging European Identity', *European Journal of Social Theory*, 9(4): 501–23.

Kantola, J. (2010) *Gender and the European Union*, Basingstoke: Palgrave Macmillan.

Kendall, G. Woodward, I. and Skrbis, Z. (2009) *The Sociology of Cosmopolitanism: Globalization, Identity, Culture and Government*, Houndmills, Basingstoke: Palgrave.

Keohane, R. (2002) *Power and Governance in a Partially Globalized World*, London: Routledge.

Keukeleire, S. and MacNaughtan, J. (2008) *The Foreign Policy of the European Union*, Basingstoke: Palgrave Macmillan.

Kielmannsegg, P. G. (1996) 'Integration und Demokratie', in M. Jachtenfuchs and B. Kohler-Koch (eds) *Europäische Integration*, Opladen: Leske and Budrich.

Kitus, A. (2008) 'Europeanization, Democratic Deficit and the Constitutional Debate in Estonia', *Innovation: The European Journal of Social Science Research*, 21(2): 111–29.

Kraus, P. A. (2008) *A Union of Diversity. Language, Identity and Polity-building in Europe*, Cambridge: Cambridge University Press.

Krzyzanowski, M. and Oberhuber, F. (2007) *(Un)Doing Europe (Multiple Europes)*, Brussels: Peter Lang.

Kumm, M. (2005) 'To be a European Citizen: Constitutional Patriotism and the Treaty Establishing a Constitution for Europe', in E. O. Eriksen, J. E. Fossum, M. Kumm and A. J. Menéndez *The European Constitution: The Rubicon Crossed?*, ARENA Report No 2005/03, Oslo: ARENA.

Kurasawa, F. (2007) *The Work of Global Justice: Human Rights as Practices*, Cambridge: Cambridge University Press.

Kymlicka, W. (1998) *Finding our Way*, Oxford: Oxford University Press.

—— (2007) *Multicultural Odysseys: Navigating the New International Politics of Diversity*, Oxford: Oxford University Press.

Laclau, E. (2005) *On Populist Reason*, London: Verso.

Landfried, C. (2002) *Das politische Europa: Differenz als Potential der Europäischen Union*, Baden-Baden: Nomos.

Larsen H. (2004) 'Discourse Analysis in the Study of European Foreign Policy', in B. Tonra and T. Christiansen (eds) *Rethinking European Union Foreign Policy*, Manchester: Manchester University Press.

LaSelva, S. V. (1996) *The Moral Foundations of Canadian Federalism*, Montreal: McGill-Queen's University Press.

Lerch, M. and Schwellnus, G. (2006) 'Normative by Nature? The Role of Coherence in Justifying the EU's External Human Rights Policy', *Journal of European Public Policy*, 13(2): 304–21.

Levy, J. (2004) 'National Minorities without Nationalism', in A. Dieckhoff (ed.) *The Politics of Belonging: Nationalism, Liberalism and Pluralism*, Lanham, MD: Lexington Press.

Liebert, U. (2007a) 'Europe in Contention: Debating the Constitutional Treaty', *Perspectives on European Politics and Society*, 8(3): 235–60.

—— (2007b) 'Transnationalising the Public Sphere? The European Parliament, Promises and Anticipations', in J. E. Fossum and P. R. Schlesinger (eds) *The European Union and the Public Sphere: A Communicative Space in the Making?*, New York, NY: Routledge.

—— (2010) 'Contentious European Democracy: National Intellectuals in Transnational Debates', in J. Lacroix and K. Nicolaïdis (eds) *European Stories: Intellectual Debates on Europe in National Contexts*, Oxford: Oxford University Press.

Liebert, U. and Trenz, H.-J. (2008a) 'Mass Media and Contested Meanings: EU Constitutional Politics after Popular Rejection', Robert Schuman Centre for Advances Studies (RSCAS) Working Papers 2008/28, Florence: European University Institute (EUI). Available at: http://cadmus.eui.eu/bitstream/handle/1814/9147/RSCAS_2008_28.pdf?sequence=1htt

—— (2008b) 'Mediating European Democracy: Methods of Comparative Media Analysis and Empirical Findings on EU Treaty Reform Discourses in 14 Member States (2004–2007)', RECON Restricted Research Report WP 5, Oslo: ARENA. Available at: http://www.reconproject.eu/projectweb/portalproject/ResearchReportWP5.html

—— (eds) (2009a) 'Civil Society and the Reconstitution of Democracy in Europe', *Policy and Society*, 28(1): 1–9.

—— (2009b) 'Between Norms and Practices of the Public Sphere: Assessing the Infrastructures for Democracy in Europe', in E. O. Eriksen and J. E. Fossum (eds) *RECON: Theory in Practice*, RECON Report No. 8, Oslo: ARENA.

—— (2010) *The New Politics of European Civil Society*, London: Routledge.

Liebert, U., Maatsch, A. and Packham, K. (2011) 'Comparative Political Discourse Analysis: A Qualitative-Quantitative Approach', Online ConstEPS Working Paper 2011/01, University of Bremen.

Liebert, U., with S. Maatsch, K. Packham, A. Wyrozumska, P. Rakusanova and T. Evas (2007) "Europe in Contention: Debating the Constitutional Treaty". Special Issue of *"Perspectives on European Politics and Society"*, 8(3), September.

Lijphart, A. (1984) *Patterns of Democracy: Patterns of Majoritarian and Consensus Government in Twenty-One Countries*, New Haven, CT: Yale University Press.

Lipset, S. M. (1990) *Continental Divide: The Values and Institutions of the United States and Canada*, New York, NY: Routledge.

Livingstone, S. (2003) 'On the Challenges of Cross-national Comparative Media Research', *European Journal of Communication*, 18(4): 477–500.

Lord, C. (2008) 'Some indicators of the Democratic Performance of the European Union and how They Might Relate to the RECON Models', RECON Online Working Paper 2008/11, Oslo: ARENA. Available at: http://www.reconproject.eu/main.php/RECON_wp_0811.pdf?fileitem=5456276htt

—— (2009) 'A RECON-inspired Democratic Audit', in E. O. Eriksen and J. E. Fossum (eds) *RECON: Theory in Practice*, RECON Report No. 8, Oslo: ARENA.

Lord, C. and Beetham. D. (2001) 'Legitimising the EU: Is there a "Post-Parliamentary" Basis for its Legitimation?' *Journal of Common Market Studies*, 42(1): 443–62.

Lord, C. and Harris, E. (2006) *Democracy in the New Europe*, Basingstoke: Palgrave Macmillan.

Lord, C. and Pollak, J. (2010) 'The EU's Many Representative Modes: Colliding? Cohering?' *Journal of European Public Policy*, 17(1): 117–36.

Lord, C. and Tamvaki, D. (2011) 'The Politics of Justification? Applying the Discourse Quality Index to the Study of the European Parliament', RECON Online Working Paper 2011/03, Oslo: ARENA. Available at: http://www.reconproject.eu/main.php/RECON_wp_1103.pdf?fileitem=5456448ht

Lucarelli, S. and Manners, I. (eds) (2006) *Values and Principles in European Union Foreign Policy*, New York, NY, Routledge.

Luhmann, N. (1997) *Die Gesellschaft der Gesellschaft*, Frankfurt: Suhrkamp.

—— (2000) *Die Politik der Gesellschaft*, Frankfurt: Suhrkamp.

Luttwak, E. (1994) 'Franco-German Reconciliation: The Overlooked Role of the Moral Re-Armament Movement', in D. Johnston and C. Sampson (eds) *Religion, the Missing Dimension of Statecraft*, Oxford: Oxford University Press.

Maatsch, A. (2010) 'Between an Intergovernmental and a Polycentric European Union. National Parliamentary Discourses on Democracy in the EU Ratification Process', RECON Online Working Paper 2010/18, Oslo: ARENA. Available at: http://www.reconproject.eu/main.php/RECON_wp_1018.pdf?fileitem=5456416htt

—— (forthcoming) 'Mainstreaming Euroscepticism? Contestation of the European Union in Reform Treaty Ratification by National Parliaments', RECON Online Working Paper, Oslo: ARENA.

—— (forthcoming) 'Where Do We Go From Here? Discursive Legitimation and De-Legitimation of the EU Polity in the Media Based 2009 European Election Campaigns', RECON Online Working Paper, Oslo: ARENA.

Maatsch, S. (2007) 'The Struggle to Control Meanings: The French Debate on the European Constitution in the Mass Media', *Perspectives on European Politics and Society*, 8(3): 261–80.

MacCormick, N. (1999) *Questioning Sovereignty*, Oxford: Oxford University Press.

Mach, Z. (1993) *Symbols, Conflict and Identity*, Albany, NY: State University of New York Press.

—— (1998) *Niechciane Miasta*, Krakow: Universitas.

MacIver, R. M. (1928) [1964] *The Modern State*, London: Oxford University Press.

Macpherson, C. B. (1977) *The Life and Times of Liberal Democracy*, Oxford: Oxford University Press.

Magnette, P. (2007) 'How Can One Be European? Reflections on the Pillars of European Civic Identity', *European Law Journal*, 13(5): 664–79.

Majone, G. (1998) 'Europe's "Democratic Deficit": The Question of Standards', *European Law Journal*, 4(1): 5–28.

—— (2005) *Dilemmas of European Integration: The Ambiguities and Pitfalls of Integration by Stealth*, Oxford: Oxford University Press.

Mancini, G. F. (1998) 'Europe: The Case for Statehood', *European Law Journal*, 4(1): 29–42.

Manin, B. (1997) *The Principles of Representative Government*, Cambridge: Cambridge University Press.

Manners, I. (2002) 'Normative Power Europe: A Contradiction in Terms?' *Journal of Common Market Studies*, 40(2): 235–58.

Mansbridge, J. (2003) 'Rethinking Representation', *American Political Science Review*, 97(4): 515–28.

March, J. and Olsen, J. P. (1995) *Democratic Governance*, New York, NY: Free Press.

Marchetti, R. (2006) 'Global Governance or World Federalism? A Cosmopolitan Dispute on International Models', *Global Society*, 20(3): 287–305.

Markell, P. (2000) 'Making Affect Safe for Democracy? On "Constitutional Patriotism"', *Political Theory*, 28(1): 38–63.

Marsh, M. (1998) 'Testing the Second-Order Election Model After Four European Elections', *British Journal of Political Science*, 28(4): 591–607.

Maurer, A., Kietz, D. and Völkel, C. (2005) 'Interinstitutional Agreements in CFSP: Parliamentarisation Through the Back Door?', *European Foreign Affairs Review*, 10(2): 175–95.

Mendelberg, T. and Karpowitz, C. (2006) 'How People Deliberate about Justice: Groups, Gender and Decision Rules', seminar paper at the Department of Politics, University of Princeton, 2 August.

Mendes, E. (2008) 'Canada's "Diversity Gene" and its Constitution: An Evolving Global Template for Reconciling Diversity, Collective Rights of National Minorities and Individual Rights?', paper presented at the RECON Workshop 'Global Transnationalisation and Democratisation Compared', Florence, 17 May 2008.

Menéndez, A. J. (2004) 'Three Conceptions of the European Constitution', in E. O. Eriksen, J. E. Fossum and A. J. Menéndez (eds) *Developing a Constitution for Europe*, London: Routledge.

—— (2005) 'Between Laeken and the Deep Blue Sea: An Assessment of the Draft Constitutional Treaty From a Deliberative-Democratic Standpoint', *European Public Law*, 11(1): 105–44.

—— (2009) 'The European Democratic Challenge: The Forging of a Supranational *Volonté Générale*,' *European Law Journal*, 15(3): 277–308.

Meyer, C. (2007) 'The Constitutional Treaty Debates as Revelatory Mechanisms: Insights for Public Sphere Research and Re-launch Attempts', RECON Online Working Paper 2007/06, Oslo: ARENA. Available at: http://www.reconproject.eu/main.php/RECON_wp_0706.pdf?fileitem=5456963htt

Mill, J. S. (1861) [1972] *Utilitarianism: On Liberty and Considerations on Representative Government*, London: Dent.

Miller, D. (1995) *On Nationality*, Oxford: Oxford University Press.

Milward, A. S. (1992) *The European Rescue of the Nation State*, London: Routledge.

Mitzen, J. (2006) 'Anchoring Europe's Civilizing Identity: Habits, Capabilities and Ontological Security', *Journal of European Public Policy*, 13(2): 271–85.

Mokre, M., Brüll, C. and Pausch, M. (eds) (2009) *Democracy Needs Dispute: The Debate on the European Constitution*, Frankfurt: Campus.

Moravcsik, A. (1994) 'Why the European Community Strengthens the State: Domestic Politics and International Cooperation', paper presented at the annual meeting of the American Political Science Association (APSA), New York, 1–4 September 1994.

—— (1998) *The Choice for Europe*, London: University College London (UCL) Press.

—— (2001) 'Federalism in the European Union: Rhetoric and Reality', in K. Nicolaïdis and R. Howse (eds) *The Federal Vision: Legitimacy and Levels of Governance in the US and the EU*, Oxford: Oxford University Press.

—— (2002) 'In Defence of the "Democratic Deficit": Reassessing Legitimacy in the European Union', *Journal of Common Market Studies*, 40(4): 603–24.

—— (2005) 'The European Constitutional Compromise and the Legacy of Neofunctionalism', *Journal of European Public Policy*, 12(2): 1–37.

—— (2006) 'What Can We Learn from the Collapse of the European Constitution Project?', *Politische Vierteljahresschrift*, 47(2): 219–41.

Morgan, G. (2005) *The Idea of a European Superstate: Public Justification and European Integration*, Princeton, NJ: Princeton University Press.

Morton, F. L. and Knopff, R. (2000) *The Charter Revolution and the Court Party*, Peterborough, Ontario: Broadview Press.

Mouffe, C. (2000) *The Democratic Paradox*, London: Verso.

Müller, J.-W. (2006) 'On the Origins of Constitutional Patriotism', *Contemporary Political Theory*, 5(3): 278–96.

Nagel, T. (2005) 'The Problem of Global Justice', *Philosophy and Public Affairs*, 33(2): 113–47.

Neunreither, K. (1994) 'The Democratic Deficit of the European Union: Towards Closer Cooperation Between the European Parliament and the National Parliaments', *Government and Opposition*, 29(3): 299–314.

Nielsen, K. (2004) 'Are Nation-states Obsolete? The Challenge of Globalization', in M. Seymour (ed.) *The Fate of the Nation State*, Montreal: McGill-Queen's University Press.

Nordenstreng, K. (2000) 'The Structural Context of Media Ethics: How Media Are Regulated in Democratic Society', in B. Pattyn (ed.) *Media Ethics: Opening Social Dialogue*, Leuven: Peeters.

—— (2010) 'Searching for the Constituents of Media Systems', presentation in the International Association for Media and Communication Research (IAMCR) panel 'Comparative Global Media Research: Issues and Case Studies', European Communication Research and Education Association (ECREA) Conference, Hamburg, 14 October.

Norman, P. (2003) *The Accidental Constitution: The Story of the European Convention*, Brussels: EuroComment.

Norman, W. (2001) 'Justice and Stability in Multination States', in J. Tully and A.-G. Gagnon (eds) *Struggles for Recognition in Multinational Societies*, Cambridge: Cambridge University Press.

—— (2006) *Negotiating Nationalism: Nation-building, Federalism and Secession in the Multinational State*, Oxford: Oxford University Press.

Norris, P. (2000) *A Virtuous Circle: Political Communications in Postindustrial Societies*, Cambridge: Cambridge University Press.

Offe, C. (2000) 'The Democratic Welfare State in an Integrating Europe', in M. Greven and L. Pauly (eds) *Democracy Beyond the State?* Toronto: University of Toronto Press.

—— (2003a) '"Homogeneity" and Constitutional Democracy: Coping with Identity Conflicts through Group Rights', in C. Offe (ed.) *Herausforderungen der Demokratie: Zur Integrations- und Leistungsfähigkeit politischer Institutionen*, Frankfurt, Campus.

—— (2003b) *Herausforderungen der Demokratie. Zur Integrations- und Leistungsfähigkeit politischer Institutionen*, Frankfurt: Campus.

Olsen, J. P. (2007) *Europe in Search of Political Order*, Oxford: Oxford University Press.

Packham, K. (2007) 'From the Contentious Constitution to the Awkward Other . . . Social Model: The Constitutional Debate in the British Print Media', *Perspectives on European Politics and Society*, 8(3): 281–313.

Pateman, C. (1989) *The Disorder of Women: Democracy, Feminism and Political Theory*, Cambridge: Polity Press.

Pernice, I. (2009) 'The Treaty of Lisbon: Multilevel Constitutionalism in Action', *Columbia Journal of European Law*, 15: 349–407.

Peters, B. (2005) 'Public Discourse, Identity and the Problem of Democratic Legitimacy', in E. O. Eriksen (ed.) *Making the European Polity: Reflexive Integration in the EU*, London: Routledge.

Peters, D., Wagner, W. and Deitelhoff, N. (2008) 'Parliaments and Security Policy: Mapping the Parliamentary Field', in D. Peters, W. Wagner and N. Deitelhoff (eds) *The Parliamentary Control of European Security Policy*, RECON Report No. 6, Oslo: ARENA.

Phillips, A. (1991) *Engendering Democracy*, Cambridge: Polity Press.

—— (1993) *Democracy and Difference*, Cambridge: Polity Press.

—— (1995) *The Politics of Presence*, Oxford: Clarendon Press.

Pijpers, A. (1996) 'The Netherlands: The Weakening Pull of Atlanticism', in C. Hill (ed.) *The Actors in Europe's Foreign Policy*, London: Routledge.

Pinder, J. (1999) *Foundations of Democracy in the European Union: From the Genesis of Parliamentary Democracy to the European Parliament*, Basingstoke: Palgrave MacMillan.

Plamenatz, J. (1973) *Democracy and Illusion: An Examination of Certain Aspects of Modern Democratic Theory*, London: Longman.

Pollack, M. A. (1994) 'Creeping Competence: The Expanding Agenda of the European Community', *Journal of Public Policy*, 14(2): 95–145.

—— (2003) *The Engines of European Integration: Delegation, Agency and Agenda Setting in the EU*, Oxford: Oxford University Press.

Pollak, J., Batora, J. Mokre, M., Sigalas, E. and Slominski, P. (2009) 'On Political Representation: Myths and Challenges', RECON Online Working Paper 2009/03, Oslo: ARENA. Available at: http://www.reconproject.eu/projectweb/portalproject/AbstractRECONwp0903.html

Powell, W. and DiMaggio, P. (eds) (1991) *The New Institutionalism in Organizational Analysis*, Chicago, IL: University of Chicago Press.

Preuss, U. (1996) 'Two Challenges to European Citizenship', in R. Bellamy and D. Castiglione (eds) *Constitutionalism in Transformation: European and Theoretical Perspectives*, Oxford: Blackwell.

Putnam, H. (2002) *The Collapse of the Fact/Value Dichotomy and Other Essays*, Cambridge, MA: Harvard University Press.

Raabe, J. (2008) 'Kommunikation und soziale Praxis: Chancen einer praxistheoretischen Perspektive für Kommunikationstheorie und -forschung', in C. Winter, A. Hepp and F. Krotz (eds) *Theorien der Kommunikations- und Medienwissenschaft*, Wiesbaden, VS Verlag.

Rakušanová, P. (2007) 'The Constitutional Debate: A One Man Show? Vaclav Klaus and the Constitutional Discourse in the Czech Republic', *Perspectives on European Politics and Society*, 8(3): 342–73.

Rawls, J. (1993) *Political Liberalism*, New York, NY: Columbia University Press.

Reif, K. and Schmitt, H. (1980) 'Nine Second Order National Elections: A Conceptual Framework for the Analysis of European Election Results', *European Journal of Political Research*, 8(1): 3–44.

Reilly, N. (2007) 'Cosmopolitan Feminism and Human Rights', *Hypatia*, 22(4): 180–98.

Resnick, P. (1994) 'Toward a Multinational Federalism: Asymmetrical and Confederal Alternatives', in L. Seidle (ed.) *Seeking a New Canadian Partnership*, Ottawa: Institute for Research on Public Policy (IRPP).

Risse, T. (2001) 'A European Identity? Europeanisation and the Evolution of Nation-States Identities', in M. Green Cowles, J. Caporaso and T. Risse (eds) *Transforming Europe: Europeanisation and Domestic Change*, Ithaca, NY: Cornell University Press.

—— (2004) 'European Institutions and Identity Change: What have we Learned?', in R. Herrmann, T. Risse and M. B. Brewer (eds) *Transnational Identities: Becoming European in the EU*, Lanham, MD: Rowman and Littlefield.

—— (2010) *A Community of Europeans? Transnational Identities and Public Spheres*, Ithaca, NY: Cornell University Press.

Rittberger, B. (2005) *Building Europe's Parliament: Democratic Representation beyond the Nation-State*, Oxford: Oxford University Press.

Rokkan, S. (1975) 'Dimensions of State Formation and Nation Building: A Possible Paradigm for Research on Variations Within Europe', in C. Tilly (ed.) *The Formation of National States in Western Europe*, Princeton, NJ: Princeton University Press.

Ruggie, J. G. (1993) 'Territoriality and Beyond: Problematizing Modernity in International Relations', *International Organizations*, 47(1): 139–74.

Rumford, C. (2005) 'Cosmopolitanism and Europe: Towards a new EU Studies Agenda?', *Innovation* 18(1): 1–9.

Russell, P. H. (1993) *Constitutional Odyssey: Can Canadians Become a Sovereign People?*, Toronto: University of Toronto Press.

Ryan, A. (1998) 'Political Philosophy', in A. Grayling (ed.) *Philosophy*, Oxford: Oxford University Press.

Sabel, C. and J. Zeitlin (2007) 'Learning from Difference: The New Architecture of Experimentalist Governance in the European Union', European Governance Papers (EuroGov) No. C-07-02. Available at: http://www.connex-network.org/eurogov/pdf/egp-connex-C-07-02.pdf

Sanders, L. (1997) 'Against Deliberation', *Political Theory*, 25(3): 347–66.

Saward, M. (2006) 'The Representative Claim', *Contemporary Political Theory*, 5(3): 297–318.

Scharpf, F. W. (1988) 'The Joint-Decision Trap: Lessons from German Federalism and European Integration', *Public Administration*, 66(3): 239–78.

—— (1994) 'Community and Autonomy: Multi-level Policy-making in the European Union', *Journal of European Public Policy*, 1(2): 219–42.

—— (1999) *Governing in Europe: Effective and Democratic?*, Oxford: Oxford University Press.

—— (2010) 'The Asymmetry of European Integration, or why the EU cannot be a "Social Market Economy"', *Socio-Economic Review*, 8: 211–50.

Schmalz-Bruns, R. (2005) 'On the Political Theory of the Euro-polity', in E. O. Eriksen (ed.) *Making the European Polity: Reflexive Integration in the EU*, London: Routledge.

Schmidt, V. A. (2006) *Democracy in Europe: The EU and National Polities*, Oxford: Oxford University Press.

Schmitter, P. C. (1996) 'Imagining the Future of the Euro-Polity with the Help of New Concepts', in G. Marks, F. W. Scharpf, P. C. Schmitter and W. Streeck (eds) *Governance in the European Union*, London: Sage.

—— (2000) *How to Democratize the European Union . . . And Why Bother?*, Oxford: Rowman and Littlefield.

Schmitter, P. C. and Kim, S. (2005) 'Prospects for Northeast Asian Integration: Lessons from Europe', paper presented at the conference 'The European Union and the World: Asia, Enlargement and Constitutional Change', Beijing, 5–6 May 2005.

Seidendorf, S. (2010) 'Contesting Europe: the Constitutive Impact of Discursive Dynamics on National Referendum Campaigns', *European Political Science Review*, 2(3): 423–50.

Sen, A. (2011) 'It Isn't Just the Euro: Europe's Democracy Itself Is at Stake', *The Guardian*, 22 June. Available at: http://www.guardian.co.uk/commentisfree/2011/jun/22/euro-europes-democracy-rating-agencies

Shapiro, I. and Hacker-Cordón, C. (1999) *Democracy's Edges*, Cambridge: Cambridge University Press.

Shelley, M. and Winck, M. (eds) (1995) *Aspects of European Cultural Diversity*, London: Routledge.

Siedentop, L. (2000) *Democracy in Europe*, London: Penguin.

Sifft, S., Brüggemann, M., Kleinen-von Königslöw, K., Peters, B. and Wimmel, A. (2007) 'Segmented Europeanization: Exploring the "Communication Lag" in the European Union', *Journal of Common Market Studies*, 45(1): 127–55.

Siim, B. (2000) *Gender and Citizenship: Politics and Agency in France, Britain and Denmark*, Singapore: Cambridge University Press.

Sjøstedt, G. (1977) *The External Role of the European Community*, Farnborough: Saxon House.

Sjursen, H. (2006a) 'What Kind of Power? European Foreign Policy in Perspective', *Journal of European Public Policy*, 13(2): 169–81.

—— (ed.) (2006b) *Questioning EU Enlargement: Europe in Search of Identity*, London: Routledge.

—— (2006c) 'The EU as a "Normative Power": How Can This Be?', *Journal of European Public Policy*, 13(2): 235–51.

—— (2007) 'Integration without Democracy? Three Conceptions of European Security Policy in Transformation', RECON Online Working Paper 2007/19, Oslo: ARENA. Available at: http://www.reconproject.eu/projectweb/portalproject/AbstractRECONwp0719.htmlht

—— (forthcoming) 'Not so Intergovernmental After All? On Democracy and Integration in European Foreign and Security Policy', *Journal of European Public Policy*.

Slaughter, A. M. (2004) *A New World Order*, Princeton, NJ: Princeton University Press.

Smith, A. D. (2001) *Nationalism: Theory, Ideology, History*, Cambridge: Polity Press.

Smith, K. E. (2000) 'The End of Civilian Power EU: A Welcome Demise or Cause for Concern?', *International Spectator*, 35(2): 11–28.

Smith, M. E. (2004) *Europe's Foreign and Security Policy: The Institutionalization of Cooperation*, Cambridge: Cambridge University Press.

Smith, W. (2008) 'A Cosmopolitan Sociology: Ulrich Beck's Trilogy on the Global Age', *Global Networks*, 8(2): 253–9.

Sparks, C. S. with Reading, A. (1997) *Communism, Capitalism and the Media in Eastern Europe*, London: Sage.

Splichal, S. (1994) *Media beyond Socialism: Theory and Practice in East-Central Europe*, Boulder: Westview Press.

Statistics Canada (n.d.) 'Canada's Ethnocultural Portrait: The Changing Mosaic'. Available at: http://www12.statcan.ca/english/census01/products/analytic/companion/etoimm/canada.cfm

Stein, E. (1981) 'Lawyers, Judges and the Making of a Transnational Constitution', *American Journal of International Law*, 75(1): 1–27.

Stephens, P. (2011) 'Europe's Return to Westphalia', *Financial Times*, 23 June. Available at: http://www.ft.com/cms/s/0/e019ba34-9dc9-11e0-b30c-00144feabdc0.html#axzz1QdxwydYx

Stie, A. E. (2010) *Co-decision – The Panacea for EU Democracy?* ARENA Report No 2010/01, Oslo: ARENA.

Stone Sweet, A. (2004) *The Judicial Construction of Europe*, Oxford: Oxford University Press.

Streek, W. (2000) 'Competitive Solidarity: Rethinking the "European Social Model"', in K. Hinrichs, H. Kitschelt and H. Wisenthal (eds) *Kontingenz und Krise*, Frankfurt: Campus.

Sükösd, M. and Bajomi-Lázár, P. (eds) (2003) *Reinventing Media: Media Policy Reform in East Central Europe*, Budapest: Central European University (CEU) Press.

Supreme Court of Canada (1998) 'Reference Re Secession of Quebec', 2 S.C.R. 217, 20 August. Available at: http://www.sfu.ca/~aheard/827/SCC-Que-Secession.html

Tamir, Y. (1993) *Liberal Nationalism*, Princeton NJ: Princeton University Press.

Tamvaki, D. (2009) 'Using Eurobarometer Data on Voter Participation in the 2004 European Elections to test the RECON Models', RECON Online Working Paper 2009/13, Oslo: ARENA. Available at: http://www.reconproject.eu/main.php/RECON_wp_0913.pdf?fileitem=3555643http

Tiilikainen, T. (2001) 'To Be or Not to Be? An Analysis of the Legal and Political Elements of Statehood in the EU's External Identity', *European Foreign Affairs Review*, 6(2): 223–41.

Tocci, N. (2007) 'Can the EU Promote Democracy and Human Rights through the ENP? The Case for Refocusing on the Rule of Law', in 'The European Neighbourhood Policy: A Framework for Modernisation?', European University Institute Working Paper, Florence: European University Institute (EUI).

Tonra, B. (2003) 'Constructing the CFSP: The Utility of a Cognitive Approach', *Journal of Common Market Studies*, 41(4): 731–56.

Trenz, H.-J. (2005) *Europa in den Medien: Die europäische Integration im Spiegel nationaler Öffentlichkeit*, Frankfurt: Campus.

—— (2008) 'Understanding Media Impact on European Integration: Enhancing or Restricting the Scope of Legitimacy of the EU, *Journal of European Integration*, 30(2): 291–309.

—— (2010) 'In Search of the Popular Subject: Identity Formation, Constitution-making and the Democratic Consolidation of the EU', *European Review*, 18(1): 93–115.

Trenz, H.-J., Conrad, M. and Rosén, G. (2009) 'Impartial Mediator or Critical Watchdog? The Role of Political Journalism in EU Constitution-making', *Comparative European Politics*, 7(3): 342–63.

Trenz, H.-J., de Wilde, P. and Michailidou, A. (2010) 'Contesting EU Legitimacy. The Prominence, Content and Justification of Euroscepticism during 2009 EP Election Campaigns', RECON Online Working Paper 2010/22, Oslo: ARENA. Available at: http://www.reconproject.eu/main.php/RECON_wp_1022.pdf?fileitem=5456424http

Turner, B. (2008) *Rights and Virtues*, Oxford: Bardwell Press.

Tyler, T. R. (1990) *Why People Obey the Law*, New Haven, CT: Yale University.

Vetters, R., Jentges, E. and Trenz, H.-J. (2009) 'Whose Project is it? Media Debates on the Ratification of the EU Constitutional Treaty', *Journal of European Public Policy*, 16(3): 412–30.

Wagner, W., Peters, D. and Glahn, C. (2010) 'Parliamentary War Powers Around the World, 1989–2004: A New Dataset', Democratic Control of Armed Forces (DCAF) Occasional Paper No. 22, Geneva: Geneva Centre for the Democratic Control of Armed Forces. Available at: http://www.isn.ethz.ch/isn/Digital-Library/Publications/Detail/?ots591=0c54e3b3-1e9c-be1e-2c24-a6a8c7060233&lng=en&id=123931

Waldron, J. (2010) 'What is Cosmopolitan?', in G. W. Brown and D. Held (eds) *The Cosmopolitanism Reader*, Cambridge: Polity Press.

Walker, N. (2004) 'The Legacy of Europe's Constitutional Moment', *Constellations*, 11(3): 368–92.

Wallace, H. (1993) 'Deepening and Widening: Problems of Legitimacy for the EC', in S. García (ed.) *European Identity and the Search for Legitimacy*, London: Pinter.

—— (2005) 'An Institutional Anatomy and Five Policy Modes', in H. Wallace, W. Wallace and M. Pollack (eds) *Policy-making in the European Union*, Oxford: Oxford University Press.

Weale, A. (1999) *Democracy*, London: Palgrave Macmillan.

Webber, J. (1994) *Reimagining Canada: Language, Culture, Community, and the Canadian Constitution*, Montreal: McGill-Queen's University Press.

Weber, M. (1921) [1978] *Economy and Society: An Outline of Interpretive Sociology*, Berkeley: University of California Press.

Weiler, J. H. H. (1999) *The Constitution of Europe: 'Do the New Clothes Have an Emperor?', and other Essays on European Integration*, Cambridge: Cambridge University Press.

—— (2001) 'European Democracy and the Principle of Toleration: The Soul of Europe', in F. Cerutti and E. Rudolph (eds) *A Soul for Europe. On the Political and Cultural Identity of the Europeans, vol. 1, A Reader*, Leuven: Peeters.

Wendt, A. (2003) 'Why a World State is Inevitable', *European Journal of International Relations*, 9(4): 491–542.

World Economic Forum (2011) 'Euro Will Never Be Abandoned Says France's President Nicolas Sarkozy', news release. Available at: http://www.weforum.org/news/euro-will-never-be-abandoned-says-france's-president-nicolas-sarkozy?fo=1

Wyrozumska, A. (2007) 'Who Is Willing to Die for the Constitution? The National Debate on the Constitutional Treaty in Poland', *Perspectives on European Politics and Society*, 8(3): 314–41.

Young, I. M. (2000) *Inclusion and Democracy*, Oxford: Oxford University Press.

Zürn, M. (1998) *Regieren jenseits dea Nationalstaates: Globalisierung und Denationalisierung als Chance*, Frankfurt: Suhrkamp.

INDEX

Lightning Source UK Ltd.
Milton Keynes UK
UKOW051022241112

202698UK00002B/23/P

9 780415 690720